New Approaches to Early Child Development

CRITICAL CULTURAL STUDIES OF CHILDHOOD

Series Editors:
Marianne N. Bloch, Gaile Sloan Cannella, and Beth Blue Swadener

This series will focus on reframings of theory, research, policy, and pedagogies in childhood. A critical cultural study of childhood is one that offers a "prism" of possibilities for writing about power and its relationship to the cultural constructions of childhood, family, and education in broad societal, local, and global contexts. Books in the series will open up new spaces for dialogue and reconceptualization based on critical theoretical and methodological framings, including critical pedagogy, advocacy and social justice perspectives, cultural, historical and comparative studies of childhood, post-structural, postcolonial, and/or feminist studies of childhood, family, and education. The intent of the series is to examine the relations between power, language, and what is taken as normal/abnormal, good and natural, to understand the construction of the "other," difference and inclusions/exclusions that are embedded in current notions of childhood, family, educational reforms, policies, and the practices of schooling. *Critical Cultural Studies of Childhood* will open up dialogue about new possibilities for action and research.

Single authored as well as edited volumes focusing on critical studies of childhood from a variety of disciplinary and theoretical perspectives are included in the series. A particular focus is in a re-imagining as well as critical reflection on policy and practice in early childhood, primary, and elementary education. It is the series intent to open up new spaces for reconceptualizing theories and traditions of research, policies, cultural reasonings and practices at all of these levels, in the United States, as well as comparatively.

The Child in the World/The World in the Child: Education and the Configuration of a Universal, Modern, and Globalized Childhood
  Edited by Marianne N. Bloch, Devorah Kennedy, Theodora Lightfoot, and Dar Weyenberg; Foreword by Thomas S. Popkewitz

Beyond Pedagogies of Exclusion in Diverse Childhood Contexts: Transnational Challenges
  Edited by Soula Mitakidou, Evangelia Tressou, Beth Blue Swadener, and Carl A. Grant

"Race" and Early Childhood Education: An International Approach to Identity, Politics, and Pedagogy
  Edited by Glenda Mac Naughton and Karina Davis

Governing Childhood into the 21st Century: Biopolitical Technologies of Childhood Management and Education
  By Majia Holmer Nadesan

Developmentalism in Early Childhood and Middle Grades Education: Critical Conversations on Readiness and Responsiveness
  Edited by Kyunghwa Lee and Mark D. Vagle

New Approaches to Early Child Development: Rules, Rituals, and Realities
  Edited by Hillel Goelman, Jayne Pivik, and Martin Guhn

NEW APPROACHES TO EARLY CHILD DEVELOPMENT

Rules, Rituals, and Realities

Edited by

*Hillel Goelman,
Jayne Pivik,
and Martin Guhn*

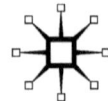

NEW APPROACHES TO EARLY CHILD DEVELOPMENT
Copyright © Hillel Goelman, Jayne Pivik, and Martin Guhn, 2011.
Softcover reprint of the hardcover 1st edition 2011 978-0-230-10543-0
All rights reserved.

First published in 2011 by
PALGRAVE MACMILLAN®
in the United States—a division of St. Martin's Press LLC,
175 Fifth Avenue, New York, NY 10010.

Where this book is distributed in the UK, Europe and the rest of the world, this is by Palgrave Macmillan, a division of Macmillan Publishers Limited, registered in England, company number 785998, of Houndmills, Basingstoke, Hampshire RG21 6XS.

Palgrave Macmillan is the global academic imprint of the above companies and has companies and representatives throughout the world.

Palgrave® and Macmillan® are registered trademarks in the United States, the United Kingdom, Europe and other countries.

ISBN 978-1-349-28989-9   ISBN 978-0-230-11933-8 (eBook)
DOI 10.1057/9780230119338
Library of Congress Cataloging-in-Publication Data

   New approaches to early child development : rules, rituals, and realities / edited by Hillel Goelman, Jayne Pivik, Martin Guhn.
     p. cm.—(Critical cultural studies of childhood)
     1. Child development. 2. Educational psychology. I. Goelman, Hillel, 1951– II. Pivik, Jayne. III. Guhn, Martin.

HQ772.N473 2011
305.231—dc22   2010049341

A catalogue record of the book is available from the British Library.

Design by Newgen Imaging Systems (P) Ltd., Chennai, India.

First edition: June 2011

To our parents, families, teachers, and ancestors who nurtured, mentored, taught, and inspired us emotionally, socially, physically, intellectually, and spiritually. To the children and families who shared their experiences, knowledge, and wisdom. To our children, grandchildren, and future generations of children in British Columbia and beyond, for whom we wish to create a healthy, optimistic, and sustainable future.

Contents

List of Figures and Tables	ix
Series Editors' Preface	xi
Foreword	xiii
Preface	xvii
Acknowledgments	xix

1 Introduction to the CHILD Project — 1
   Hillel Goelman

2 The Theoretical Framework(s) That Guided the CHILD Project — 17
   Hillel Goelman and Martin Guhn

3 From Theory to Practice: Implementing the CHILD Project — 33
   Hillel Goelman

4 What We Learned about Poverty and Vulnerability — 53
   Mary Russell

5 Lessons from Community-University Partnerships with First Nations — 69
   Jessica Ball and Lucy Le Mare

6 What We Learned about Early Identification and Screening — 95
   Hillel Goelman, Laurie Ford, Mari Pighini, Susan Dahinten, Anne Synnes, Lillian Tse, Jessica Ball, and Virginia E. Hayes

7 Nurturant Environments for Children's Social, Emotional, and Physical Well-Being — 117
   Jayne Pivik, Susan Herrington, and Michaela Gummerum

8	What We Learned about Interdisciplinarity *Hillel Goelman and Martin Guhn*	141
9	Lessons in University-Community Collaboration *Jayne Pivik and Hillel Goelman*	155
10	Graduate Student Experiences in the CHILD Project: The Invaluable Contribution of Interdisciplinary, Collaborative Research to Young Academics and Professionals *Martin Guhn, Suretha Swart, Mari Pighini, and Silvia Vilches*	179
11	Conclusions and New Beginnings: What We Have Learned about the Rules, Rituals, and Realities of Interdisciplinary Research *Hillel Goelman, Jayne Pivik, and Martin Guhn*	201

References	219
List of Contributors	247
Index	251

Figures and Tables

Figures

5.1	The Hook and Hub Model in Indigenous Communities	89
6.1	Continuum of Screening Models in the CHILD Project	108
6.2	Proposed Integration of Screening and Intervention Services in British Columbia Based on the CHILD Project	110

Tables

1.1	The Studies, Academic Disciplines, and Community Partners in the CHILD Project	4
2.1	Interconnected Ecological Systems in the 10 Studies in the CHILD Project	24
3.1	Excerpts from CHILD*Talk* Papers	38
3.2	Summary of Research Methods in the 10 Studies in the CHILD Project	43
4.1	Excerpts from the CHILD*Talk* Papers for *The Income Assistance* and *The Parent Counselling Studies*	54
6.1	Current (2010) Early Childhood Screening and Early Identification Procedures in British Columbia: Who Gets Assessed, By Whom, When, and Why?	99
6.2	Four Questions about Screening in the Four Studies	103
6.3	Current and Proposed Early Screening and Identification Procedures in British Columbia	109
8.1	Interconnected Ecological Systems in the 10 Studies in the CHILD Project	143
8.2	Relative Emphases in the 10 Studies in the CHILD Project	144
9.1	The Studies, Academic Disciplines, Community Partners, and Methods Represented from the CHILD Project	160

Series Editors' Preface

*Marianne Bloch, Beth Blue Swadener,
and Gaile S. Cannella*

New Approaches to Early Child Development: Rules, Rituals, and Realities by Hillel Goelman, Jayne Pivik, and Martin Guhn is a welcome addition to the book series on *Critical Cultural Studies of Childhood* for Palgrave Press. In the series, we emphasize interdisciplinary and multitheoretical ways of examining childhood, and this book describing the dilemmas of research and results of research in a large interdisciplinary, multimethod/theory project, directed by and conducted by the authors, and many others, is an excellent example of types of work we wanted to publish in the series. Goelman, Pivik, and Guhn embrace the critical cultural studies of childhood orientation of our series in multiple ways by drawing in new critical theories into their research framework; they also highlight the ways in which alternative frameworks for theory and research help us to interrogate as well as understand childhood differently.

The book is written by the authors and their interdisciplinary team of researchers to illustrate how one project can be done by a large multibackground team, from multiple disciplinary backgrounds, and one that draws on different methodological and theoretical frameworks to understand childhood within diverse and nested contexts. By including chapters from a variety of the projects done by their team of interdisciplinary researchers (including graduate student authors/teacher/parents as co-researchers), the authors present an example of the ways in which a long-term collaborative group can come together to understand how children and families thrive under varying circumstances, and at the same time, ways in which social policies that affect children and their families could be envisioned differently. The research illustrates the utility of "mixed methods" in which empirical, statistical and qualitative/ethnographic research together better illustrate how knowledge can be constructed in different ways, illuminating different aspects of childhood. This again forces us to deconstruct the hyperindividualism and the emphasis on only positivist and a certain narrow view of empirical research that is at the core of most American research on children, and the ways in which we come to think about their child development and learning. We are pleased to have our series with Palgrave where this type of study, with its multiple dimensions, can be published as an illustration of how to do research differently.

Foreword

Kofi Marfo

This is a timely publication in the context of significant ongoing shifts in the way we think about the nature of inquiry, the research mission of modern universities, and the relevance of institutions of higher education to their local publics. For a wide variety of reasons, including both a growing sense of moral imperative and perhaps an unspoken desire to push back against the deeply entrenched societal image of universities as Ivory Towers, research institutions are increasingly and explicitly embracing *community engagement* as a core mission. In North America, the past two decades in particular have seen an upswing of university-community partnerships, some of them supported initially by substantial leveraging of institutional resources in anticipation of long-term sustainability through payoffs in increased extra-mural grant generation. While community engagement initiatives across institutions may vary in their underlying values, operational models, breadth of focus, or success in garnering broad institutional involvement, they share one thing in common: the goal of using the intellectual capital and research machinery of the modern university not only to fulfill the traditional universal mission of knowledge advancement but to also make a demonstrably positive difference in the economic and social circumstances of local communities and constituent groups closer to home.

On a related level, continuing discourse and contemplation on the vexing challenges of disciplinary insularity in the academy appear to be ushering in an era marked by concerted institutional efforts to build bridges across disciplines. We are witnessing significant shifts in the valuing of interdisciplinary inquiry, and there is a growing commitment to interdisciplinary advanced graduate and postgraduate research education, even as this trend continues to be impeded by structural and operational barriers endemic to the administrative organization and funding of academic units and their teaching and research programs. Within the behavioral and social sciences, in particular, the hegemonic paradigm wars of yesteryears are gradually giving way to increased openness to epistemological and methodological pluralism. When such pluralism, in combination with an interdisciplinary intellectual climate, succeeds in fostering a pragmatic ethos of multilevel research collaboration on important societal problems, the stage is set for meaningful and sustainable university-community engagement in which the voices and experiences of communities and community-based professionals are as valued as those from the academy.

This book is simultaneously a significant scholarly contribution to early child development research and a primer on what can be learned about interdisciplinarity, methodological boundary-crossing, multilevel collaboration, and the pursuit of community-based policy-responsive inquiry from a highly multifaceted program of applied research. The volume embodies the exciting possibilities waiting to be realized fully as the changing intellectual traditions and values identified in these opening paragraphs approach an ideal point of convergence. This is the stage at which *interdisciplinary inquiry as realistic problem solving in community contexts* (as was the case with the CHILD Project) necessitates not only the harnessing of expertise and synergy across disciplines and methodologies, or the building of collaborative alliances beyond the academic environment, but also the courage on the part of researchers to interrogate within their own specialized fields the worldviews, assumptions, and conventions informing all aspects of inquiry.

Beyond the many policy insights and the high level of theoretical integration within and across disciplines—accomplished comprehensively in the opening chapters and complemented so well in the chapters reporting on specific projects—the scholarly appeal of this volume lies also in the kaleidoscopic assembling and interweaving of findings on questions so wide-ranging that only an innovative and unconventional project like CHILD can unite them in one forum. Throughout the book, Goelman, Pivik, Guhn, and their collaborating authors also provide valuable education, implicit as well explicit, about the challenges and benefits of inquiry in which space for culture-building and continuous in-situ interrogation of mindsets, methods, and tools are an integral part of the research implementation process. What happens when working closely with research participants and communities results in insights that are not consistent with previously held assumptions and understandings that informed the choice of research design and instrumentation in the original proposal? Should a research team see such a scenario as an opportunity to explore the authentic, and thus be open to a rethinking of the original plan, or should it push ahead with preplanned procedures in the name of "scientific" and procedural integrity? What would methodological integrity mean in this context? What deliberative processes would guide the resolution of such a problem within a collaborative research team, and what considerations would inform the nature of the resolution(s) reached? Finally, how does a research team negotiate the boundaries of flexibility with the funding agency and the local Institutional Review Board?

Collectively, these questions coalesce around fundamental values on conceptions of knowledge and its production, cultural/contextual variation, professional ethics, and personal and institutional accountability. Above all, they are questions that should be of interest to the research community's core constituencies: professional researchers and their community-based collaborators, advanced graduate research education programs and the students in whose hands lies the future of inquiry, institutional research review boards with oversight and adjudicatory responsibility for the conduct of inquiry, and funding agency staff and blind reviewers who are often among the first to make decisions about the knowledge value of proposed projects. Those interested in these and related questions would find in this volume an invaluable reference companion as refreshingly informative as it is provocative.

As a member of the small group of advisors who participated in the steering of the CHILD Project, I have looked forward to seeing and reading a project-spawned publication that could particularly give future collaborative research teams the benefit of the lessons learned from the design, review, implementation, and monitoring of the project. It is a delight, therefore, to see this hope not only realized but also fulfilled as part of a book that also reports the substantive findings from the various projects. On the basis of my deep conviction that research education must *simultaneously* foster knowledge and competencies in the technical tools of design and analysis *and* prepare students to be able to think through applied behavioral and social science research as a socioculturally negotiated enterprise with profound ethical and moral ramifications, I consider this book a must-read resource in research education and invite those who teach research courses at the graduate and advanced undergraduate levels to give their students the benefit of the book's unique contributions.

Preface

In the fall of 2002, a partnership of academic and community researchers submitted a grant proposal to a national funding council in Canada. A four-person team representing the partnership was invited to meet with the council's adjudication committee to defend the proposal. Numerous members of the review panel complimented the research team on the strength of the research proposal, but there were many questions that focused on whether the project was really feasible in the real world of research. In other words, the committee thought the proposal was a good idea, but had doubts as to whether it could actually be implemented. The team members tried to reassure the committee as best they could by pointing to the quality of the academic and community professionals on the project; to the research design and the harmonization of quantitative and qualitative methods; to the enthusiastic support for the project from the communities in which the work would be conducted; to the involvement of community researchers; and to the track records of the coinvestigators. Despite these repeated assurances, the review panel remained concerned. It reminded us of the old science fiction movies when one of the heroes (usually a teenager) devises a creative, daring, and even outlandish way to defeat the invading Martians, and the response from all of the high-powered military men is something like: "It sounds crazy—but it just might work."

When the "can you really do it" question was repeated for the fifth or sixth time, I tried a different tack. I pointed out that there were many different approaches to interdisciplinary research but that our project was somewhat unique in that it included 10 different studies all within one overall interdisciplinary framework. I said that if there existed a handbook that described exactly how to conduct this kind of collaborative, interdisciplinary research in early child development, I would buy multiple copies of this text, distribute it to my coinvestigators and use it to implement the CHILD Project. Such a text, if I could find one, would serve as a roadmap, pointing out the benefits of certain pathways and the challenges of others. In our experience, however, this particular handbook did not exist. I then said that I was confident that by the end of the five-year period our project would be in an excellent position to produce a book on the strengths, weaknesses costs, and benefits of a collaborative interdisciplinary research project in early child development. Days later we were informed that our proposal was funded.

I am hopeful that the rules, rituals, and realities of research described in this book can be of assistance to those on their own journeys into new, complex, and challenging questions about children, families, research, and themselves.

HILLEL GOELMAN
Vancouver, British Columbia

Acknowledgments

There are many people to thank for supporting the CHILD Project and the publication of this book. The CHILD International Advisory Committee contributed many hours of consultation, advice, and guidance over the five years of the Project and we thank (in alphabetical order) Willie Charley, Mary Clifford, Dr. Judith Duncan, Dr. Gosta Esping-Andersen, Dr. Emmet Francoeur, Dr. Robert Glossop, Dr. Kofi Marfo, Sherri Torjman, and Dr. Andrew Wachtel.

We thank the two Project Coordinators Barbara Goyer and Eileen Grant for serving as virtual "air traffic controllers" in managing the large longitudinal study. We also want to thank the administrative team in the Human Early Learning Partnership at the University of British Columbia for their overall implementation of the CHILD Project. The administrative teams at the other participating universities—the University of Victoria, Simon Fraser University, the University of Northern British Columbia, and the University of Lethbridge—also contributed to the collaborative efforts that supported the Project.

The CHILD Project could not have succeeded without the active and patient support of our many community partners: Susan Anstett, Pam Best, Dana Brynelsen, Dianne Cameron, Sarah Chapman Chen, Michael Goldberg, Tammy Harkey, Dianne Liscumb, Megan Tardiff, and Lillian Tse. We are also indebted to the following community organizations and groups for their support:

- BC Centre for Ability
- Canadian Centre for Policy Alternatives
- City of Vancouver Social Planning Department
- Family Services of Vancouver
- HIPPY Canada
- Infant Development Program of BC
- Katzie First Nation
- Kermode Friendship Society
- Laichwiltach Family Life Society

- Lil'wat First Nation
- Musqueam First Nation
- Sechelt First Nation
- Sliammon First Nation
- Social Planning and Research Council of BC;
- Tla'Amin Community Health Services Society
- Tsawwassen First Nation
- Tsleil Waututh First Nation
- Westcoast Child Care Resource and Referral

On a personal level we thank our families for their sustained interest and support throughout the Project: Sheryl Sorokin, Zachary Goelman, and Nadav Goelman (HG); Robert Baker, Jesse Baker, and Joshua Baker (JP); and Annette Guhn and Ekkehard Guhn, and Anne Maria Gadermann (MG).

This book would never have seen the light of the day without the patience, the dedication, and the skilled, compassionate, and critical editorial eye, hand, and mind of Adam Wilton. Finally, we thank Samantha Hasey, Burke Gerstenschlager, Erin Ivy and Rohini Krishnan at Palgrave Macmillan for their trust in this book and the support that they gave us throughout the writing and editing process.

CHAPTER 1

Introduction to the CHILD Project

Hillel Goelman

This book describes the theoretical framework, the implementation, and the research findings of the interdisciplinary, five-year (2003–2008) Consortium for Health, Intervention, Learning, and Development (CHILD) Project. The purpose of the CHILD Project was to study children and childhood within the multiply embedded and interactive contexts that frame and influence early child development. The CHILD Project was made up of 10 interconnected research studies, which were conducted by interdisciplinary teams of researchers from a wide range of university-based health, medical, and social sciences in collaboration with community-based professionals. The CHILD Project has generated much rich information on the determinants of the developmental trajectories of typical and atypical children and has thus contributed to a better understanding of the social determinants of development for all children. The CHILD Project has provided community-based organizations with access to the research process and, as a whole, has made deliberate attempts to inform child and family public policy.

This introduction attempts to lay the groundwork for two levels of critical analysis in the book. At one level of analysis, the book discusses the design, implementation, and findings of the 10 studies and what they contribute to our understanding of early child development. At another level, it attempts to describe what we learned about interdisciplinarity, about collaboration, and, ultimately, what we learned about ourselves as researchers by conducting the CHILD Project. Both levels of analysis require a "numbers and narratives" strategy that permits the presentation of the research findings that, in some cases, are reported by statistics and quantitative analyses. In other cases, the research findings are based on qualitative data and are presented as stories of children, families, and/or communities in which they live. We draw upon both the numbers and the narratives in order to weave together the epistemologies, methodologies, and findings from 10 different studies into a meaningful understanding of the many different and complex factors that contribute to early child development.

Overview of Goals and Objectives

The major goal of the CHILD Project was "to study early childhood development (ECD) through a series of linked, interdisciplinary, multi-methodological, and longitudinal research projects involving both academic researchers and community-based organizations" (Goelman et al., 2002). Taken together, the 10 studies of the CHILD Project, which are described below, were designed to inform and complement one another by casting light on common themes as well as on the subtle nuances and major variations that emerged within and across the 10 studies. The CHILD Project attempted to bridge the distinct cultures and discourses that frequently inhibit collaboration between researchers in different disciplines and between university-based researchers, community-based practitioners, and government-based policymakers (Shonkoff, 2000). The construction of this bridge was dependent upon all of the research being conducted within the social, political, economic, and policy contexts of the province of British Columbia, over the five-year period from 2003 to 2008, and by all the 10 studies subscribing to the following eight specific objectives:

1. To study the development of typical and atypical children, across different domains of development, from birth through the early years.
2. To study early child development within the programmatic, community, and policy contexts that frame the lives of children and families.
3. To examine how shifts and changes in the policy environment impact children and families.
4. To support interdisciplinary research in early child development across the biological, medical, health, and social sciences.
5. To support collaborative work among university researchers and community service professionals.

6. To support community service professionals and advocates to engage in research, public education activities, and possibly graduate study in universities; and, likewise, to support researchers to engage in community practice and professional activity, in order to meaningfully inform their research.
7. To expose graduate students to collaborative, interdisciplinary research.
8. To disseminate the research findings in ways that are accessible to a wide audience of policy officials, community professionals, parents, and other citizens.

The 10 Studies in the 4 Thematic Clusters of the CHILD Project

The 10 studies in the CHILD Project can be grouped into 4 general clusters although there are a number of alternative ways that the 10 studies could be organized (table 1.1). The clusters were created by considering a range of factors including a commonality of research questions and research methodologies and the populations of children and families who were the foci of the studies. Each cluster served as an immediate "community of discourse" where common issues were first voiced and discussed prior to being raised within the consortium as a whole.

The first cluster, *Policy Studies in Early Child Development*, consisted of research projects, which addressed child and family policy in the province. The *Income Assistance Study* investigated the impact of changes in family assistance policies on lone-parents by conducting econometric (i.e., quantitative) and content (i.e., qualitative) analyses of official income assistance policies, and by also conducting a series of interviews and focus groups with single mothers with young children who were living in poverty (Fuller, Kershaw, & Pulkingham, 2008; Kershaw, Pulkingham, & Fuller, 2008). The *Child Care Policy Study* examined the development and implementation of child care policies in regard to government-funding allocations, child care subsidy payments for low-income families, and the viability, sustainability, and quality of child care services (Goelman, 2000; Goelman et al., 2006). In both policy studies, researchers drew on federal and provincial administrative databases as well as on consultations with key stakeholders in the areas of income assistance and child care.

While all 10 of the studies included some children of Indigenous descent, the 2 studies in the second cluster, *Early Childhood Development in Indigenous Communities*, focused exclusively on

Table 1.1 The Studies, Academic Disciplines, and Community Partners in the CHILD Project

The 10 Studies and Their Main Objectives	Academic Disciplines	Community Partners
Cluster 1: *Policy Studies in Early Child Development*		
The Income Assistance Study To assess the impact of changes in income assistance policy on lone-parent families with young children.	Sociology & Anthropology; Community & Regional Planning; Women's Studies	Social Planning and Research Council of BC; Canadian Centre for Policy Alternatives
The Child Care Policy Study To investigate the impact of child care policy changes on communities, child care facilities, families, and children.	Early Childhood Education; Policy Analysis; Measurement and Evaluation	City of Vancouver Social Planning Department; Westcoast Child Care Resource and Referral
Cluster 2: *Early Childhood Development in Indigenous Communities*		
The Indigenous Child Project To obtain the perspectives of Indigenous communities on child development and measurement.	Child and Youth Care	Four on-reserve Indigenous communities
The Aboriginal HIPPY Documentation Project To explore the 'Home Instruction for Parents of Preschool Youngsters' program as implemented in Indigenous communities.	Early Childhood Education	Three on-reserve Indigenous communities; HIPPY Canada
Cluster 3: *Early Identification and Screening Studies*		
The Developmental Pathways Study To follow the long-term development of highly at-risk infants.	Neonatology; Developmental Pediatrics	Infant Development Program of BC; BC Centre for Ability
The Infant Neuromotor Study To explore the effectiveness of two types of training models for the early identification of children with neuromotor delays.	Rehabilitation Sciences; Nursing	Infant Development Program of BC; BC Centre for Ability
The Community-Based Screening Study To determine the effectiveness of a universal, community-based, developmental screening program.	Nursing; Child Development	Public Health Nurses in Chilliwack, BC

Continued

Table 1.1 Continued

The 10 Studies and Their Main Objectives	Academic Disciplines	Community Partners
Cluster 4: *Early Childhood Intervention Programs*		
The Outdoor Criteria Study To analyze how outdoor play spaces are utilized by children, and to investigate any differences that emerge.	Landscape Architecture; Policy Analysis; Child Development	City of Vancouver; BC Council for Families
The Parent Counselling Study To assess the impact of counselling on parents whose children are at risk for apprehension by child protection authorities.	Social Work and Family Studies	Family Services of Vancouver
The Safe Spaces Study To examine the short- and long-term effectiveness of a preschool antibullying program.	Child Development	Westcoast Child Care Resource and Referral

Indigenous children. The *Indigenous Child Project* focused on the traditional and contemporary perceptions of First Nations communities on the definitions of optimal developmental outcomes for First Nations children and explored the communities' perspectives on different approaches to the measurement of early development. This study drew on the voices of parents, child care staff, health, medical, and educational professionals as well as First Nations Elders in the participating communities (Ball, 2004, 2005a, 2005b). The *Aboriginal HIPPY Documentation Project* evaluated the impact of *Home Instruction for Parents of Preschool Youngsters* (HIPPY), a home-based, parent-directed intervention program for First Nations children (Lombard, 1981). This study monitored the lived experiences of the participating mothers, the family support workers who supported the participating mothers, and the perceived impacts of the program on the children. The Indigenous content and context of the program were major considerations in the study of the effectiveness and utility of the HIPPY program (Beatch & Le Mare, 2007).

The third cluster, *Early Identification and Screening Studies,* consisted of three studies that focused on the early identification of children with challenges to their development and community-based screening programs designed to assist in these early identification efforts (Goelman & the CHILD Project, 2008). The *Developmental Pathways Study* examined the developmental trajectories of children who were treated in neonatal intensive care units (NICUs) after their births. This study collected longitudinal data on the biological, medical, familial, and societal factors that contribute to the developmental outcomes of these children in their preschool and early school years (Schiariti, Matsuba, Houbé, & Synnes, 2008a; Schiariti et al., 2008b). The *Infant Neuromotor Screening Study* assessed the validity and reliability of a new measure designed to identify neuromotor delay in infants and toddlers. This study also assessed face-to-face and computer-assisted training techniques to teach a wide range of health and human service professionals in the use of the measure (Harris, Megens, Backman, & Hayes, 2003; Tse et al., 2008). The *Community-Based Developmental Screening Study* evaluated the efficacy and broader impacts of a community-based preschool screening program and examined the specificity and sensitivity of a screening measure of child development for this purpose (Dahinten, 2007a, 2007b).

The fourth cluster was made up of three *Early Childhood Intervention Studies* designed to foster positive developmental outcomes for young children and, in one case, their families as well. *The Outdoor Criteria Study* worked closely with a number of child care centers in the design and evaluation of outdoor play spaces. This involved studying the design features of the centers' play spaces and how the design influenced children's play (Herrington & Lesmeister, 2006; Herrington & Nichols, 2007). The *Parent Counselling Study* evaluated the short- and long-term effects of a program designed to support and strengthen family functioning among families whose children were being considered for nonparental foster care settings. Qualitative analyses were conducted on interviews and focus groups of participating parents both while they were in the program and after they had left the program (Russell, Harris, & Gockel, 2008; Harris, Russell, & Gockel, 2007; Russell, Gockel, & Harris, 2007). The *Safe Spaces Study* evaluated the implementation and impact of a prosocial development and antibullying program that was designed specifically for preschool-aged children. Research was conducted on the fidelity, integrity, and consistency of program implementation and the outcomes for children who participated in those programs (Smith, Schonert-Reichl, Lawlor, & Jaramillo, 2008; Jaramillo, Schonert-Reichl, & Gummerum, 2007).

These 10 studies were the original studies in the CHILD Project but over the course of the 5 years, another 5 studies developed out of these 10, largely with the help and direction of graduate students and postdoctoral fellows. One was the *Playground Study*, which integrated the work of the *Outdoor Criteria Study* and the *Safe Spaces Study* in order to examine children's social behaviors in different kinds of playground environments. The *Child and Youth Well-Being Study* examined the perspectives of young people on resources and safety of their home communities. The *University-Community Collaboration Study* focused on the positive and challenging aspects of the collaborations within the CHILD Project. The *Developmental Pathways Study* spawned two spin-off studies: The *NICU Study* included longitudinal and retrospective examinations of the developmental trajectories of graduates of Neonatal Intensive Care Units (NICU) by using linked administrative databases in the provincial ministries of Health and Education. The second was *A Multiple Case Study of the Children and Families in the Infant Development Program*, which examined the experiences of families with children with special needs. These five studies are also discussed in this book.

An Overview of the Book

The book does not present a study-by-study breakdown of each of the 10 studies in the CHILD Project. The book contains sufficient references to the published findings of each individual study. It focuses on the integrative, collaborative interdisciplinary features of the CHILD Project. Chapter 2 gives the theoretical background of the CHILD Project; Chapter 3 details the practical ways in which the CHILD Project strove to create a community of discourse from all of its disparate parts. The second part of the book includes chapters on cross-cutting themes, which emerged from the different studies. Chapter 4 focuses on the impacts of poverty on children and families, and Chapter 5 reflects on what we learned about Indigenous children and families. Chapter 6 addresses the findings and implications of the studies which examined different approaches to early screening and identification. Chapter 7 discusses what we learned about nurturant communities for children from a number of different studies. The third part of the book includes chapters that reflect on what we learned about collaborative interdisciplinary research while conducting the CHILD Project. Chapter 8 discusses the theory, practice, and outcomes of interdisciplinarity in the CHILD Project. Chapter 9 analyzes what we learned about university-community partnerships, and Chapter 10 gives voice to the experiences of the graduate students who were involved in the CHILD Project. In Chapter 11 we offer our closing remarks on the most important learnings from the CHILD Project and its implications for future research, practice, and training.

Rules, Rituals, and Realities: Why This Book Was Written

In addition to reporting data and findings, this book is about a journey and the stories that illuminate and animate that journey. The stories of the CHILD Project emanate from the *rules, rituals,* and *realities* that guided the journey. By rules we refer to the accepted procedures that establish the credibility of the programs of disciplined inquiry (Shulman, 1988) within and across the 10 studies of the CHILD Project. The 10 studies in the CHILD Project were conducted through different research traditions and, therefore, according to the rules of those respective disciplines. We are not, however, privileging any one research tradition, or set of rules, over another. Rather, we are saying that whatever research tradition that is being used must be conducted according to the criteria that establish rigor within that particular discipline. That is, the researchers in the CHILD Project were expected to conduct their work within the ontologies, epistemologies, and methodologies of the paradigm best suited to their research questions. Paradigms articulate specific approaches to the ontology or the assumptions on the nature of the knowledge. For example, in some disciplines knowledge is seen as an objective mirror of reality—as in many positivist research paradigms. At the other end of the continuum, knowledge is seen as a subjective, constructed reality—as in many postpositivist paradigms. In many mixed-methods studies researchers can draw successfully on a combination of ontological positions. Rules of epistemology determine the relationship between the researcher—or, the "knower"—and the knowledge that is being acquired in some traditions or constructed in others. Finally, disciplined inquiry also articulates standards that help to govern the appropriate selection and use of specific research methodologies. The CHILD Project included a wide range of approaches and methods to the study of early child development within multiple individual, familial, societal, policy, and values contexts. This book attempts to specify the rules of inquiry that guided, facilitated, and constrained the 10 linked programs of research in the CHILD Project.

Following the *rules* of disciplined inquiry would only give the Consortium partial assistance in weaving together the findings from different research traditions. It was critical that we create opportunities, activities, and interactions—in other words, *rituals*—that would help us to link the research findings across the research traditions represented in the 10 studies. We discovered no a priori rules that would govern this ongoing interactive and collaborative process and so we created a number of rituals of interaction that would facilitate the continuing co-construction of knowledge across the boundaries of the 10 individual studies. Our work in this area echoes Wolin and Bennet's (1984) recommendation of "family rituals" as a means of contributing to healthy family functioning. Such rituals can serve three key purposes for the family or, in our case, for the Consortium: communication, stabilization, and transformation. Our rituals took both oral and written form and provided a scaffolding within which all 10 studies could communicate their current status, progress, and findings. This contributed to a sense of stabilization by which all 10 studies kept abreast of developments within the other studies. Through these interactive rituals, the individual studies and the CHILD Project as a whole were transformed into a community of discourse that we continuously strove to create. As is shown in detail in Chapter 3, these rituals included a combination of self-reflection within each study, the production of written documents, and the distribution and discussion of these documents in large and small group settings. Each of these ritualized interactions had their own set of expectations and a consistent framework to help ensure a sense of continuity and shared purpose across the 10 studies. These rituals proved to be the lifeblood of the collaboration.

These rules and rituals did not, however, serve as a checklist of criteria for the implementation of collaborative interdisciplinary research in early child development. Rather, for the CHILD Project as a whole, the presentation of both the rules and rituals led to a new understanding of the *realities* of collaborative research. On a continuing basis, the researchers in the CHILD Project had to either find new applications of old rules or develop new rituals to deal with changing realities. These changing realities included, for example, major cuts to the funding of the community partners' programs; changes to government policies in the middle of data collection; attrition of participants; and new or revised procedures and policies of the funding agency. All of these challenges mandated the creation of a culture including rituals, which carried meaning and symbolic force at different points in the evolution of the five-year research project. By describing the flexible rules and rituals of the CHILD Project, this book diverges from many texts on research methodology, which are replete with checklists and flow charts. Many traditional research methodology textbooks suggest a uniformity, homogeneity, and linearity of the research process, and attempt to systematize what is essentially a complex, nonlinear, and iterative process of inner and outer dialogue among the research participants.

In addition, the changing realities of the CHILD Project paralleled significant changes in the lives of the many research and community partners: marriage, childbirth, death, retirement, resignations, graduations, and all kinds of life course and life cycle changes. We grew, changed our opinions, and created new ones. The book describes how we proceeded on this journey and how we attempted to build a collaborative community of discourse across different disciplines and professions with participants who were engaged in different parts of their personal journeys and career paths. This aspect of the book owes much to the autoethnographic descriptions of Ellis (2004) and Richardson (1997), in which they illustrate how they and their research collaborators constructed knowledge and were, in turn, transformed by that knowledge at critical junctures in their lives.

Ellis describes how she worked with a diverse group of graduate students with very different research interests. The common theme among those research interests was the researchers' attempt to use reflective and empirical methods to construct meaningful perspectives on and interpretations of their own lived experiences and the lived experiences of their research participants. Ellis does a masterful job of integrating theory and method, and she also shows how such a book can be used to describe the iterative process of building, refining, revising, adapting, and implementing programs of research.

Richardson discusses her professional and political struggles in academic life, her attempts to create new intellectual spaces for her work in traditional university departments and, most importantly, how the trajectory of her academic career was profoundly impacted by a series of early childhood experiences. Although neither Ellis' nor Richardson's books deal with academic research in child development, they do provide insightful examples of what we came to call the "rules, rituals, and realities" of collaborative interdisciplinary research.

This book thus aims to provide important findings in the field of childhood studies through a collaborative, interdisciplinary process that draws upon a number of different quantitative and qualitative research paradigms. Our task was not just to present the findings of the individual studies conducted under the umbrella of the CHILD Project, but to weave them together into a fabric of understanding;

to explore where the findings complement and extend one another; and to identify points of contention and gaps in our understanding. The insights from the CHILD Project presented in this book include what we learned about young children and what we learned about ourselves in the process of learning about young children. When we reflect carefully on our roles within the research process, we learn about our respective roles in the co-construction of knowledge about the lives and development of young children and about the ways in which dynamic research partnerships participate in the co-construction of knowledge about early child development. This book is as much about what we learned by peering through our respective academic and professional lenses as it is about what we learned about the nature, structure, possibilities, and limitations presented by the lenses themselves.

One of the key learnings that we aim to convey is that the process of interdisciplinary, collaborative research, as it interacts with researchers' lives over time, is much like the development of the children whom we were studying. We were witness to developmental transitions—in the children and in ourselves—that were nonlinear, nonuniform, and subject to varied influences.

For Whom Was This Book Written?

In Chapter 2 we discuss the different theoretical and empirical influences in this book. It is our hope that readers from this broad continuum of influences will find this book useful and provocative. The study of early childhood development used to be the exclusive domain of fields like pediatrics and developmental psychology. In recent years, a wider range of disciplines including, but not limited to, sociology, anthropology, women's studies, gender relations, history, cultural studies, economics, literature, and landscape architecture have begun to ask and pursue new questions about child development through their respective lenses. The CHILD Project is made up of a wide range of disciplines and our intention is to produce a volume that will invite and engage readers from this wide range of disciplines. For this reason we are pleased that this book is presented as part of Palgrave Macmillan's *Critical Cultural Studies of Childhood* Series, which publishes books designed to enlighten, engage, and provoke intellectual reflection on the lives of children.

A primary audience for this book, then, are child development researchers in many different disciplines including the medical sciences (e.g., pediatrics, family medicine, and health care and epidemiology), the health sciences (e.g., nursing, rehabilitation sciences, and speech and language therapy), the social sciences (e.g., psychology, sociology, anthropology, economics, and public policy), and professional schools (e.g., education, social work, and landscape architecture). The 10 studies within the CHILD Project involved an interdisciplinary and interprofessional team both within and across the 10 studies. This book is an attempt to recreate the cross-disciplinary dialogue within the CHILD Project by reaching out to and including the many different disciplinary and professional groups that have worked together to gain a more fully contextualized understanding of child development trajectories.

In addition to readers from different academic disciplines, we hope to draw the attention of scholars who adopt explicitly postmodern or reconceptualist perspectives on childhood studies. For example, we believe that the work presented in this book from feminist theoretical and empirical frameworks will speak to audiences for whom gender is both a focus of study and an approach to the construction of knowledge on child and family life. Similarly, the book raises questions regarding the systemic poverty, cultural diversity, ability diversity, and, in the Canadian context, the history and long-lasting effects of colonialism on Canada's First Nations. We feel that this book would extend and complement other books on reconceptualist and postmodern approaches to early childhood and will raise challenges across both sides of the modernist and postmodernist divide by proposing ways of weaving together findings from diverse disciplinary traditions while maintaining the intellectual integrity of these traditions.

The book is aimed at researchers who are specifically interested in interdisciplinary and collaborative research. This work differs considerably from the traditional model of individual scholars establishing their research credentials by conducting research that is seen as the fruit of their individual efforts and resulting in single-authored research papers that support their bids for recruitment, hiring, tenure, and promotion. In addition, this book provides researchers (1) with critical insights about the challenges and barriers that often characterize the communication and collaboration between researchers and professionals/practitioners, and (2) with stories about the processes in the CHILD Project that overcame such challenges and barriers. Even more importantly, the book illustrates that child development research, which is intended to be translated into practice and to be applied by practitioners and policymakers, critically depends on being informed by practitioners and policymakers engaged in the research process.

We also hope to reach out to researchers who have strong interests in policy development, analysis, and implementation. "Evidence-based practice" is a current mantra in government, community-based service, and academia, and the concept of evidence-based practice suggests that academics should strive to conduct policy-relevant research, which government officials can use in their work and decisions on child and family public policies. The work within CHILD placed a strong emphasis on the "transfer" and "dissemination" of research findings, with varying degrees of success. In some cases, government policy offices actually served as community-based partners for the work. In other cases, researchers attempted to access government information in order to conduct analyses of the impacts of public policy on children and their families. The stories that emerge from the CHILD Project echo and give greater detail to Shonkoff's (2000) description of the different languages and cultures of researchers, community partners, policymakers, and government officials, so that researchers interested in public policy will hopefully find these stories instructive.

Another target audience for the book is graduate students with an interest in child development. In particular, graduate students may benefit from obtaining insights into the different models of graduate student education, which were represented in the CHILD Project, and which were, at the same time, significantly shaped by the CHILD Project. Faculty members from different academic programs in different universities were involved, and graduate student education was largely shaped by the curriculum and programs of study within these different academic programs. The graduate students' involvement in the CHILD Project added new dimensions and value to their graduate work. It gave them exposure to a very wide range of research methodologies and opportunities to learn new skills, knowledge, and insight. For these graduate students, there was an added dimension of being drawn into an interdisciplinary program of research, enabling them to meet academics and graduates from other disciplines. While not all graduate students learned the identical set of skills and knowledge, it is fair to say that their involvement in the CHILD Project contributed to the development of a certain level of literacy and competence in their ability to understand child development research conducted in other disciplines. While the faculty members were trying to build cross-disciplinary bridges that had not been open to them in their own training, their graduate students were introduced to different theoretical and empirical lenses on child development to which they would not have had access if they had stayed within the confines of their own discipline or department.

Community professionals who provide programs and services on behalf of young children and their families are another audience for this book. By targeting this audience, the intention is to support community professionals in their attempts to access relevant firsthand research in their areas of interest and expertise. The book also provides examples of how community professionals can partner with academic researchers in identifying significant research questions for their communities and help in developing research methodologies that can generate findings in order to strengthen their communities. The community partners in the CHILD Project demonstrated their interest in applying research findings in their work and to using these kinds of research efforts as vehicles for professional development in their agencies. Reaching this audience is facilitated by the range of professionals represented in the CHILD Project. The community partners included clinicians and early intervention specialists who worked directly with children on an individual basis; child care providers and early childhood educators who worked with groups of young children; and executive directors and provincial coordinators of large multifaceted umbrella organizations that included advocacy, training, resource, and referral functions. There were also individuals who worked at the municipal, regional, and provincial levels of government and public health nurses who visited children and families in their homes to monitor and consult on aspects of the children's development. There was no one dominant pattern or template into which all of these university-community collaborations neatly fit. While certain overarching principles guided each of these collaborations (e.g., trust, respect, shared resources), the precise ways in which these principles were manifested provide multiple case studies for those community professionals who are considering research partnerships with academic researchers.

This book is also intended for policy officials who deal with child and family policy at local, regional, provincial, and federal levels. Shonkoff (2000) describes the ways in which the culture of policy differs from, or conflicts with, the culture of research. Shonkoff argues that researchers place a high value on empirical evidence in drawing conclusions and supporting theory whereas policymakers emphasize values, political expediency, financial, and other pragmatic considerations. Researchers tend to be most interested in following up their most recent research project with their proposed *next* research project. In contrast, policy officials tend to place heavier emphasis on the *most recent* findings from the last research project rather than on hypotheses regarding the next research project. The CHILD Project provided numerous opportunities for interaction, discussion, and dialogue among policy officials, researchers, and community service providers. In addition, the stories from the CHILD Project illustrate the processes that allowed researchers and policy officials to engage in their common interest in child and family issues, despite differences in the rules of evidence in the policy and research spheres. Furthermore, the book presents examples (1) of how the collaboration between policy officials, community professionals, and researchers contributed to the formation and refinement of research questions; and (2) that illustrate the mutual appreciation of policy officials and researchers who, despite limited time and resources, engaged in a process that aims to generate information to the benefit of both sides.

Finally, we believe that this book is also of interest to public and private funding agencies. The CHILD Project was funded in its entirety by one of the more progressive funding programs of the Social Sciences and Humanities Research Council of Canada (SSHRCC). The Major Collaborative Research Initiatives (MCRI) program of SSHRCC supports highly innovative collaborations with a strong emphasis on interdisciplinarity and the creation of new knowledge. Yet, even while operating within the guidelines of this funding program, there were numerous instances in which the funders and the researchers had different perspectives on some of the fundamental aspects of the processes and expected outcomes of both "collaboration" and "interdisciplinarity." There are stories in the CHILD Project that deal with the positive aspects of our relationship with the funding council, and that reflect some of the inherent tensions that came to the surface in the course of the five-year academic and fiduciary relationship. We believe that the lessons learned in this regard can have a positive benefit for funding agencies that issue requests for proposals and that allocate research funds, and also for the researchers who depend on these grants to conduct interdisciplinary and collaborative research.

CHAPTER 2

The Theoretical Framework(s) That Guided the CHILD Project

Hillel Goelman and Martin Guhn

> *When you look at a child, you shouldn't just see that child today. You should see that child seven generations back into the past and seven generations forward into the future.*
>
> Chief Willie Charlie, Chief of the Chehalis Indian Band,
> Member of the CHILD Advisory Committee

Is it possible to describe a single, unitary theoretical framework for a collaborative project with 10 studies from multiple disciplines? The 10 studies in the CHILD Project represent a wide range of epistemologies and methodologies that includes genetic and cellular within-child factors to broad, community-based policies and programs. Some of the studies drew upon quantitative data collection techniques while others collected and analyzed qualitative data. The studies also included a mix of traditional research designs, postmodern perspectives, gender, culture, methodological, and policy lenses. In this chapter, we describe how the CHILD Project as a whole created and drew upon an overarching theoretical framework, which enabled us to incorporate diverse conceptual orientations and different approaches to data collection, analysis, and interpretation.

As a starting point for this discussion, we quote Chief Willie Charlie, who implies a number of the shared underlying principles for the CHILD Project. These principles do not, in and of themselves, constitute a theoretical framework but they do lay the groundwork for such a framework. The first shared principle is that any research or work with children must begin with looking at the child herself—not at her test scores, not at her observed behaviors, not at her medical or health restrictions, but to look at who she is as an autonomous human being. The second principle is that a fuller understanding of this child's life is enhanced by understanding her personal history and the history of her family, clan, people, community, and culture over time. The third principle is that this child's life—and in particular her early formative years— will have far-reaching ripple effects in her lifetime and in the lives of future generations.

The Growth of Interdisciplinary Research on Children

There were a number of major challenges to articulating an overarching theoretical framework for the CHILD Project. One challenge was that traditional studies of early childhood have focused on studying aspects of development that were seen as dichotomous or mutually exclusive; for example, by exclusively studying social or cognitive domains of development. While the medical sciences tended to focus on biological or physical characteristics of the child, psychology emphasized language, cognition or social relations. Further, while some researchers studied child-specific variables in isolation, others focused on the impact of different social environments on children's development. Studies of the influence of social environment could be further divided between those that focused on the specific, immediate environments in which children live and grow up (e.g., families) and those that focused on broader, more general environmental influences (e.g., social class, social policy). Further, as noted above, there are also strong disciplinary differences in focus, methodology, analysis, and interpretation of data, the attribution of causation, and the construction of meaning based on a wide range of different kinds of quantitative and qualitative data. Thus, while different disciplines operated within their respective theoretical frameworks, the co-construction of a meaningful theoretical framework that could not only accommodate but also support a collaborative research effort like the CHILD Project would require substantial theoretical model building.

As Bloch (1992; Bloch et al., 2006) and others have pointed out, until very recently psychology has held a hegemonic control over the discourse, methods, research questions, and knowledge claims in the areas of child development and early childhood education.

Emphases on sampling strategies, instrumentation, and forms of data analysis helped to construct a psychological view of the child to the near exclusion of other disciplinary approaches. Increasingly, however, different disciplinary voices and perspectives are emerging in various research literatures. Super and Harkness (2002) took the lead in articulating the ways in which anthropology could describe and explain differences in developmental patterns across cultures. In their wake came studies of differences of early infant care in Africa, Asia, and Europe (Keller et al., 2005) and cultural variations in neuropsychological development (Braga, 2007). Studies of "universal" behaviors such as infant crying were conducted in a wide range of different countries and cultural settings, exploring parental perceptions of, and responses to, infant crying (e.g., Abdulrazzaq, Kendi, & Nagelkerke, 2009; Alvarez, 2004; St. James-Roberts, 1989; St. James-Roberts et al., 2006).

A number of researchers in the CHILD Project contributed to this growing literature through an invited lecture series later published as an edited volume (Goelman, Marshall, & Ross, 2004). By presenting different lenses on child development, the intent of the lecture series/book was to draw attention to both what was being learned about children through these lenses and what we were learning about the disciplinary lenses themselves. Research on the history of childhood (e.g., Benzaquen, 2004) drew attention to the ways in which the "idea" and the "ideal" of childhood are created and recreated in different historical epochs. Building on this perspective, legal scholars such as McGillvray (2004) have demonstrated that children's legal rights and restrictions—and adult responsibilities to children—have also gone through many iterations based on perceptions of children's needs and the "best interests of the child." Sokoloff (2004) explored representations of children's thought in literature, and Herrington (2004) discussed the history of outdoor play spaces from the perspective of landscape architecture. Hanson (2004) examined constructions of "ability" and "disability" and how definitions of both impacted on children and their families. Scott (2004) considered the ways in which adults framed and conceptualized children's internal spiritual and religious lives, while Mistry and Diaz (2004) studied the various constructions of childhood across different cultural settings. Taken together, these varied research initiatives serve to demonstrate the many different ways in which childhood studies could be conducted from many different disciplinary perspectives. Despite the increase in childhood studies in different disciplines, however, there were still relatively limited attempts to develop theoretical frameworks that could accommodate interdisciplinary or multidisciplinary approaches to the study of early childhood development.

The simplistic dichotomies of the past have begun to give way to research efforts that recognize the interaction of biological, psychological, social, and cultural factors that affect children and their families. For example, the concept of "biological embedding" (as distinct from "biological determinism") from the discipline of population health (Keating & Hertzman, 1999) sought to bridge the "nature versus nurture" debate by emphasizing the importance of the interaction of biological and environmental factors on children's developmental trajectories throughout the life-course (Shonkoff & Phillips, 2000). Similarly, the field of early intervention (Ramey & Ramey, 1997) has developed the concept of "bio-social developmental contextualism" as a way of capturing a child's biological status within the specific social environments in which he or she develops. Advances in neuroscience (Cynader & Frost, 1999) have acknowledged the interaction of neurobiological aspects of the child's development with the environment, demonstrating that environmental factors help to shape the physiological development of the brain by affecting the processes of neural sculpting and pruning. Drawing upon techniques from social geography and population health, researchers (e.g., Kershaw, Irwin, Trafford, & Hertzman, 2005) have begun to study the ecology of child development through community asset mapping that visually displays the social determinants of early development in communities with differing socioeconomic characteristics. These approaches have contributed to an emerging understanding of the interrelationships of individual, familial, community, and policy factors that impact early childhood development.

The interdisciplinary study of the social determinants of child health and development has made great progress in the past 10–15 years by drawing on contributions from pediatrics, epidemiology, rehabilitation science, nursing, developmental psychology, and other health and social sciences. Shonkoff and Phillips (2000) have emphasized the importance of adopting a "neurons to neighborhoods" approach to capturing the complex and nuanced interactions of the biological, psychological, and environmental factors that influence early childhood development. Examples of this work include studies of the relationship between sociodemographic variables and, for example, congenital anomalies (e.g., Cordier, 2004; Vrijheid et al., 2000); cerebral palsy (e.g., Sundrum, Logan, Wallace, & Spencer, 2005; Raina et al., 2005); health care utilization (e.g., Leventhal & Brooks-Gunn, 2000); asthma (e.g., Chen, Fisher, Bacharier, & Strunk, 2003);

cortisol levels of children in child care settings (e.g., Watamura, Donzella, Alwin, & Gunnar, 2003); chronic disease (e.g., Kuh & Ben-Shlomo, 2004); and research on training opportunities within medicine and related health care professions (e.g., Browning & Solomon, 2005; Strelnick et al., 1988). The Canadian Institute for Advanced Research has taken the lead in developing a similar "cell to society" approach to studying the interaction of medical, psychological, social, educational, economic, and community influences on the developmental trajectories of young children (e.g., Heymann, Hertzman, Barer, & Evans, 2006; Keating & Hertzman, 1999). In short, researchers have not shied away from complex, interdisciplinary questions. While these studies all validated the importance of the inclusion of multiple disciplinary perspectives, what remained elusive was the articulation of a theoretical framework that could meaningfully harmonize these diverse disciplinary voices and provide a coherent set of understandings that could both predict and explain the diverse set of research questions, methods, analyses, and results that the CHILD Project would generate.

Bronfenbrenner, Bioecological Theory, and the CHILD Project

The original proposal for the CHILD Project drew from Urie Bronfenbrenner's bioecological theory of human development (1977, 1979, 2005; Bronfenbrenner & Morris, 2006). A number of core tenets from Bronfenbrenner's bioecological theory particularly resonated with the CHILD Project. Bronfenbrenner's bioecological theory emphasizes the importance of *proximal processes* on children's development. Bronfenbrenner considered proximal processes the "engines of children's development" (Bronfenbrenner & Morris, 2006, p. 798), and defined them as "processes of progressively more complex reciprocal interaction between an active, evolving biopsychological organism and the persons, objects, and symbols in its immediate external environment" (p. 797). In line with this emphasis, the CHILD Project focused, in a number of its studies, on examining a variety of proximal processes, such as play and child-parent interactions.

A second emphasis of the bioecological theory is the notion that proximal processes do not occur in isolation, but within specific spatial, relational, emotional, and temporal contexts—and that the developmental significance of any proximal processes may differ from one context to the next, and that the significance of proximal processes can be understood only if they are interpreted jointly with the context characteristics. This notion of interdependence between proximal processes and context factors is reflected in Bronfenbrenner's statement that "in human development, the main effects are likely to be found in the interactions" (Bronfenbrenner & Morris, 2006, p. 802). Accordingly, in order to examine development as a joint function of proximal processes and the characteristics of contextual, personal, and temporal factors, Bronfenbrenner proposed the *person-process-context-time* (PPCT) model as a research design model. This research model captures the importance of jointly studying multiple system variables that are hypothesized to jointly influence children's development. In fact, Bronfenbrenner specifically noted that such a model is necessary to detect synergistic effects of multiple developmentally relevant factors.

What resonated especially powerfully with the researchers in the CHILD Project was the sense that the "scientific power of the process-person-context model lies in its capacity not so much to produce definitive answers as to generate new questions by revealing the inadequacies of existing formulations in accounting for observed complexities" (Bronfenbrenner & Morris, 2006, p. 811). As a collaborative, interdisciplinary research project, the CHILD Project was driven much more by a search for novel and compelling research questions rather than a search for definitive answers. In fact, the CHILD Collaborative subscribed to Bronfenbrenner's impression that (re)search for "definite answers" in the field of child development has repeatedly led to "inadequacies of existing formulations" about developmental questions (p. 119).

Bronfenbrenner described the ways in which proximal processes, personal characteristics, temporal factors, and context factors at different ecological levels might influence children's development. He proposed a series of nested systems, which contextualized the child in different layers of familial, institutional, community, and ideological factors. Within the nested systems, the *microsystem* refers to the environment in which proximal processes exert their effects on children's development; in Bronfenbrenner's words, the microsystem "involves the structures and processes taking place in an immediate setting containing the developing person" (e.g., home, classroom, playground) (2005, p. 80). The 10 studies in the CHILD Project included many different microsystems in children's lives. These comprised (1) the homes of single-mother families living in poverty; (2) child care centers and family child care homes where children received nonparental child care; (3) Indigenous families/homes both on- and off-reserves; (d) hospital-based Neonatal Intensive Care Units (NICU); (4) community-based health and mental health clinics; (5) home-based and center-based early intervention programs; (6) outdoor play spaces; (7) parent drop-in centers; and (8) gatherings of First Nations Elders where traditional stories and ceremonies are described and explained.

Whereas much of the previous research has focused exclusively, or primarily, on specific microsystems in isolation, many of the CHILD Project studies acknowledged the children's participation in multiple microsystems and the relationships among those microsystems. Bronfenbrenner referred to these as *mesosystems*, "which comprise the linkages and processes between two or more settings containing the developing person (e.g., the relations between home and school, school and the workplace, etc.). In other words, a mesosystem is a system of microsystems" (p. 38). One example of this would be that in documenting the developmental trajectories of children born with medically complex profiles, data would be gathered from their experiences in hospitals, family settings, doctors' offices, Aboriginal Head Start Programs, and Infant Development Programs. One of the research questions to be addressed would be to determine the additive and/or multiplicative effects of participation in different microsystem settings—and the outcomes when children and families are faced with restricted options in terms of the kinds and quality of microsystem environments that exist in their communities.

While microsystems and, by definition, mesosystems are immediate environments that frame proximal processes involving children and others in their lives, the next systemic level, the *exosystem*, includes a broader range of settings that do not contain the developing child him/herself.

> The *exosystem* encompasses the linkages and processes taking place between two or more settings, at least one of which does *not* ordinarily contain the developing person, but in which events occur that influence processes within the immediate setting that does contain that person (e.g., for a child, the relation between home and the parent's workplace, for a parent, the relation between the school and the neighborhood peer group). (pp. 38–39, italics in original)

Table 2.1 shows which factors pertaining to the different micro-, meso-, and exosystems were examined in the CHILD studies. For example, the *Aboriginal HIPPPY Documentation Project* focused to a large extent on the proximal process of parent-child interactions

Table 2.1 Interconnected Ecological Systems in the 10 Studies in the CHILD Project

Study in the CHILD Project	Ecological systems		
	Microsystems	*Exosystem*	*Macrosystem*
Cluster 1: Policy Studies in Early Child Development			
The Income Assistance Study	Lone mothers and their preschool children on Income Assistance	Income Assistance policies	The feminization of poverty
The Child Care Policy Study	Survey of characteristics of child care settings	Child care regulations, funding	Women in the paid labor force; government support for nonparental care
Cluster 2: Early Childhood Development in Aboriginal Communities			
The Indigenous CHILD Project	First Nations children, families, communities	Government policy toward First Nations	Historical and cultural oppression of First nations
The Aboriginal HIPPY Documentation Project	First Nations children, families, communities	Government policy toward First Nations; School readiness policies	Historical and cultural oppression of First nations
Cluster 3: Early Identification and Screening Studies			
The Developmental Pathways Study	Infants in NICUs	Medical policy, health priorities	Lowering mortality rates, lowering disability rates
The Infant Neuromotor Study	Children with neuromotor delays/disabilities	Early screening and intervention programs	Early identification leads to early intervention and remediation
The Community-Based Screening Study	Preschool children at home	Capacity building for programs for young children	Population health approach to healthy child development
Cluster 4: Early Childhood Intervention Programs			
The Outdoor Criteria Study.	Children in outdoor play spaces in child care centers	Government regulations on play spaces	Value of play, safety and security, and the fear of litigation
The Parent Counselling Study.	Children perceived as at risk by child welfare authorities	Government policies and regulations on child welfare; effectiveness of training programs	Child safety, family stability
The Safe Spaces Study	Children in child care centers	Effectiveness of training programs	Importance of social, and emotional self-regulation in young children

Note: Bronfenbrenner's "mesosystem" level is not presented in this table because it is comprised of relationships among the various microsystems under study.

around child-centered activities, which were observed in the child's home. The parent-child interactions, however, were embedded in the framework of certain education, health, and family support policies that were made available through a complex combination of federal and provincial government policies, programs, and funding vehicles for Indigenous peoples.

The *Income Assistance Study* gave voice to the stories of single mothers living in poverty to better understand the lived experiences of these women and their children. The stories were shared in the privacy of the women's homes, and the women described their experiences in microsystems in which they and their children participated, such as child care programs, drop-in centers, and food banks. At the same time, it was possible to interpret these women's stories of their vulnerability with regard to the effects of government policies, as the stories illustrated the government's role in monitoring the mothers' compliance with a wide range of restrictions on their ability to work for pay, to volunteer, or even to receive gifts.

The *Safe Spaces Study* sought to enhance children's social skills in general and their ability to empathize particularly in the group child care centers in which the training programs were being offered. The children's play interactions in these centers were the main focus of this study. The training program itself had been created in response to a perceived lack of emphasis on this area of child development in both provincial regulations and in child care training programs. The Safe Spaces program was implemented by a community-based child care resource and referral agency, which was fighting for its financial survival throughout most of the five years of the CHILD Project, due to a series of government cuts.

In sum, all of the 10 studies in the CHILD Project examined a combination of process, person, context, and/or time characteristics to generate new, more refined questions about the multiple factors' joint, synergistic effects on children's development.

There were two major political developments that coincided with the CHILD Project and in some ways created conflict within the team. The CHILD Project itself was funded by the federal government of Canada's *federal* Liberal Party as part of a much larger initiative known as the "National Children's Agenda," which had prioritized policies and programs designed to actively support child development. At the same time, the provincial (state) government of British Columbia (led by the *provincial* Liberal Party—no relationship to the *federal* Liberals) was engaged in major restructuring and cutbacks in all social programs, including those for children and families. Thus, as the academic researchers on the team were enthused about this infusion of federal research funds to support the CHILD Project, many of the community researchers who had just had their provincial budgets slashed were faced with difficult decisions regarding staff layoffs and/or the curtailment of needed services. This development became even more problematic when two of the community partners in the CHILD Project were competing with one another for one specific provincial contract. Thus, it was important for the entire team to remain aware of and sensitive to the various discrepancies and disparities that existed within the project itself due to the nature of federal and provincial political decisions that affected the processes within the different exosystems studied in the CHILD Project.

Bronfenbrenner (1989) asserts that there is one overarching system, which further contextualizes the micro-, meso-, and exosystems: the *macrosystem*. In his original formulation of this idea, Bronfenbrenner wrote:

> The *macrosystem*...is defined as an overarching pattern of ideology and organization of the social institutions common to a particular culture or sub-culture. In other words, the *macrosystem* comprises the pattern of micro-, meso-, and exosystems characteristic of a given society or segment thereof. It may be thought of as a societal blueprint for a particular culture or subculture. (p. 39, italics in original)

These "overarching patterns of ideology" could refer to societal expectations regarding women's participation in the paid labor force outside of the home, the extent to which the society tolerates or encourages income disparities, or the role of the state in providing family support service. As a "blueprint," the macrosystem broadly defines the parameters of what is possible, what is impossible, and what is encouraged through the instruments of the exosystem. These instruments, in turn, frame the possibilities and limitations that either support or impinge upon early child development. Bronfenbrenner's original definition, however, was considered as lacking in detail, and he responded to this criticism by generating a revised definition of the macrosystem:

> The *macrosystem* consists of the overarching pattern of micro-, meso-, and exosystem characteristic of a given culture, sub-culture, or extended social structure, *with particular reference to the developmentally instigative belief systems, resources, hazards, lifestyles, opportunity*

structures, life course options, and patterns of social interchange that are embedded in such overarching systems. (2005, p. 101, italics added)

This (revised) definition of the macrosystem has become particularly helpful for understanding the broader contextualization of the studies in the CHILD Project: As we describe in more detail in Chapter 3, all of the studies were asked at different times over the course to articulate "the developmentally instigative belief systems" that guided their selection of study participants, their choice of methodologies, and their expectations and assumptions around optimal, expected, or anticipated child development outcomes. The purpose of this process as well as other sharing rituals that were used throughout the CHILD Project was to confront our own beliefs about and lenses on critical aspects of early child development, and to reconcile our findings with different theoretical, methodological, and disciplinary lenses.

In later chapters, the insights resulting from this process are illustrated. For example, the Indigenous studies in the CHILD Project compelled the other eight studies to confront questions about "normative" child development and about the frequent mismatch between Indigenous "cultures" and "social structures" and the "culture(s)" or "social structures" of the politically dominant society with regard to understandings and goals for children (see Chapter 5). Similarly, the studies in the CHILD Project, which examined the effects of poverty—and the associated "[lack of] resources, resources, hazards, lifestyles, opportunity structures, life course options" (Bronfenbrenner, 1989)—on children's and families' development, compelled the other studies to consider the pervasive effects of poverty on every aspect of development (see Chapter 4). Finally, the CHILD Project's studies on early identification and screening compelled the other studies to critically examine the ways in which our language and other *patterns of social interchange*—for example, the usages, practices, and connotations of "screening" and "surveillance"—shape our perspectives and discourse on child development, and affect the lived experiences of children and families (see Chapter 6).

In addition to the four interconnected ecological systems, the bioecological theory defines the *chronosystem*. The chronosystem refers to a lifespan perspective on development, stating that developmental effects of proximal processes may critically depend on *when* and *in which order* they happen in a person's life, as well as on when they happen within the historical context. The notion of chronosystem is a helpful way of conceptualizing the impact of events at specific times, for example, in the life of the child (e.g., starting child care), the life of the mother or father (e.g., postdivorce or onset of illness), or the life of the family (e.g., the birth of twins with special needs). On a broader chronosystem canvas, many of the studies explicitly embedded their analyses within the historical context in which their current studies were situated. In the two studies involving Indigenous community partners, for example, the histories as well as the aspirations for the future of their children's development were among the most salient themes (see Chapter 5). In other words, the Indigenous participants' accounts of the importance of embedding theory and practice regarding child development within a temporal horizon echoed the proverbial wisdom, shared with us by Chief Willie Charlie, to "see the child seven generations back into the past and seven generations forward into the future."

The awareness of the previous seven generations called to mind the traditional wisdom, knowledge, and strengths of the Indigenous nations as well as the history of oppression, racism, and colonialism that has inflicted such great damage on present-day Indigenous peoples. The concurrent focus on the next seven generations is an expression of hope and optimism that by recovering their voice and control over their own destiny, these Indigenous nations will develop the means to ensure a more positive future.

Bronfenbrenner and His Discontents

Readers of other books in the *Critical Cultural Studies of Childhood* series likely share a healthy skepticism of the discipline of developmental psychology in general, and potentially of Bronfenbrenner's bioecological theory. In recognition of criticisms by many postmodernist and reconceptualist scholars, we review these criticisms and provide our suggestions for reconciling these differences with the bioecological theory and with the design and implementation of the CHILD Project.

Based on increasing numbers of multidisciplinary and interdisciplinary approaches to the study of child development, a strong consensus emerged beginning in the 1980s that the traditional dominance of developmental psychology in the study of child development tended to overemphasize individual traits and did not sufficiently acknowledge the social and contextual influences on development. Early childhood educator Marianne Bloch, and one of the founders of the reconceptualist approach to early childhood studies, has given voice to these concerns by referring to "the century-long domination of psychological and child development perspectives in the field of early childhood" (1992, p. 3). In response to this, she called for "*alternative* ways of thinking, including other disciplinary knowledge (e.g., anthropology, sociology, history, political economics, philosophy) and methodologies (e.g., qualitative and ethnographic research, action research, teacher narratives, oral history, autobiography, and so on)" (Bloch, 2000, p. 57). From a different disciplinary perspective, psychiatrist Leon Eisenberg (1998) argued against what he saw as traditional dichotomies in psychology: "Nature and nurture stand in reciprocity, not opposition. Offspring inherit their parents' genes, their parents, their peers, and the places they inhabit. Development is at one and the same time a social and a psychological and a biological process" (p. 213). These approaches reflect dissatisfaction with traditional psychological models of research—a dissatisfaction shared by many in the CHILD Project and reflected in the diverse set of research questions and methodologies in the CHILD Project studies.

One of the few reconceptualists or postmodernists to acknowledge and discuss Bronfenbrenner's bioecological theory is Alan Prout, one of the leaders of the "new sociology of childhood" group. He summarized the model in this way:

> Briefly stated, the social-ecological approach makes the assumption that development is a reciprocal process of interaction and accommodation across the life cycle involving the individual in increasingly large contexts. Although depicted as separate circles, users of this approach are urged to think of it as entailing reciprocity and interaction between individuals and their multiple environments. (Prout, 2005, p. 65)

While Prout feels that Bronfenbrenner begins to deal with some of the traditional limitations of psychological research, he questions both the theoretical and empirical usefulness of the model. He feels that the model's systems are more like "containers" that hold the child, and which, in his view, prevent rather than facilitate mutual influences within and across the systemic levels.

> Thus, while bidirectional reciprocity between levels is urged, it is in practice often left unconceptualized and unexamined. When it is done it is often done in such a way that context is reduced to a supposedly objective, static and relatively crude set of indices such as demographic variables (Linney, 2000)..... For these reasons I believe that the ecological approach, although an advance in that it poses some essential questions, does not adequately deal with the question of context. One

might say that it is a good diagram of the problem – but not of the solution. It highlights the need to look at the interactions and mediations between different spheres (which, misleadingly, in my view, it calls "levels") but provides few conceptual tools for doing so. Its focus is not on what connects the different spheres of social life, or indeed, how, if at all, they are constituted as separate but on the spheres ("levels") themselves. This not only renders the spheres rather static but also takes the existence of these spheres as given rather than produced through practice within certain historically circumscribed conditions. (p. 66)

This is an argument probably best left to Bronfenbrenner (to explain what he meant) and to Prout (to explain the limitations that he saw in the model). For the CHILD Project, Prout's views are a useful reminder that Bronfenbrenner's theory has repeatedly been oversimplified by child development researchers in their attempts to operationalize spheres or levels of "context" as influences on children's development. In line with Bronfenbrenner's and Prout's cautionary suggestions, the studies in the CHILD Project accordingly undertook deliberate steps to enhance the clarity and quality of the data collected from the different systemic levels. Our approach thus coincided with both Bronfenbrenner's and Prout's call to look for the "the interactions and mediations" across the systems. As discussed above, we were not interested in categorizing or classifying children, families, or their experiences into different, mutually exclusive containers. Rather, we sought to operationalize the very bidirectional reciprocity that Bronfenbrenner's framework is calling for, and that Prout is also emphasizing. It is also important to point out that Bronfenbrenner did not describe one specific methodology that should be used to conduct research that is grounded in the bioecological theory. Rather, his framework was seen by the CHILD Project as a means of identifying different perspectives on early child development that, taken together, could facilitate the construction of knowledge across disciplines.

Another powerful voice for change in the style and substance of early childhood studies is Glenda Mac Naughton (2006). Mac Naughton has contributed a very useful analysis of how the work of Foucault can inform a new generation of research in this area. Mac Naughton points out the importance and the implications of the language used in research discourses:

[Foucault and others] have argued that language is connected intimately with the politics of knowledge and that those politics are evident in the language we use to think of ourselves (our subjectivities) and to describe our actions and our institutions. Poststructuralists have also challenged the idea that individuals can think and act freely outside of the politics of knowledge...Consequently, identifying the stories of (individuals or societies) that are silenced or marginalized and then sharing them is a political act. (p. 4)

Woven throughout the planning, data collection, and data analysis stages of the CHILD Project was an explicit awareness of what one of our colleagues referred to as "the power of words and the words of power." Accordingly, in our explorations of the lived realities of marginalized families, parents, and children, we listened with the intent to bring out the underlying meaning of the stories that were being told to us in different ways. It also forced the CHILD Project as a whole to interrogate our own language, our terminologies, our turns-of-phrase, our shorthands, and sometimes the sloppiness of our language. This was a challenge precisely because we came from so many different disciplines, each with their own linguistic coding. In one major example—to which we return more than once in this book—the CHILD studies which were screening young children in order to identify children with significant health risks referred to their work by using the term "surveillance," meaning to measure and follow children over time. The researchers in the Indigenous and poverty studies were aghast. For them, the term "surveillance" conjured up images of government control, monitoring, and manipulation; activities that had been extensively used with these populations. Our debate over this issue echoed Mac Naughton's and the poststructuralists' identification of language itself as a source and instrument of power.

Furthermore, a number of Mac Naughton's recommendations for research were organically adopted in the CHILD Project. For example, Mac Naughton encourages researchers to be open to different, alternative minority perspectives on the phenomena and experiences that are the object of study, so that they are in a better position "to develop meanings and actions that are more equitable and just." This is especially true, she says, when dealing with "groups and individuals who experience discrimination and/or marginalization in a specific regime of truth" (p. 47). In the CHILD Project, the inclusion of multiple disciplines and academic and community researchers ensured that a multiplicity of perspectives and interpretations were brought to these studies and to the CHILD Project as a whole. The discourse of the research community who constructed and implemented the CHILD Project was continually focused on alternative perspectives. Each of the research teams were required to articulate what they had learned from, and contributed to, the other nine studies in the CHILD Project. The construction of meaning that was drawn from the data was informed by the diversity of perspectives and underlying principles that sought both *equity* and *justice* in reporting the results.

While these theorists do differ with one another, the CHILD Project draws upon the diverse lessons and insights provided by Bronfenbrenner, Bloch, Prout, and Mac Naughton. A common core of values and perspectives among these individuals can be seen in their emphases on both the content and context of early childhood development, the importance of multiple perspectives and disciplines in conducting childhood studies, and the importance of listening carefully and respectfully to the voices of research participants. The 10 studies in the CHILD Project adopted and implemented these principles into a wide range of different methodologies. The following chapter describes some of the specific ways in which these principles were implemented in the CHILD Project.

CHAPTER 3

From Theory to Practice: Implementing the CHILD Project

Hillel Goelman

> *In this view, ritual is more complex than the mere communication of meanings and values; it is a set of activities that construct particular types of meanings and values in specific ways.*
>
> Bell (1997, p. 82)

The phrase "collaborative interdisciplinary research" is used increasingly in the health and social sciences but there was little to guide us in the process of operationalizing and implementing the coordination of the 10 distinct studies under one organizational framework. While each of the studies was keen to get under way in setting out and implementing its own program of research, it was also important to create the ways in which the 10 studies would communicate with one another. In this chapter we review the different approaches we took to enable each of the 10 studies to both contribute to and learn from the other studies in the CHILD Project. In a Piagetian sense, we were asking each study to begin the process of decentring in order to understand more about the other studies in the CHILD Project. In this chapter we discuss how these rituals evolved in response to various challenges in different phases of the project.

Groark and McCall (1996) and others have suggested some general principles to help overcome the obstacles to interdisciplinary collaboration. They emphasize the importance of positive and respectful attitudes, effective communication strategies, and a shared research focus, which reflects not just the interests of the different disciplines and professions, but a respect for different theoretical and methodological approaches to studying the problem at hand. However, beyond these generalities, the question remained regarding how to implement Bronfenbrenner's bioecological model of human development in the real world of time, space, and money, with researchers from different disciplines and with community leaders in different professions. Breaking down and speaking across disciplinary boundaries is a major undertaking and we explore the important but difficult process of breaking down the "tribes of academe" (Becher, 1989, p. 24) in greater detail in Chapter 8.

This chapter identifies what we would describe as our own critical patterns of communication and how we see them as expressions of ritual in our community of discourse within CHILD. The term "ritual" is often associated with rote and repetitious activities, which may have long lost their original meanings. We prefer to see ritual as a particularly mind*ful* activity. The communication and community-building aspects of the CHILD Project—the rituals we developed—provided all participants with opportunities to articulate, to share, and to question what they were learning in predictable formats and at regular intervals. Some of these opportunities were in large group settings, some in smaller group settings and some in one-on-one settings. Some involved verbal presentations and others were based upon papers that encouraged introspection and reflection. The quotation from Catherine Bell's *Ritual: Perspectives and Dimensions,* with which we opened this chapter, captures this strong sense of ritual as a means of constructing shared meaning and purpose.

Thus, every study conducted their own inquiry according to the *rules* of their discipline as they encountered the *realities* of their own research. Mediating the encounter between the rules and the realities were the *rituals* we developed to frame and facilitate meaningful interactions among all participants. These 3 Rs framed the central empirical question facing the CHILD Project that was what will emerge when researchers from different disciplines are asked (encouraged, pushed, prodded) to answer two important related questions: What can my own study of early child development learn from these other studies? What can my own study contribute to the other studies in the CHILD Project?

A number of management and administrative structures were established from the beginning of the program to help structure and implement the various collaborative rituals that wove the Consortium's work together. First, in addition to the Project Director who was the faculty member serving as Principal Investigator of the CHILD Project, a full-time Project Coordinator was hired whose portfolio included all administrative, financial, and communication responsibilities for the CHILD Project. The Director and the Coordinator, along with a number of graduate research assistants and the postdoctoral fellows from different fields, helped coordinate the integrative activities of "CHILD Central" that came to be described as the "11th of the 10 CHILD studies." The specific roles of the Postdoctoral Fellows in the collaborative rituals is discussed later in this chapter. In addition, two committees were struck to help monitor and guide the Consortium's work. The CHILD Executive Committee was set up, which included a mix of university and community participants whose primary responsibility was to provide policy and planning guidance to the Consortium. The CHILD International Advisory Committee included representatives from the health and social service sectors, policy think tanks, First Nations leaders, directors of social service agencies, and providers of health and medical care. Their role is also described in this chapter.

Over the course of the CHILD Project, a number of rituals of information sharing evolved. In the following, we describe each type of information sharing ritual. To some extent, these information sharing rituals represent forms of communication that are commonplace in any organizational structure (e.g., group meetings, newsletters). At the same time, the interdisciplinary nature of the CHILD Project made it necessary to use communication strategies and media that are typically not part of the communication process among researchers or community professionals.

Opening Rituals: Milestone and CHILD*Talk* Reports

Early in the project, when the CHILD researchers, graduate students, and community professionals were being introduced to one another, each study was asked by the funding agency to write a *Milestone Report* that outlined their expectations. The report was in the form of a grid with the following information required:

1. Timeline;
2. Research activities;
3. Mechanisms to achieve optimal integration of team members, research activities and anticipated research results and mechanisms to achieve cross-fertilization and exchange between units;

4. The stakeholders beyond the immediate range of the project;
5. The dissemination of research results to scholars, stakeholders, and the public
6. Training students and monitoring their research;
7. The management structure: Roles and responsibilities.

These milestone reports served two functions. First, the reports fulfilled one of our formal obligations to the funding agency. Second, and more importantly, the reports provided thumbnail descriptions of the essential ingredients of each study within the CHILD Project. The reports served as an introduction for each study and point of departure for further discussion on the theoretical and professional contexts of each study and how each study related to the aims, goals, and objectives of the CHILD Project as described in Chapter 2. In a sense, the writing and sharing of the milestone reports served as a rite of passage through which the participants gained entry to our community of discourse, from which point on, more meaningful and substantive interactions would take place.

It was clear early on that the skeletal structure of the milestone reports did not fully convey the detail, nuance, and complexity of each of the 10 studies. In response to this need, we introduced a series of CHILD*Talk Papers* as a way of stimulating meaningful dialogue connections among the participants. In the first issue of CHILD*Talk* we introduced the series and the expectations we had for it:

> You are looking at the first issue of what we hope will become a useful and meaningful way of reflecting on and discussing what we are learning through our research. The CHILD Executive Committee and CHILD Central Staff feel that it is important that we have a number of different communication vehicles through which we can communicate not just what we are doing in our respective projects but to also share the learnings, the new questions and emerging insights that we are gaining through our work. We see "CHILD*Talk*" as a series of discussion papers rather than as a newsletter. We will be explaining more in the new year about how we will be inviting (expecting!!) each project to produce their own discussion paper in this series... (CHILD*Talk* Number 1, December, 2003).

That first CHILD*Talk* Paper at the end of Year 1 of the Project presented a series of understandings and learnings about interdisciplinarity and university-community collaboration that emerged in the first year of the CHILD Project. That initial paper also proposed a consistent format for this series that would help each team to communicate the goals, objectives, and methods of their study and to also explain some of the underlying and perhaps implicit aspects of the study. In particular, each paper in the series addressed the following specific issues and questions:

1. What is this study about?
   a. The community agency's perspective;
   b. The researchers' perspectives;
2. How does the study advance CHILD's overall as mandate/vision articulated in the original grant proposal?
3. What is the one key analytic concept that drives the study?
4. What are the important data sources for the study?
5. How might the study findings inform the production of child environment impact statements?

Each issue of CHILD*Talk* was produced as a result of extensive consultation among the faculty, community, and graduate student partners within each study.

Excerpts from the CHILD*Talk* Papers illustrate the range of responses these papers generated. Table 3.1 provides selections from the university perspectives and the community perspectives, roles and responsibilities in all 10 studies. The papers also revealed the different kinds of community partners and agencies that partnered on these research projects. For example, the community partner in *The Community Screening Study* was not a single agency as in the case of Parent Counselling, but a local coalition of early childhood organizations ("Kids First"). Among the goals of the coalition was to implement a screening program and to test out a specific screening instrument. In this case it was the coalition that approached the researchers and invited them to participate in the research and evaluation component of their work. In their CHILD*Talk* paper, the coalition defined their roles and responsibilities in the CHILD Project.

The studies were also asked to explain how they saw their study contributing to the overall mandate and vision of the CHILD Project. *The Parent Counselling Study* described the ways in which their study was consistent with the CHILD Project's theoretical perspective, the emphasis on training graduate students, and the importance of university-community collaboration. *The Outdoor Criteria Study* situated its work within the CHILD Project's ecological framework, which included the possibilities and limitations presented by the actual neighborhood settings in which the studies were conducted,

Table 3.1 Excerpts from CHILD*Talk* Papers

	University Research Perspective	Community Researcher Perspective
Cluster 1: Policy Studies in Early Child Development		
The Income Assistance Study	The study's multiyear timeline allows the research team to examine how lone mothers and their young children negotiate the consequences of these policy changes over time.	For the past seventeen years, SPARC BC has produced periodic reports on the adequacy of income assistance rates in meeting the costs of daily living in BC. The results for this research will greatly aid us in our public policy work.
The Child Care Policy Study	The project aims to investigate the ecology of nonparental child care services across the province of BC. We are examining how policy changes, particularly since 2001, have impacted child care services, families, and children.	As the provincial child care resource center, participation in this project facilitates Westcoast's access to systematically collected data that helps to tell the whole story that comes with implementation of changing child care policies over time.
Cluster 2: Early Childhood Development in Indigenous Communities		
The Indigenous CHILD Project	The overall goal of the project is to explore new approaches for gathering information and designing assessment strategies that ensure the cultural and community relevance, or ecocultural validity, of procedures used for determining service needs and impacts in early childhood learning and development.	The Indigenous CHILD project offers the opportunity to identify dimensions of child development and indicators of well-being that are important to Aboriginal parents and ECD practitioners and that could be used to inform the development or adaptation of tools for (1) assessing Aboriginal children's development; and (2) impacts of Aboriginal ECD programs.
The Aboriginal HIPPY Documentation Project	The project focuses on the process of doing research within Aboriginal communities and the development of researcher-community relationships. It focuses on the process of introducing, implementing, and maintaining a program for families of preschoolers in Aboriginal communities.	We hope that the research will inform us about what in the Program is working, what isn't, and what needs to be changed in both the HIPPY curriculum and methodology to better meet the needs of Aboriginal families.

Continued

Table 3.1 Continued

	University Research Perspective	Community Researcher Perspective
Cluster 3: Early Identification and Screening Studies		
The Developmental Pathways Study	To study the longitudinal development of children recruited from the Special Care Nursery of British Columbia's Children's Hospital and for all provincial recruits who are either extremely low-birth weight, extremely low-gestational age, severe retinopathy of prematurity requiring treatment, have suffered an intraventricular hemorrhage or periventricular leukomalacia, neonatal stroke, or born with a congenital diaphragmatic hernia.	The objectives of these studies are to define the incidence of various aspects of developmental delay in various groups of at-risk neonates. The results of this study will help us target and triage at-risk newborns referred to the Infant Development Program by classifying the degree of risk.
The Infant Neuromotor Study	This research has two main purposes: 1) to examine whether or not early screening for at-risk and healthy infants for motor development has positive outcomes for infants and their families by age 3 years, and 2) to compare two methods of training child professionals to use the Harris Infant Neuromotor Test (HINT) and the Alberta Infant Motor Screen (AIMS).	The organization's strategic goals aim for community partnerships and for high-quality services that are guided by research. We value the role we are able to play with the CHILD Project and with the Early Identification project specifically. Our Center is committed to pursuing opportunities to collaborate in research activities, which may have an impact on the services we provide.
The Community-Based Screening Study	The purpose of this five-year project is to determine the effectiveness of a universal, community-based, developmental screening system at the child, family, and community levels. The project consists of four separate but related components or phases. Different samples and sampling strategies will be used for each part of the study, although children and families may participate in more than one part of the study	This project will help CHILD, the Chilliwack community, and the broader community to understand the effectiveness of screening young children with the Nipissing District Developmental Screen. Will increase Public Health and MCFI Screening Task Group's knowledge of the impact that screening has had for the children, families, care-givers, and professionals in our community.

Continued

Table 3.1 Continued

	University Research Perspective	Community Researcher Perspective

Cluster 4: Early Childhood Intervention Programs

The Outdoor Criteria Study	The goal of this project is to assess the different types of physical outdoor design in licensed child care centers for young children in Vancouver. In this study we ask what types of outdoor play spaces currently exist at child care centers in Vancouver, and what are the benefits and setbacks of these designed environments in regard to children's development?	The majority of the early childhood educators and directors from 12 participating child care centers envision this study as an opportunity to contribute their knowledge to further the understanding of the importance of the outdoor environment in child care and child development. Their aim is to affect change to current policy design guidelines and improve the conditions of play spaces for young children.
The Parent Counselling Study	This study, therefore, follows parents and explores their perceptions as they progress through an intensive, multicomponent intervention, and for two years postentry. It is anticipated that compilation and analysis of parent perceptions over time will have relevance for future program delivery.	A database of program demographics and outcomes over the past three years has been developed, and a draft analysis of this data has been produced. Results from initial focus groups have been reported to staff at meetings. The change in program delivery will also provide an opportunity to monitor impact on families.
The Safe Spaces Study	The overall objective of the study is to examine both the short-term and long-term effectiveness of the Safe Spaces program in promoting young children's social and emotional competence. This study is the first attempt to examine empirically the impact of this multifaceted universal primary preventive program designed to promote social-emotional competence and reduce aggression/antisocial behaviors (e.g., bullying) among preschool-aged children.	Westcoast Child Care Resource Centre provides experienced early childhood educators with fifteen hours of specialized training to support their implementation of the Safe Spaces approach in their child care settings. The objective of Safe Spaces is to teach young children the key social/emotional vocabulary and skills that have been identified as essential for preventing bullying behavior.

with their respective building and safety codes—and the impacts of these possibilities and limitations on child development.

It is fair to say that all of the CHILD*Talk* papers struggled with the section in which they were asked to describe "one key analytical concept" that guided their work. The struggle involved both identifying the analytical concepts in the study and then nominating one of those as "the key" analytical concept. The intention of the request was to try and compel the partners (primarily the academic partners) to focus and limit their response. This section presented each of the studies with the challenge of reflecting on and articulating some of their foundational assumptions and motivations to be involved in this research project. *The Outdoor Criteria Study*, for example, discussed their key analytic concepts in this way:

> CHILD's mandate includes the study of the "physical, intellectual, social and emotional development of the child." During each observation session and review of videotapes, we are looking for examples of the relationship between these aspects of development and the child's physical environment. We observe how certain features of the designed play space facilitate different realms of the child's development. We are working to help translate these observations into the City's design guidelines and we advocate for designing play spaces that provide a range of developmental opportunities.... In the second phase of our study we plan to investigate the differences between child care play spaces at different geographic locations. We also plan to map the urban fabric surrounding the project child care sites to show availability of child accessible green spaces and street character. (Outdoor Criteria Study, CHILD*Talk* Paper, May 19, 2004)

In contrast, *The Community Screening Study* articulated a very different key analytic concept in their CHILD*Talk* paper, which drew upon a model of community capacity building rather than notions of individual interventions.

> This project is based on the conceptual framework of Health Determinants developed by Stoddard and Evans (1994). This model describes the interrelationships of physical and social environment with genetics, biology and disease in ultimately affecting use of medical care and population health, function and well-being. In our analytic model, we are targeting aspects of the interrelationships between disease and biology with health and medical care in determining the

health and functional outcomes in infants born prematurely or with other serious health risks.

The key aspects of this project are its descriptive design and the utilization of longitudinal data to assess temporal trends in outcomes. We seek to describe the associations between biological risk factors including birth weight, gender and gestational age with disease incidence and health outcomes that include visual impairment and brain injury. In looking longitudinally at health care utilization at 4 years of age, we seek to understand the associations between known risk factors and health outcomes with utilization of physician and hospital services. (Community Developmental Screening Study, CHILD*Talk* Paper, May 19, 2004)

The CHILD*Talk* papers also provided a summary of the specific methodological approaches that each of the studies had adopted, and excerpts from these sections are presented in table 3.2.

Regularly Scheduled Rituals

If the Milestone Reports and the CHILD*Talk* Papers served as the point of departure for more detailed and substantive conversations, the *CHILD Learning Forums* (CLFs) were the primary vehicles for those conversations. The CHILD Learning Forums were quarterly gatherings that all community, academic, and graduate student participants were expected to attend and contribute to. In the first two years of the Consortium, each team was responsible for providing a detailed presentation on the aims, goals, objectives, methods, and early findings of their study. They were asked to focus on two key questions in their presentations: What they felt that their study could contribute to the other studies in the CHILD Project, and how they felt that their study benefitted from the other studies in the CHILD Project. The CLFs were major and highly anticipated gatherings. These forums provided opportunities for clarification around theory and methodology and also opportunities to explore the policy and programmatic implications of the data. As discussed in greater detail in Chapters 8 and 9, the CLFs also generated disagreements over language, conceptual frameworks, and societal priorities over universal versus targeted programs for children and families. After the first two years, the CLFs shifted from project-by-project updates to a more thematic focus.

One CLF each year was held as the *Annual Retreat*, a two-day gathering of all participants. The retreats were opportunities to step back and gain perspective on the developments both in the Consortium

Table 3.2 Summary of Research Methods in the 10 Studies in the CHILD Project

The Ten Studies	Research Methods
The Income Assistance Study To assess the impact of changes in income assistance policy on lone-parent families with young children.	Qualitative analyses of multiple interviews and focus groups with lone mothers on Income Assistance with preschool children. Also, documentary and econometric analyses of Income Assistance policies.
The Child Care Policy Study To investigate the impact of child care policy changes on communities, child care facilities, families, and children.	Analyses of government policies and programs on child care use patterns and the accessibility, affordability, and quality of child care services.
The Indigenous CHILD Project To obtain the perspectives of Aboriginal communities on child development and measurement.	Interviews and focus groups with Aboriginal parents, child care professionals, elders in on-reserve Aboriginal communities. Evaluation, critique, and possible adaptation of standardized child development assessment measures.
The Aboriginal HIPPY Documentation Project To explore the 'Home Instruction for Parents of Preschool Youngsters' program as implemented in Aboriginal communities.	Interviews and focus groups with Aboriginal parents, child care professionals, elders in on-reserve Aboriginal communities on the impact of the HIPPY program in their communities. The administration of child development outcome measures to assess children's school readiness upon completion of the program.
The Developmental Pathways Study To follow the long-term development of highly at-risk infants.	Analyses of child development status of survivors of neonatal intensive care units using standardized child development outcome measures at 6, 12, 24, 36, 48, 60 months.
The Infant Neuromotor Screening Study To explore the effectiveness of two types of training models for the early identification of children with neuromotor delays.	Screening infants, toddlers, and preschoolers for neuromotor delays/disorders using two different screening measures at 6, 12, 24, 36, 48, 60 months. Also, an evaluation of two methods of training staff to administer these measures.
The Community-Based Developmental Screening Study To determine the effectiveness of a universal, community-based, developmental screening program.	Administration and analyses of a battery of child development screening measures for all children in one municipality at ages 6, 12, 24, 36, 48, and 60 months.
The Outdoor Criteria Study To analyze how outdoor play spaces are utilized by children, and to investigate any differences that emerge.	Observations and analyses of children's play in a range of outdoor play spaces. Interviews and questionnaires in with key informants including child care staff, municipal social planning departments.
The Parent Counselling Study To assess the impact of counselling on parents whose children are at risk for apprehension by child protection authorities	Interviews and focus groups with parents participating in a mandatory parent counselling program to prevent child abuse/neglect.
The Safe Spaces Study To examine the short- and long-term effectiveness of a preschool antibullying program.	Observing and evaluating children's levels of social and emotional development before, during, and after completing the Safe Spaces training program.

as a whole and within the 10 individual studies. The extended time frame and the use of both formal and informal discussions enabled the participants to update one another on developments within their respective studies and to review the progress on the objectives of the CHILD Project. It also served as a useful opportunity for all partners in the studies (academics, community researchers, and graduate students) to explore issues that were of primary importance to these respective constituencies.

There were other forms of information sharing and documentation, which were held throughout the five-year CHILD Project. As part of their budget submission for each subsequent year, all studies were required to submit *Annual Summaries of Activities* that reviewed their progress and challenges during the previous twelve months. A regularly updated *Data Inventory* was created that reported on methodological aspects of each study's data collection, including such information as sample size and characteristics, research instruments, standardized child development outcome measures, qualitative data collection and analysis, and software programs.

Rituals of Writing and Reflection: Cluster Reports and the Midterm Report

During the first two years of the CHILD Project, the 10 studies were busy conducting their respective research, and although the milestone reports, CLFs and CHILD*Talk* papers provided useful information to the other studies, meaningful collaboration was relatively underdeveloped. It is fair to say that initially the individual studies were concerned primarily with the disciplinary rigor of their individual studies. Since they were focused on issues around sampling, instrumentation, training graduate students, and data collection the collaboration component was typically assigned a lower priority. In Year 3 we began to push the envelope, to encourage more active forms of interdisciplinary collaboration across the 10 studies. To encourage more active reflection on the interdisciplinary nature of the CHILD Project and possible avenues for further integration across the studies, we decided to commission four graduate students in the CHILD Project to conduct a self-study of the CHILD Project itself. The academics, community partners, and graduate students of the CHILD Project now became the subjects of study. The Cluster Reports were designed to elicit the perceptions, hopes, and fears of the researchers and to suggest specific ways of stepping up to a higher level of collaboration. Graduate students from a wide range of disciplines conducted the interviews and wrote the Cluster Reports, which were discussed at the Annual Retreat.

The broad consensus in the Cluster Reports was that in the first two years of the CHILD Project, the CLFs, retreats, and CHILD*Talk* papers provided some useful but very basic information on the 10 studies. The priority within each study was, understandably, its own program of research, and relatively little effort was put into planning collaborative work with the other studies. The Cluster Reports helped each study and each cluster to focus specifically on what each study could contribute to or learn from the other studies and on the administrative and disciplinary obstacles to collaboration. The administrative and logistical obstacles included limited time to pursue collaborative efforts and geographic distances between potential collaborators. Time was also a factor in that some of the studies were forced to adapt their original research plan after their original CLF and CHILD*Talk* paper. These changes were made necessary for a variety of reasons: including changes in provincial policies and programs; the inability to use certain methods or government data bases; and shifting priorities within the research team. Thus, by the time some of the studies caught up with each other, the original methodology and design may have changed. While issues around the implementation of complex research designs are common in most programs of research, these issues were multiplied exponentially in the CHILD Project due to the implementation of 10 distinct programs of research with the added expectation that they consciously collaborate across disciplinary boundaries.

With further discussion, however, the interviewees began to see possibilities of using the same, similar, or complementary research instruments that were used in other studies in their cluster. Perhaps the most powerful set of understandings that emerged went beyond the sharing of methods and data and focused upon the identification of cross-cutting themes that were emerging within each of the studies and across the designated clusters. For example, most of the studies encountered issues around "culture" in their work, both in terms of specific ethnic or immigration issues but also broader concepts dealing with "health cultures" and "organizational cultures." Similarly, issues of targeted and universal programs provided both contrast and similarity when examined within the clusters. Some studies intentionally addressed issues that impact on entire populations while others focused exclusively on specific groups that were marginalized by income, disability, or ethnicity. Across disciplines, professions, and studies, issues of language emerged as salient and provocative. Language that was seen as descriptive and neutral in one setting was viewed as offensive and derogatory in another. For the CHILD Project it was, therefore, important to jointly confront these issues and to search for language that would bridge research inquiry instead of blocking it.

The process of interviewing ourselves, reading draft reports, responding, and often critiquing the reports resulted in a number of new collaborative initiatives. Within the screening cluster a decision was made to write a collaborative paper that would describe the ways in which different approaches to screening and early identification could complement one another within a spectrum of early childhood services. With the leadership of one of the postdoctoral fellows *The Safe Spaces Study* and *The Outdoor Criteria Study* decided to adapt the observation schemes used in *The Safe Spaces Study* and to apply them to children's interactions in *The Outdoor Criteria Study*. An interdisciplinary research seminar for graduate students was planned and implemented. The research seminars provided an opportunity for the graduate students and research fellows to discuss results, research methods, and analyses across different disciplines.

One retreat focused on discussions of the Cluster Reports (see below), which reviewed the state of collaboration within each of the thematic areas, and others included presentations by the Project Director and others regarding specific strategies for collaborative data collection and analysis.

The writing of the Cluster Reports occurred during Year 3 of the CHILD Project, and marked a critical tipping point with regard to collaboration in the CHILD Project. Shortly thereafter three postdoctoral fellows with backgrounds in community psychology and developmental psychology were hired for the CHILD Project. These individuals were hired specifically to assist in the collaborative, interdisciplinary research of the CHILD Project by facilitating communication and planning across the 10 studies. By joining CHILD Central they added fresh eyes to the CHILD Project and were successful in implementing new strategies for collaboration and in encouraging the 10 studies to "think outside the box" regarding their programs of research. The fellows also took the lead in writing collaborative papers and submitting proposals to academic and professional conferences in both disciplinary and interdisciplinary settings.

One of the postdoctoral fellows conducted a process evaluation of the collaborative relationships between the academic and community partners (see Chapter 9). The principal investigator and community partners from eight of the 10 studies were interviewed and discussed the importance of training and educational supports, required resources, organizational support requirements, communication strategies, interpersonal factors, and decision-making strategies from the perspective of both community and academic research partners. Also, the benefits, barriers, facilitators, and recommendations for collaboration within their individual studies at their respective institutions and across the CHILD Project were explored in detail. The results of this evaluation were presented at an annual retreat and provided opportunities for further detailed discussion on the facilitators and barriers to collaboration between academics and community service providers.

Midway through the five-year project, the federal funding agency conducted its required midterm review that focused on the extent to which the Project had achieved its goals. In preparation for the review, the CHILD Project as a whole and the individual studies provided updates on the ways in which the CHILD Project was meeting its commitments from the original grant proposal and the overall objectives of the MCRI program. The result of working together on the CHILD*Talk* papers, the CLFs, the Annual Retreats, and the Data Inventories from the first half of the CHILD Project provided the vehicle to both report our progress and to describe the substantive accomplishments to date. The concluding paragraph of the midterm review summarized our current status at the time and our plans for the future:

> The success of the CHILD Project to date is not attributable only to the talents and knowledge brought to the Project by the academic, community and graduate student partners who are conducting these exciting programs of research. It is successful because these individuals share both a vision of what collaborative interdisciplinary work can be, and a commitment to work hard with others to operationalize their visions. The partners in CHILD have demonstrated this commitment, both with their work and with their patience. It is much more difficult to co-construct a model of research than it is to fit into a pre-existing template. We state with confidence that in the remaining 2 ½ years, the individual CHILD studies will reach their individual milestones and the collaborative process that we have put into place will result in the new and innovative understandings of early child development that can only be obtained through this kind of very difficult and very rewarding work.

The Review Committee met with all CHILD researchers over a three-day period, eliciting rich conversation. Of particular interest to the Review Committee were the ways in which such diverse disciplinary and community partners found common cause and vision in their collective work.

As indicated above, in each year of the CHILD Project there were two-day Annual Retreats for all CHILD participants. The retreat was to assess the current progress of the CHILD Project, to identify areas of opportunity and concern, and to strategize ways of further strengthening and expanding the collaborative nature of the CHILD Project. While the early retreats in Year 1 were, however, designed to introduce the 10 studies to all members of the CHILD Project, all subsequent retreats were used as opportunities to review the collaborative process to date and to suggest new avenues of collaboration. In the second half of the CHILD Project, the Annual Retreats were usually held in conjunction with meetings of the CHILD International Advisory Committee. The Advisory Committee members helped in a number of critical ways. They helped to place our findings in the research literatures with which they were familiar; they helped to contextualize our work with current policy developments in Canada and internationally; they encouraged the research teams to speak to the implications and potential applications of their results; and they assisted in identifying common or complementary themes across the 10 studies.

It was actually at one of the CHILD retreats where we encountered an individual whom we subsequently invited to join the Advisory Committee. It is now current practice in British Columbia to acknowledge the First Nations people of the province and specifically the nation on whose grounds our meetings are held. As part of this acknowledgment, an Elder comes to the gathering, welcomes the guests, shares historical anecdotes of the place, and offers a blessing. At this particular retreat, the Elder was highly interested in the topic of our discussions, and in his opening remarks, he gave us an overview of how children were perceived and treated in his Nation. It was part in this speech that we heard Chief Willie Charlie give over the teaching with which we opened Chapter 2: "When you look at a child, you shouldn't just see that child today. You should see that child seven generations back into the past and seven generations forward into the future." These simple but powerful words struck a deep chord in everyone who was present and set the tone for our discussions.

The meeting with Willie Charlie was serendipitous. As one of our postdoctoral fellows later pointed out, however, there was more to the meeting than serendipity. Willie Charlie spoke to us at a time when the members of the research consortium were perhaps more receptive to his words than they might have been earlier in the process. After all, Willie Charlie shared a narrative that represented a powerful and elegant illustration of the "chronosystem" and of its significance for conceptualizing human development (see Chapter 2). Willie Charlie's story illustrated how developmental progress is captured not just in terms of individuals, families, and communities, but how it is also contextualized within specific historical periods. He did this in convincing language to which everyone could easily relate—and in a way that seemed, at that moment, more accessible than Bronfenbrenner's description of the chronosystem. What it made us realize is that the way in which, and the moments at which, stories (and theories) are told, matters a great deal. In academia, we do not necessarily have the opportunity to regularly create these "teachable moments" and to tell stories that capture the essence of a worldview or philosophy on child development.

In the following days as we discussed the effect of Willie Charlie's words on us, we came to a strong consensus that the Project needed to have precisely this historical, ethical, and cultural perspective informing the work of the CHILD Project and Chief Willie Charley agreed to serve as a member of our Advisory Committee.

The Closing Ritual

One of the key goals from the very beginning of the planning of the CHILD Project was a final, closing conference in which the results would be presented to key professional, academic, and government stakeholders in early child development in British Columbia. The province had provided a dynamic and meaningful context for our work and we felt obligated to give back to the province what we saw as the implications and applications of our work. We also saw the conference as a crucial opportunity for the stakeholders to pose questions, to challenge our interpretations and our data, and to try and create what might be an ongoing forum for discussion between academics, community professionals, politicians, and government officials. The title of the conference was "*Opportunities and Challenges in Translating Early Child Development Research into Policy and Practice: The CHILD Project 2003–2007.*" The invitation was issued in the name of the university and community research partners of the CHILD Project and read in part:

> Since 2003, the CHILD Project has conducted extensive research on different aspects of early child development in British Columbia and

we see this upcoming "working" conference as an opportunity for the researchers to give something back to the province. Your presence will help us to interpret and understand the research findings and provide an opportunity to explore how this research might contribute to the work you and your colleagues do.

The conference will include two keynote presentations, but the major activity of the conference will be conducted in a series of small, roundtable discussions. These roundtables will include academic researchers and community partners from a wide range of professional and disciplinary backgrounds involved with CHILD and representatives of provincial ministries, school districts and community representatives.

The goal of this gathering is to share our respective perspectives in order to enrich our understanding of early child development in BC and to help inform a public policy agenda regarding programs that will help children thrive. This event is inspired by the words of developmental pediatrician, Dr. Jack Shonkoff (author of *Neurons to Neighborhoods*) who wrote that the purpose of research is to *generate new social strategies and build broad-based public will that transcends political partisanship and recognizes the unique and complementary responsibilities of family, community, school, workplace, and government to promote the healthy development of all children.* (Shonkoff, 2000)

Over 150 participants were invited to the conference, including elected officials, government bureaucrats, academics, community professionals, and children's advocates. This gathering allowed the CHILD Project to present not just the outcomes of our research studies but to also present and model the rules of our respective disciplines, the rituals that enabled us to come together to construct new understandings of early child development, and the energy that is created when the rules and the rituals are summoned to confront the pressing realities of the day.

Summary

In the Preface to this volume we pointed out that there was no manual, handbook, map, or substantive guide to the journey we were undertaking. Along the way, we developed a variety of planning and communication tools to facilitate collaboration and cooperation across disciplinary boundaries, professions, and 10 different studies. The strategies we developed grew out of equal parts of intuition, prior experience, and a large measure of commitment to an evolving shared vision of what was possible and what was desirable. All relationships depend upon commitment and communication, and this particular complex set of relationships was challenging. The ritual that evolved out of the CHILD Project as the most effective tool to elevate the level of interdisciplinarity and collaboration was the ritual of asking the questions "What can we learn from this?" and "What can we contribute to this?" This ritual put the CHILD Project members into the roles of both teacher and learner, of an expert and a novice, of a speaker and a listener. This ritual supported our ability to critically examine paradigms that were established in one discipline, but that were unknown in another. The ritual helped to open up new questions, since the methods and perspectives of one field were applied to another. Finally, the ritual helped to gain new insights, because the synthesis of knowledges, perspectives, and experiences combined into understandings that were more than the sum of individual parts.

This chapter brings to a close the first section of this book, where we introduced the background and operating principles, which guided the program's inception and progress over time. In the next section, we present select findings from the CHILD Project, not in a study-by-study analysis, but by considering the integrative themes, which emerged from our collaborations. The coming chapters thus illustrate in what ways we were able to learn from one another, contribute to one another, and gain from the collective knowledge and wisdom that was being cocreated by the CHILD Project.

CHAPTER 4

What We Learned about Poverty and Vulnerability

Mary Russell

Both *The Income Assistance Study* (IA) and *The Parent Counselling Study* (PC) were concerned with lone-parent families and their preschool-age children and both used interviews with the children's mothers over the five years of the Project to collect their data. There were similarities and differences between the two studies that allowed for the strengthening of certain common research findings and the complementarity and extension of other findings. Both programs of research involved multiple case studies of lone-parent mothers on income assistance with preschool children, both used an ecological orientation to their work and both used the family as the unit of analysis. There were also differences in the aims and key analytic concepts of the two studies as shown in the excerpts from their respective CHILD*Talk* papers (table 4.1). *The Income Assistance Study* started out with the goal of studying child poverty while in *The Parent Counselling Study* the attention to mothers in income assistance emerged from the interviews themselves. The *Income Assistance Study* was based on a gendered perspective that considered the mothers' poverty within the multiple layers of community, economics, and social policy. *The Parent Counselling Study* began as an evaluation of an intervention program for targeted families. These were families that had come to the attention of child protection authorities who were concerned for the health, safety, and welfare of the children. The intervention was designed to provide the parents with support, guidance, and strategies to enhance their parenting and to change family

Table 4.1 Excerpts from the CHILD*Talk* Papers for *The Income Assistance* and *The Parent Counselling Studies*

Aims of The Income Assistance Study	Aims of The Parent Counselling Study
The primary objective of the study is to advance our understanding of the environment in which families with young children live when they receive Income Assistance. Findings will supplement and contextualize existing quantitative and qualitative data about this foundational thread in BC's social safety net by documenting how changes to income assistance since 2001 affect the daily lives of lone-mother families with preschool children. For some families, recent policy changes may reduce benefits, restrict eligibility, enforce paid work obligations and/or cut child care subsidies. The study's multiyear timeline allows the research team to examine how lone mothers and their young children negotiate the consequences of these policy changes over time.	This study explores high risk parents' perspectives over time of benefits and limitations of intensive interventions aimed at improving and supporting their parenting. While ecodevelopmental interventions that provide multicomponent services had been considered to be particularly beneficial for high risk families (Thomlison, 2003; Wolfe, 2004) little exploration of parents' experiences with such interventions, and even less follow-up of parents, has taken place despite acknowledged importance of prospective longitudinal child maltreatment research (Widom, Raphael, & DuMont, 2004). This study, therefore, follows parents and explores their perceptions as they progress through an intensive, multicomponent intervention, and for two years post entry. It is anticipated that compilation and analysis of parent perceptions over time will have relevance for future program delivery.
Key Analytic Concept	**Key Analytic Concept**
A key analytic concept governing our research is the feminization of poverty, and how the ideology of the neoliberal bureaucratic structure shapes the identity of lone mothers and their families, and the strategies that they use to remain resilient. The research seeks to understand how the policies governing Income Assistance "pathologize" Income Assistance recipients and the impact that this has on their lived experience. By interpreting their lived experiences we expect to challenge the discourse around poverty in a way that could lead to reframing policies.	Bronfenbrenner's (1979) ecological model has provided a key conceptual framework for this study. Building on this model and its recent adaptations (e.g., Cash & Wilke, 2003), preliminary results have identified four intervention environments and social forms of help/support/training that parents indicated made a difference to their parenting skills, and child and family functioning.

dynamics. A significant number of these parents were on income assistance.

In this chapter we consider the ways in which the studies parallel and complement one another. While poverty was a main focus of these two studies, all 10 of the studies in the CHILD Project encountered poor families and poor children in their research. As noted in

Chapters 5 and 6, the notion of developmental surveillance, which was a cornerstone of the screening and early identification studies—the monitoring of child growth and development—were highly problematic issues in the assessment of children who were poor, of First Nations descent, or who were marginalized from the mainstream in other ways. We also see how poverty impacted on the study of child care in the province, the development of outdoor play spaces, and the provision of nurturant environments for children and families. Each of the studies within the CHILD Project contributed to and learned from these explorations of the lived experience of poverty on children and families.

Poverty and Child Development

Poverty has devastating effects on child development in that poor parents face immense challenges in providing adequately for their children. The concept of "capability deprivation" (Sen, 2000), which suggests that social exclusion deprives individuals of the opportunity to undertake important activities, applies to poor parents who have less time, resources, and energy. These parents have been found to be less "responsive" to the needs of their children as they struggle to meet the basic material needs, and cope with increased stressors in an environment of decreased social support (Evans, Boxhill, & Pinkava, 2008). Sen further indicates that poverty results not only in material deprivation but also in relational deprivation that consists of individuals feeling unworthy and not entitled to make claims upon society due to prevailing negative social attitudes. Frequently these attitudes are reinforced by helping professionals, who struggle with their own limited capacities and resources in assisting families suffering from multiple stressors and deprivations. Children being raised in poor families are, therefore, more likely to grow up in environments of multiple stressors; to have less material resources, including books and computers (Evans, 2004); to suffer from social condemnation, particularly if the parents are dependent upon Income Assistance; and to come to the attention of child protection agencies.

A considerable number of studies have demonstrated an association between poverty and negative influences on child development. Several comprehensive reviews of this literature (Bradley & Corwin, 2002; Brooks-Gunn & Duncan, 1997; Evans, 2004) indicate that children raised in poverty are prone to have low birth weight, diminished cognitive development, and higher likelihood of both physical and mental health problems. These disadvantages frequently are cumulative and interrelated (Caragata, 2009; Evans, 2004), and child development is most adversely affected when families in poverty suffer from cumulative and prolonged adverse social and physical environmental conditions. Many of these conditions result from social policies that fail to provide adequate protection or support for poor families. Lone-mother families, particularly those in receipt of Income Assistance (IA), experience the multiple disadvantages associated with lone parenting and insufficient income. Lone mothers on income assistance have been described as the "poorest of the poor" as they strive, sometimes against seemingly insurmountable odds, to care adequately for their children.

This chapter describes the experiences of mothers on Income Assistance in British Columbia. While the main focus of the chapter is on lone mothers who had come to the attention of child protection agencies and been referred to a parenting program (i.e., *The Parent Counselling Study*), there were a number of parallels with *The Income Assistance Study* and these will be noted as well. The main focus of *The Parent Counselling Study* was the perceived effectiveness of a parenting program for mothers, but as the mothers were interviewed, it became apparent that a constant theme was the effect of poverty on their parenting experiences, and these results are provided here. To provide a background for these studies, we begin with a review of what is known about poverty and child development, poverty and child protection, and about lone-mother families in the Canadian context.

Previous Research on Poverty and Child Development

The negative effects of poverty on child development have been demonstrated across a wide range of developmental outcomes. These effects are most pronounced when poverty is prolonged, severe, and when children experience it in early childhood. Reviews of developmental studies have indicated that negative effects of poverty are marked in children's cognitive abilities and school achievement, with grade repetition and school drop-out significantly higher in children of low-income families. Health outcomes associated with poverty include prematurity, low birth weight, higher rates of infant mortality, growth stunting, higher rates of illness and injuries, and negative emotional and behavioral outcomes, including psychiatric disturbances and maladaptive social functioning (Brooks & Gunn, 1997; Bradley & Corwin, 2002; Evans, 2004). Evans (2004) further argues that the environment of poverty provides poor children with a daunting array of suboptimal psychosocial and physical conditions including poor air and water quality, exposure to toxins and noise pollution. Substandard housing quality further increases exposure to rodents, inadequate heating, overcrowding, and generally unsafe conditions.

The exposure to multiple risks increases the likelihood of adverse physical, socioemotional, and cognitive outcomes (Evans, 2004). This cumulative environmental exposure to risk is particularly high for lone parents subsisting on minimal state financial support, or Income Assistance, as it is known in British Columbia.

Lone-Parent Families

Lone-parent families are the fastest increasing family constellation in Canada, the United States, and most of the Western countries, with lone-mother families, especially unmarried lone-mother families, constituting the vast majority of these families (Bradshaw & Harland, 2006; Statistics Canada, 2007). Disadvantages accrue to all lone-parent families and these are magnified in lone-mother families. These mothers face physical and temporal burdens of being solely responsible for their children, while also being expected to provide adequate care for their children with limited resources (Hardley & Crowe, 1991). In addition, prevailing neoliberal social attitudes regard lone mothers as a growing social problem, a drain on the economy, and poor role models for their children (Baker & Tippin, 1999). Lone mothers are at risk of being considered inadequate parents (Roseneil & Mann, 1996), "bad mothers" (Swift, 1995), or "feckless" and willfully responsible for the poverty in which they are raising their children (Phoenix, 1996). While social attitudes are becoming somewhat more accepting, lone-mother families have nevertheless been considered to constitute an "underclass" prone to violent crime and unemployment (Roseneil & Mann, 1996). Not all lone-mother families suffer from this same constellation of negative conditions and attitudes. In cases where lone mothers were able to find gainful employment with a sufficient income, they had no difficulty in describing themselves and their families as successful (Morrison, 1995). Sadly, it is the poor lone mothers who, by virtue of their need to seek government financial assistance (i.e., Income Assistance), also face a heightened risk of coming to the attention of child protection authorities.

Poverty and Child Protection

Poverty is the common thread that unites the majority of families involved with child protection services (Pelton, 1989). Living in poverty results in a substantial increase in the likelihood that parents will have their parenting subject to scrutiny by child protection services. Pelton (1989) indicates that 90 percent of reported incidents of child abuse or neglect involved families living below the mean income level. Brooks-Gunn (1997) reported that families living in poverty are seven times more likely to be subject to child protection investigations than affluent families. Lone mothers, who are most likely to be the poorest of the poor, are overrepresented in child protection investigations (DiLauro, 2004). Studies in the United States have indicated that the main predictor of out-of-home placement following a child protection investigation is parental poverty, and the second highest related factor is lone motherhood (Kamerman & Kahn, 1990). In addition, poverty is frequently accompanied by substance misuse and domestic violence. As these conditions become chronic and result in a downward spiraling of family functioning, child protection services increasingly rely on out-of-home placement as a solution. While most of these studies reflect the United States context, the situation is very similar in Canada.

Canadian Context

Canada is one of the wealthiest nations in the word (according to its GDP), yet more than 15 percent of children, that is one out of every six, live in poverty. In a recent UNICEF (2007) study ranking child well-being in wealthy countries, Canada ranked only 12th out of 24 countries listed. The Canadian child poverty rate reaches a high of 18.8 percent in British Columbia. Lone-mother families have a much higher rate of poverty (43.4 percent) compared with two parent families (12.5 percent). Lone mothers with children living on Income Assistance in British Columbia find that only about 60 percent of their basic living expenses are covered by the benefits they receive (First Call, 2009). Income Assistance rates thus ensure that children living with poor lone mothers will have an increased risk of malnutrition and an increased likelihood of living in substandard housing. Adequate housing is particularly difficult for lone-mother families to obtain, as such housing is increasingly unaffordable with two-thirds of low-income families in Canada spending more than 30 percent of their income on housing, and British Columbia having some of the highest housing costs in the country.

In short, lone-mother families in British Columbia, particularly those on Income Assistance, face inordinate difficulties in providing adequate care to optimize developmental outcomes for their children. The stress associated with trying to cope with inadequate income, as well as battling against negative social attitudes, present immense barriers to providing optimal levels of care for their children. In addition, when child protection agencies raise concerns about the level of parenting in lone-parent families, these mothers face the added stigma of being labeled as inadequate mothers.

The present results of *The Parent Counselling Study* are part of a larger study of parents who had been identified "at risk" by child protection authorities for child neglect or abuse, and referred to a parenting program (Gockel, Russell, & Harris, 2008; Russell, Harris, & Gockel, 2007, 2008). The aim of this larger study was to determine, from the parents' perspective, the elements of social interventions that were most useful. In the process of doing so, however, the parents described their parenting experiences in the context of poverty, and the present discussion is limited to those findings. This analysis sought to give voice to the subsample of 25 lone mothers regarding their experiences of parenting in poverty. As in *The Income Assistance Study*, this discussion aims to make visible the experiences of poor mothers who, although objects of public debate, remain largely invisible as contributors to, and participants in, society at-large (Pulkingham, Fuller, & Kershaw, 2010). All mothers were residents of the Lower Mainland region of British Columbia (Vancouver and surrounding communities) and had been referred to a parenting program because of child protection concerns. The mothers could be considered to be parenting "under duress" (Greaves et al., 2002) in that all were poor, 17 were known to misuse substances, and 16 reported having previously experienced domestic violence. The mothers ranged in age from 16 to 40 and were primarily Caucasian, with six identifying as Indigenous, three as African, and two as Asian. The level of education ranged from less than high school to some postsecondary courses. All mothers were current or former recipients of Income Assistance. Open-ended interviews were held at either the program site or at the mothers' homes at 3-month intervals over an 18 month period. All interviews were recorded, transcribed, and analyzed using grounded theory methodology (Strauss & Corbin, 1990).

As the mothers told their stories, it was evident that parenting in the context of poverty and dealing with unresponsive bureaucracies had significant impacts in terms of their capacity to meet their children's needs, their views of themselves as adequate parents, and their hopes and aspirations for the future.

The mothers in the study described their day-to-day functioning as a "constant (economic) struggle," "trying to make ends meet," and their efforts to meet their basic needs as the "hardest part" of their daily existence. Their economic situation was summed up as "money just goes—you don't get a lot of it," and typical coping strategies, such as buying on credit or leaving bills unpaid, served to exacerbate their already precarious situations when heating or electricity was cut off or their credit rating was ruined. Mothers described their daily existence as a "fight," dealing with bureaucracies that were unresponsive, making it difficult, if not impossible, to care adequately for their families. These findings echo those of Edin and Lein (1997) and are also found in an Income Assistance study report by Gurstein and Goldberg (2008) who describe the "precarious" situation of poor, struggling lone mothers. Somewhat less precarious was the financial situation of mothers who had been able to secure subsidized housing, which was similar to that reported in Gurstein and Goldberg (2008). While subsidized housing reduced financial stress, there were other stressors noted. For example, Lillian[1] described the overcrowding in her two-bedroom apartment where she lives with two growing adolescent boys. She reported that she found herself sleeping on the couch in a living room cum kitchen amidst a pile of cardboard boxes storing the family's belongings. Also, Miranda spoke of the noise and illegal behaviors of her neighbors and her fears that these would negatively influence her young and impressionable daughter. Similarly, in *The Income Assistance Study*, mothers described neighbors' behaviors as problematic. Nevertheless, as Gurstein and Goldberg (2008) conclude, the financial security provided by social housing more likely helped mothers to move forward in their lives toward meeting educational and/or employment goals.

In contrast, the 12 mothers who found it necessary to rent on the commercial market expressed considerable concern about housing costs and reported that they found it necessary to utilize their food allowance to cover housing costs and to obtain food from food banks and community kitchens. The lack of sufficient units of subsidized housing in part reflects the federal government's abandonment of its role in social housing and the subsequent off-loading of this responsibility to the provincial governments, with resultant curtailment of this provision (Cohen & Pulkingham, 2009). For the mothers, the result of this sense of financial marginality or precariousness, together with the effort of obtaining necessary resources to meet daily needs, left mothers exhausted, often demoralized, and aware that they were not attending sufficiently to their children—leaving them to question their mothering capacity.

Mothers indicated that financial hardship affected their perception of their mothering competence. Debra, a highly self-reflective mother, indicated how her children's deprivation contributed to her sense of inadequacy: "I got caught up in thinking that if I can't bring the income in, then I am not really a great [mother]."

Mothers' self-worth was further compromised by self-blame that was commonly reported as mothers accepted personal responsibility for mismanagement of funds or inability to budget, despite having inadequate funds to cover basic costs in the first place. Mothers described themselves as "really bad with money," or being "no good with finances." They described how they unsuccessfully tried to "make funds stretch" or be "smart about your money." In either case, when they ran out of funds before the end of the month, mothers concluded that they were incompetent or incapable of caring for their families. As Edith stated, "I put myself in this position...I made my bed and now I must lie in it. I made the mistakes and now have to suffer the consequences."

Self-blame and acceptance of personal deficiencies in family provisioning and financial management, rather than indignation about insufficient income assistance, were the common experience reported, thus providing further evidence of the internalization of poor self-worth or "relational deficiency" as described by Sen (2000). Given prevailing social attitudes regarding welfare recipients, in addition to the negative connotation of inadequate parenting resulting from child protection interventions, it is not surprising that the mothers internalized these messages and began to question their own self-worth.

Mothers also described how poverty frequently led to social isolation and depression. Mothers linked poverty to their depression with statements such as "finances, finances, we are having problems...and my mood is up and down" and "I have more than [mental health] problems...like housing and finances." Mothers thus confirmed previous findings that depression is a common adjunct to parenting in poverty (Magnuson & Duncan, 2002; Spencer & Baldwin, 2005). Social isolation was frequently associated with poverty and depression. Mothers spoke about being housebound with small children with "no place to go and no one to talk to." Funds for public transport limited access to community programs that could benefit their children. Mildred provided a typical statement relating social isolation, poverty, and depression: "I started to get really depressed at home, not being able to go anywhere...I am stretched (financially) and a lot of things are tough to do."

Several mothers described how they had investigated community programs for their children, but could not pay the nominal fees involved, contributing to their own depression, and sometimes that of their children. Other mothers indicated the lack of a telephone, either because of lack of funds or previous unpaid bills, exacerbated their social isolation from friends and relatives, increasing their already depressed affect. Mothers recognized that their social isolation interfered with their ability to provide adequate mothering, sometimes causing unpredictable mood swings, or "mean" behavior toward their children. In short, mothers recognized that, in part, their depression was linked to their limited financial circumstances and that being depressed was problematic in terms of providing adequate care for their children.

Substance misuse was a frequent concomitant of depression and the 17 mothers in *The Parent Counselling Study* who had misused substances typically linked their behavior to depression. Betty stated: "I suffer from severe depression. Heroin was my best friend—my anti-depressant, my sleeping aid. And now I have to live without it." Mothers described how substances were used to assuage depression or dull the pain of living in impoverished conditions. This substance misuse frequently led to intervention by child protection services, while the sometimes resultant child apprehensions served to exacerbate existing depression. Motivation to overcome depression, abstain from substance abuse, and demonstrate adequate mothering capacity in order to regain custody of their children was sufficient in some, but not in all instances.

Amelioration of this negative self-image was an aim of the parenting program staff, and mothers indicated how the positive attitudes of the parenting program staff served to counter the double negative messages associated with receiving Income Assistance and the involvement of child protective services. Shelley, who had a series of negative encounters with state representatives both in relation to her income and her child care, described her initial apprehension, and subsequent relief, in the face of positive staff attitudes upon entering the parenting program:

> When you walk in you are thinking what are [staff] going to look at me like? Are they going to look at me like I am this big bad bitch that's beaten my kid...you have no self-esteem, no self-confidence you think you are the rottenest parent...but they [staff] have no accusing fingers...they give you confidence.

Similarly Karen stated: "[Staff] give you the confidence to know that what you are doing is O.K., ...they give people hope."

In a parallel fashion, mothers in *The Income Assistance Study* described how their involvement in volunteer activities was partly aimed at resisting the erosion of self-respect that dominant welfare discourses called forth (Fuller, Kershaw, & Pulkingham, 2008). Mothers, through their own actions or through their interactions with helpers with positive attitudes, are engaged in actively resisting negative social stereotypes and in reconstituting their self-worth as individuals and as parents in a more positive fashion. In a separate analysis of the Indigenous mothers' interviews in *The Parent Counselling Study* (Harris, Russell, & Gockel, 2007), the Indigenous mothers described the importance of fostering their children's cultural identities as well as involving themselves in Indigenous ceremonies. These were noted as ways of increasing self-respect. Gertie spoke of "teaching [my daughter] to be proud of who she is," and several mothers described how Indigenous emphasis on spirituality and ceremony was assisting with their own "healing journey."

Mothers described their aspirations and their hopes that life would be better for their children, and spoke somewhat haltingly of what they needed to do to realize these aspirations and hopes. They spoke of their aspirations to become "a better person" and a "good role model" for their children, one who could "lead by example." They indicated that they wanted their children "to know that there is a better way of life" and "not to choose the same path as I did." This accords with McKendrick's (1998) observations that lone mothers are highly motivated to improve their quality of life through self-improvement, but feel constrained by lack of opportunities. Economic deprivation and a lack of child care were reported as primary barriers. In describing the means to reach the goal of an improved quality of life, mothers described both furthering educational efforts and acquiring experience through their volunteer labor. Sheryl spoke of "trying to figure out how to get to the next level education-wise" to improve her chances of employment. Mildred described a need to focus on self-improvement. In the past she had "constantly put all my efforts into [my child]...I must put myself first because if I don't, I won't be helping him in the long run." Similar to *The Income Assistance Study* (Fuller, Kershaw, & Pulkingham, 2008), the mothers described their volunteer efforts as providing them with additional skills and experience that could potentially make them more attractive on the labor market.

In listening to the mothers' voices it became clear that inadequate family income was perceived to be a primary factor in diminishing their parenting capacity. The struggle to meet the family's basic needs was exhausting and frequently demoralizing. While internalizing aspects of the social stereotype of the inadequate "welfare mother," the mothers nevertheless sought out experiences that countered these messages as means of maintaining a sense of hope for the future. Despite the incredible difficulties the mothers faced in raising their children in poverty, they largely accepted these as challenges to be overcome in pursuing ways to improve the situation for themselves and their children.

Lone mothers receiving Income Assistance, suffering from material deprivation, beleaguered by negative social stereotypes, as well as a sense of overwhelming individual responsibility for their families were readily able to identify their requirements for successful parenting. While they had accepted and internalized the socially prevalent sense of private responsibility for child-rearing, they nevertheless evidenced high motivation to pursue self and family improvement. Unfortunately, these ambitious goals may be difficult to realize given the difficulties of integrating the responsibilities of breadwinning and caring for children. In British Columbia lone mothers have been particularly targeted by Income Assistance regulations that reject care for preschool-aged children as a legitimate alternative to full-time employment. This contrasts with historical evidence that raising children at home was recognized as an important civic contribution for which lone mothers were perceived to be worthy of support (Chun & Gavigan, 2004). It contrasts with European social policies that accept a joint responsibility between the state and parents in securing the best conditions for child rearing—recognizing that children are social capital and that the development of active citizenship helps to secure the future for all. Gornick and Meyers (2003) describe how society generally benefits from the labor of parents, particularly mothers, through child care that enriches present society and provides economic benefit for the next generation. Women providing care pay the costs for the care of children in terms of time, energy, and foregone market wages while the rest of society benefits but does not necessarily share in this cost. As Land (2001) has suggested, there is a need for the work of caring for children (and others) to be transformed from being a private virtue to a public concern. European nations, particularly the Nordic nations, have evidenced their commitment to a shared state-family responsibility for rearing children for decades. In the UNICEF (2007) rankings of child well-being, Northern European countries claimed the top four places, with child poverty levels below 10 percent. Furthermore, there was no obvious relationship between levels of child well-being and GDP per capita, or between the proportion of children being raised by lone parents and child poverty, but higher government spending on family and social benefits was associated with lower child poverty rates. Variations in government policy appeared to account for most of the variation in child poverty levels. It is time for Canadian family policies to be developed that incorporate this shared vision for promoting the well-being of all children, regardless of family structure.

The material deprivation identified by mothers in the present study exists to a much diminished level in European countries that have instituted programs such as mother benefits, guaranteed minimum child support, and housing and transportation subsidies. Universal benefits, rather than targeted benefits, have been found to be most effective in reducing child poverty in European countries. Such benefits have included both direct economic payment and material aid. Direct financial benefits that are provided to European families, and recommended for inclusion in Canadian family policies, include child and/or mother allowances (Polakow, 1993), and guaranteed minimum child support benefits (McLanahan & Sandefur, 1994). While the Canadian Child Tax Credit provides some necessary financial relief to impoverished lone-mother families, the income-testing basis of such a benefit takes away from the message of universal support for the cost and work of raising children. Kamerman and Kahn (1998) conclude that family allowances are an effective income redistribution mechanism, and the absence of child poverty observed in some European countries is attributable to these and other child-related income transfers.

Canadian laws regarding payment of child support have been of questionable benefit to low-income families. Recommendations have been made that governments be responsible for collecting child support obligations and guarantee a minimum child support benefit (McLanahan & Sandefur, 1994). Guaranteed advance of child support or child maintenance is found in a number of European countries (e.g., Denmark, Sweden, Austria, Germany, and France) with the objective of assuring more adequate provision of child support (Kamerman & Kahn, 1989). Similar measures need to be instituted in Canada. Parents in numerous European countries benefit from public policies that distribute the cost of caring for children across society and require employees to accommodate to a parent's caring responsibilities. Gornick and Myers (2003) report that in Finland and Denmark all children have a right to care regardless of their parents' employment status. In 1992, a European Union recommendation adopted by all member states endorsed universal policies of reliable child care with a pedagogical focus and professional training. Kamerman and Kahn (1988) reported that child care services that are near to the home, reasonably priced, and of decent quality were the single most important service for lone parents and the highest priority on their "wish lists." Gornick and Myers (2003) state that American (and it could be added, Canadian) parents need and want more support from government in terms of child-rearing costs and responsibilities.

Gornick and Myers (2003) report that the European experience suggests that policies that support both earning and caring can provide an important first tier of support that actually reduces the need for targeted, welfare-based assistance. Lone mothers need to be brought into the mainstream of labor market policies with more resources attached to meeting their needs (Lewis, 2001). These resources include educational opportunities for mothers with low education to complete educational requirements that will make them competitive in the labor market. A variety of labor market policies, such as maternal leave and flexible working hours, have been advocated for those lone mothers already employed (Kamerman & Kahn, 1988). However, as with the mothers in this study, more assistance, such as the "activation policies" described by Rowlingson and McKay (2001) and including upgrading of lone mothers' education, is required. In general, the success of the Swedish system that fosters employment of lone mothers through a number of aforementioned family supports as well as flexible labor policies deserves further consideration in the Canadian context.

Poverty presents multiple barriers for lone mothers receiving Income Assistance attempting to provide the best possible care for their children. Increased likelihood of involvement with child protection authorities leave them vulnerable to state intervention in most every aspect of their lives, which may lead to feelings of inadequacy and low self-worth. Nevertheless, they seek out social interactions that help counter such negative social messages and that assist in keeping alive their hopes for a better future for their children. Policies and practices of state interventions, particularly the current neoliberal orientation of Canadian policies, engender and reinforce prevailing negative social attitudes toward poor lone mothers. Alleviation of poverty and development of more women-centered social policies as per Northern European countries, or through more radical change to the definition of financial dependence as outlined by Gurstein and Vilches (2009), would go far to improve the future well-being and development of poor Canadian children.

Note

1. All names in this chapter are pseudonyms.

CHAPTER 5

Lessons from Community-University Partnerships with First Nations

Jessica Ball and Lucy Le Mare[1]

"You'll never believe what happened".... is always a good way to start.

The Indigenous Child Project (ICP) and the *Aboriginal HIPPY Documentation Project (AHDP)* were 2 of 10 component studies in the Child Health, Intervention, Learning, and Development (CHILD) Project, funded by the Social Sciences and Humanities Research Council of Canada.[2] Jessica Ball, the university-based principal investigator for the ICP, partnered with two on-reserve First Nations communities and two urban Aboriginal community groups to deliver the project. Lucy Le Mare, the university-based principal investigator for AHDP, partnered with Aboriginal HIPPY Canada (the national office of an early education program) and five on-reserve First Nations communities to conduct the AHDP. Both studies ran from 2003 to 2007 and involved multiple Indigenous community partners with an interest in promoting children's development.

These two studies illustrate several key principles and considerations to support knowledge sharing and cultural safety (elaborated subsequently) in research and in early childhood screening, assessment, and learning programs involving Indigenous and non-Indigenous people working together on behalf of young children. The embedding of the ICP and AHDP studies within the larger collaborative CHILD Project created challenges as well as opportunities since within the CHILD project network, recognition of ethical principles and practices in research involving Indigenous partners and participants varied considerably. In both projects, the research questions and goals that framed the research at the point of applying for funding and initiating partnerships changed significantly during the first two years of the five-year studies. These shifts occurred as goals that were most pressing for the Indigenous partners became better known and as we came to terms with the need for slow and careful collaborative processes involved in laying the foundation for meaningful partnership research necessitated shifts in priorities from large, tangible outputs—such as a new developmental monitoring tool that had been envisioned for the ICP and a program impact evaluation that had been envisioned for the AHDP—to positively transformative processes. Nevertheless, testimonials from community partners demonstrate that the ICP and AHDP studies produced substantive knowledge and strengthened capacities to engage in collaborative research through community-university partnerships. At this time in the history of relations between Indigenous and non-Indigenous people in Canada, we believe, the studies yield timely insights into the sensitivities surrounding screening, assessment, and early education processes, the notion of surveillance, and the diversity of Indigenous communities' views on monitoring and supporting Indigenous children's development.

Prepare for the Unexpected Because "You'll Never Believe What Happened..."

Against the background of a paucity of research and (written) theory on Indigenous children's development, we ventured as non-Indigenous investigators into the "space between" dominant, university-based expectations and goals for research on child development and less well understood, community-based expectations and goals for the purposes, pace, process, and products of research on child development. The concept of "ethical space," originated by Roger Poole (1972) and elaborated by Cree scholar Willie Ermine (1995), captures the interpersonal, intellectual, and spiritual space within which emissaries from distal cultural origins meet. Knowledge creation transpires in this space, where no one has jurisdiction, where respect is the currency, and where reciprocal and mutual learning is possible. Given that we were traveling in uncharted territory, it is perhaps unsurprising that each study took a somewhat different route than originally planned, a development to which we allude in the chapter title, borrowed from Cree storyteller, academic, politician, and broadcaster, Thomas King (2005).

Briefly, the AHDP sought to evaluate the impact of a parent-involving early education program on Indigenous children's "school readiness," defined as the language, motor, social, and academic skills that (non-Indigenous) teachers typically expect five-year-olds to have when entering kindergarten. The AHDP's focus shifted to seeking community members' views of early childhood education and development (ECE/D) programs generally and of the Home Instruction for Parents of Preschool Youngsters (HIPPY) program in particular. The ICP sought to generate culturally based knowledge and goals for children's development and to identify environmental conditions that promote or detract from optimal developmental outcomes. The ICP came to focus on a topic of pressing concern to the partnering communities: how to improve the developmental monitoring, screening, and assessment practices of early childhood educators and allied professionals.

In this chapter, we seek to contribute to the nascent and growing movement in Canada to understand and support Indigenous communities' efforts to support the optimal health and development of children. We also suggest ways to promote collaboration in research and practice among parents, ECE/D practitioners, and allied professionals to meet children's needs. As such, we situate this chapter within the broader social agenda of restorative justice and self-determination of Indigenous Peoples in Canada, following centuries of colonial government interventions (Royal Commission on Aboriginal Peoples, 1996) and knowledge-harvesting by university-based researchers (Smith, 2002).

The chapter begins with a brief overview of the historical context and current situation of Indigenous children in Canada. We then describe the ICP and AHDP and summarize two findings that were common to both studies. Next, we discuss five interrelated themes that emerged from both studies: (1) the importance of attending to the temporal context, or "chronosystem" (Bronfenbrenner, 1979) in which Indigenous child care, education, and development play out; (2) the sociohistorical significance of "surveillance"; (3) relationship-building; (4) the primacy of interpersonal processes and the need for "cultural safety" (Papps & Ramsden, 1996) in the choice of screening, assessment, and education technologies; and (5) the challenges of integrating Indigenous Peoples' concerns about control, access, ownership, and possession of Indigenous knowledge (Snarch, 2004) or Indigenous self-determination (RCAP, 1996) into a larger research culture that is uninformed of or relatively insensitive to such concerns. As such, this chapter responds to the increasingly vocal calls of

Indigenous scholars for explicit recognition of Indigenous histories, cultures, goals, needs, and approaches to knowledge creation and knowledge sharing.

The Historical Context of Indigenous Childhood

Indigenous Peoples in Canada have withstood numerous assaults to their populations, social structures, and cultures, including a history of assimilationist education and child welfare policies that has undermined Indigenous parenting, family life, and the transmission of culture (Royal Commission on Aboriginal Peoples, 1996). Beginning in the latter half of the nineteenth century and lasting for over 100 years, Indigenous children were forcibly educated through government-sponsored, church-run residential schools designed to break the bonds between Indigenous children and their families and to assimilate children into European-heritage culture and the Christian faith (Royal Commission on Aboriginal Peoples, 1996; Trocme, Knoke, & Blackstock, 2004). By 1930, these institutions housed approximately 75 percent of all First Nations children between the ages of 7 and 15 years (Fournier & Crey, 1997) and a significant proportion of Métis and Inuit children (RCAP, 1996). Children were forbidden to speak their own languages or maintain their spiritual and cultural traditions. Distances between schools and the children's home communities prevented contact with parents and other family members. In residence, siblings were separated, abuse was common, and many children succumbed to disease. In these institutions children were traumatized and rarely encountered healthy parental role models. Consequently, as adults, many had diminished capacity to care for their own children (Bennett & Blackstock, 2002; Smolewski & Wesley-Esquimaux, 2003).

As residential schools closed in the second half of the twentieth century, the government instituted a new approach to the assimilation of Indigenous children, commonly referred to as the "Sixties Scoop." Child welfare workers were encouraged to apprehend Indigenous children and place them in the care of non-Indigenous families (Fournier & Crey, 1997; Miller, 1996), often out of province and sometimes out of country (Trocme, Knoke, & Blackstock, 2004). Between 1960 and 1990, over 11,000 children of Indian status were adopted outside their communities (Department of Indian Affairs, quoted by the Royal Commission on Aboriginal Peoples, 1996), a statistic that does not include children whose Indian status was not recorded or Indigenous children who remained in the child welfare system, but were not legally adopted.

The Current Situation for Indigenous Children in Canada

As a legacy of such colonial government interventions, Indigenous children are now among the most marginalized children in Canada (UNICEF, 2010). Despite some advances, Indigenous children are at least two or three times worse off than other Canadian children on almost any index of health and well-being. One in four Indigenous children lives in poverty, compared to one in nine Canadian children (UNICEF, 2010). The province of British Columbia, where the studies took place, has the highest child poverty rate in the country and census figures show that here Indigenous children have a poverty rate that is almost double that of non-Indigenous children, a rate that would be even higher if children living on reserves were included in the statistics (Kemp, 2008). In their early years, Indigenous children are less likely than non-Indigenous children to see a physician or other health care provider. Indigenous children remain significantly overrepresented in the child welfare system, comprising approximately 40 percent nationally—and up to 80 percent in some provinces—of children living in out-of-home care (Trocme, Knoke, & Blackstock, 2004). The educational attainment of Indigenous children is lower than that of non-Indigenous children across elementary and high schools (e.g., Morin, 2004), especially for Indigenous children in out-of-home care, whose educational attainment is less than that of Indigenous children who remain in their homes and of non-Indigenous children in their homes or in out-of-home care (Joint Special Report by the Representative for Children and Youth and the Office of the Provincial Health Officer, 2007). As teens, Indigenous youth are more likely than non-Indigenous youth to leave school before graduation, and, especially in those communities in which cultural continuity has been most disrupted, they are much more likely to commit suicide (Chandler & Lalonde, 1998).

Notwithstanding this grim picture, Indigenous Peoples regard children as cherished gifts from the Creator whose well-being is key to the social, cultural, and economic future of their communities (Greenwood, 2006). At all levels and sectors of Indigenous governance, Indigenous communities are making concerted efforts to restore, revitalize, and recreate family and community supports for children's development (Anderson & Ball, in press; Castellano, 2002). It is within this context that the ICP and AHDP studies unfolded.

Overview of the Aboriginal HIPPY Documentation Project and Indigenous Child Project

AHDP

As previously noted, the AHDP examined the views of First Nations parents, Elders, ECE/D educators, and paraprofessional educators on ECE/D programs for young Indigenous children in general, and on the HIPPY program that was implemented in the five participating on-reserve communities in particular. Often, ECE/D programs for Indigenous children do not meaningfully incorporate the cultural heritage and worldviews of Indigenous people. While perspectives on this situation range from highly critical (e.g., Kirkness, 1998) to cautiously supportive (e.g., Charters-Voght, 1999; Goulet et al., 2001), scholars and community leaders generally agree on the importance of parental and community control over educational programming for young children and the inclusion of Indigenous cultural content and heritage language learning (Beatch & Le Mare, 2007).

The HIPPY program, a 30-week, home-based, early intervention program, was developed in Israel in the late 1960s to improve the school readiness of low-income, immigrant preschoolers and to support parents as their children's first and most important teachers. In HIPPY, currently delivered in more than a dozen countries internationally (HIPPY International, n.d.), community-based, paraprofessional Home Visitors train and support parents to strengthen their children's linguistic, cognitive, and social skills. Home Visitors meet with enrolled families to introduce the curriculum and model the lessons, which parents then conduct with their children. Home Visitors also run group meetings for all the families they work with, providing further support and additional activities. A program coordinator supports the Home Visitors and oversees the program (for a detailed description of HIPPY, see Lombard, 1981 and Westheimer, 2003). Over the course of the AHDP, Indigenous Home Visitors' views of the HIPPY program and of their roles within it transformed as they strengthened their own Indigenous identities, leading them to seek out and infuse the program with Indigenous content and processes (Beatch & Le Mare, 2007).

As part of the AHDP, we also sought the views of community members and public school teachers on how young Indigenous children from urban reserves fare in off-reserve public elementary schools. Indigenous leaders and agencies have argued that Indigenous children's lower educational attainment stems from the lack of culturally appropriate services for very young children and the failure of schools to be welcoming places for Indigenous children and families (Assembly of First Nations, 1988). Accordingly, we were particularly interested in participants' perceptions of how early education and parent involvement might affect children's transitions to public school and the relationships between public schools and the on-reserve communities they serve.

Through the AHDP, we conducted 37 individual interviews with Indigenous participants (15 parents, 3 Elders, 4 ECE/D educators, 2 Band Education Coordinators, 8 HIPPY Home Visitors, and 5 Aboriginal support workers employed by public schools) and 9 individual interviews with non-Indigenous participants (5 public school kindergarten teachers, 1 public school grade-one teacher, and 3 Band employees, including a preschool teacher, social worker, and child care director). In addition, we hosted two focus groups, one with Indigenous HIPPY Home Visitors and the second with Indigenous early childhood educators in one on-reserve community. Using a version of grounded theory (Strauss & Corbin, 1990), interview responses clustered around three key themes, including (1) community members' views on, and aspirations for, ECE/D programs in their communities; (2) community members' and Home Visitors' views of the Aboriginal HIPPY program; and (3) community members' and public school teachers' views of the relationship between on-reserve communities and off-reserve public elementary schools.

ICP

The ICP examined the views of First Nations parents, Elders, and ECE/D practitioners regarding the developmental monitoring, screening, and assessment of young Indigenous children. Many Indigenous parents and ECE/D practitioners reportedly believe that formal tools and approaches to screening and assessment are culturally inappropriate or unhelpful for Indigenous children and families (Royal Commission on Aboriginal Peoples, 1996). Many find the very concept of testing, scoring, or comparing the developmental levels of children offensive (Stairs & Bernhard, 2002). Some perceive assessment to conflict with cultural values and practices that welcome the "gifts" of each child or that affirm the wisdom of waiting until children are older before making categorical attributions about them. In addition, Indigenous leaders and agencies across Canada have argued that culturally inappropriate assessment and intervention practices and lack of services often have serious negative consequences for Indigenous children (Assembly of First Nations, 1988; B.C. Aboriginal Network for Disabilities Society, 1996; Canadian Centre for Justice, 2001). These consequences include over- and underrecognition of children with developmental challenges; interpretations that focus on the individual child rather than the role of the environment; services that are introduced too late or that are directed at a misinterpretation of the primary problem; undermining of Indigenous language and cultural goals through the overvaluation of the dominant, European-heritage culture and language (English); and high rates of placement in non-Indigenous foster care.

Through the ICP, 42 community-based ECE/D practitioners contributed to group forums and questionnaires and 47 parents and 16 Elders participated in individual interviews. The study sought community members' views on early childhood development, ECE/D programs, typical and atypical development, and developmental monitoring, screening, and assessment, including what approaches had been used recently in early child care programs, which approaches were considered useful, and what could be done to improve associated tools and practices. A grounded theory approach to data analysis was conducted by an Indigenous project team, including a team leader and locally chosen members of each of the four partnering communities. Initial findings were presented to groups within each community and final interpretations and recommendations for practice were formulated, based on community members' feedback.

Broad Perspectives on ECE/D Practice

In this section, we highlight two general findings, common to both the ICP and AHDP studies that convey essential components of the community contexts in which our studies took place. These two findings set the stage for the presentation of five key, cross-cutting themes in the next section of the chapter. (For detailed findings specific to ICP, see Ball, 2004; 2005; Ball & Janyst, 2007; for AHDP, see Beatch & Le Mare, 2007; Le Mare, 2005.)

Endorsement of ECE/D Supports

As previously noted, Indigenous communities are revitalizing supports for parenting and children's development after centuries of disruptive and destructive colonial government interventions (Smolewski & Wesley-Esquimaux, 2003). Many community leaders and program staff are eager to introduce workshops, programs, media, and intervention services to promote the well-being of children, youth, families, and the community as a whole.

In the ICP, parents and practitioners confirmed a desire for ECE/D programs that engage families and that impart cultural knowledge and skills, and for early intervention services for children when necessary. However, based on their previous experiences, participants felt that formal monitoring, screening, or assessment might not be congruent with their priorities for family development and parent support. They also expressed concern that an externally designed, formalized observation and evaluation system could undermine ECE/D programs' capacity to promote knowledge of Indigenous language, spirituality, arts, and skills for living on the land, as well as traditional ways of teaching and learning, for example, through listening, quiet observation, and meaningful participation in family and community activities.

In the AHDP, participants and communities affirmed the need to invest in ECE/D programs that support young children's learning and development. Many participants saw education as key to alleviating poverty and other social issues in their communities. At the same time, community members saw a strong Indigenous identity as the foundation for children's healthy development and school success and ECE/D programs as important settings to create that foundation. Participants hoped that ECE/D programs, while promoting school readiness skills, could focus at least as strongly on local Indigenous culture, including language, spirituality, art, and subsistence practices. Parents expressed appreciation for resources provided by ECE/D programs, such as opportunities to interact with other parents, to engage in adult cultural activities, and access information that supports children's healthy development.

Parents as Children's "Most Valuable Player"

In concert with strengthening community-based supports for Indigenous children's development, families are reasserting their roles and rights with respect to their children. Parents affirmed the primacy of their perspectives on what they want for their children, the timing of supports, and the design and implementation of ECE/D programs that support their involvement.

Parents and practitioners in the ICP group forums and interviews underscored the need for policies, programs, and practices to support children within the context of their families and cultures. All participants voiced the importance of supporting families to recapture and strengthen Indigenous child-rearing skills, drawing on cultural understandings of the holistic nature of children's development, and the embeddedness of children's lives within their families, communities, mainstream institutions, and society. This larger agenda establishes the context for understanding the safety, relevance, and usefulness of screening, assessment, and early intervention practice.

AHDP participants echoed the central importance of understanding and supporting children in the context of their families and cultures. Several participants commented on the loss of parenting knowledge and skills from the Residential School era and the desire for support to promote the positive development of their children. All parents expressed a desire to be involved in their children's education in the early years and beyond. Indigenous early childhood educators commented that "ideal" ECE/D programs in their communities would include, among other things, parent involvement, Elder involvement, and support and resources for families, including parents, grandparents, aunties, uncles, siblings, extended family and friends.

In summary, participants in both the ICP and AHDP affirmed the potential for ECE/D programs not only to support the well-being of young Indigenous children but also to engage parents, families, and communities in the revitalization of Indigenous language, culture, and traditions. It is within the context of these commonly held aspirations that the five themes discussed in the next section, which present both challenges and opportunities for ECE/D research and practice with Indigenous communities, hold particular salience.

ECE/D Research and Practice: Contested Terrain It's About Time

Both the ICP and AHDP highlighted the critical importance of considering the impact of historical trauma on Indigenous families in every undertaking affecting children and families, including research, policy, and practice. Normative, universalistic concepts of child development or policymaking tend to disregard or minimize the dimension of sociohistorical time. A philosophical orientation that emphasizes contemporary child-environment interactions cannot fully accommodate the unfolding sociohistorical context of Indigenous Peoples as they came under colonial rule and as they gather the strength to engage in a still nascent process of truth and reconciliation with their colonizers, whose understanding of Indigenous realities often remains shallow and naive (Aboriginal Healing Foundation, 2008). Following Bronfenbrenner's (1979) concept of the chronosystem, it is critically important for child development scholars and policymakers to recognize the history of Indigenous childhood in Canada during and following the Indian Residential School era as part of the contemporary ecology of Indigenous child development (Fournier & Crey, 1997; Haig-Brown, 1988, Trocme, Knoke, & Blackstock, 2004).

This multigenerational view, extending both backward and forward in time, figured prominently in the accounts of many Indigenous participants in the ICP and AHDP, including the Indigenous coordinators from both projects. In the AHDP, the Indigenous coordinator initiated an explicit and systematic examination of the colonial history of Indigenous peoples in Canada, bringing the entire study team to a deeper understanding of the need to cast Indigenous parenting and child development within a historical context. Most participants across both studies explained how their own experiences of childhood, parenthood, and/or ECE/D practice were affected by colonial interventions, including residential schooling. In interviews and personal narratives, participants often highlighted the themes of personal wellness and healing, the reconstitution of family life, and the revitalization of cultural knowledge and culturally based ways of raising children. This reference to a personal and collective past and future is captured in Chief Willie Charley's encouragement to the CHILD Project group to see each child "seven generations into the past and seven generations into the future," as cited in Chapter 2.

Throughout the data collection, ICP participants expressed sensitivity and skepticism about the use, motivation, and benefits of standardized developmental screening and assessment tools and of prescriptive early intervention programs imported from non-Indigenous contexts. These views were echoed among AHDP participants, particularly older adults who had observed their children's public schooling and had seen numerous imported programs come and go from their communities, leaving little lasting impact. In explaining their skepticism, Indigenous participants referred to the historical and contemporary damage imposed on families by exclusionary practices that stigmatize and overdiagnose Indigenous people and that reflect a persistent assumption that European-heritage ways of knowing and thinking about child development are the right, best, or only ways. Against that background, many Indigenous community members, agencies, and allied professionals voiced suspicion about the perceived tendency of non-Indigenous professionals to construct profiles of Indigenous children as "at risk," "vulnerable," or "diagnostically significant" and to view Indigenous families as "uncaring" or "incompetent." As other CHILD researchers learned over the course of the project, this kind of language reflects both "words of power" and the "power of words."

To address these concerns, practitioner training must promote awareness of the sociohistorical context of Indigenous childhood. Such awareness can support a generally more sensitive approach to understanding and interacting with Indigenous families, and more particularly can inform screening, assessment, and intervention decisions, including which tools or nonstandard approaches to use with a particular child or program at a given time. This awareness must also infuse the *practice* of screening, assessment, and intervention, so that parents are kept informed at each stage. ECE/D practitioners who work with Indigenous children and families also need to be kept informed, since they often initiate the screening and assessment process through referral, and are also most likely to be positioned to provide ongoing support to children and families.

In general, awareness of the chronosphere may help to create a climate of cultural safety for Indigenous partners and research participants, as well as for Indigenous parents and children in ECE/D settings. Attunement to this broader context can help broaden discussion from an exclusive focus on the individual child or parent to include consideration of how improved social environments can better support the optimal development of Indigenous children.

Surveillance: A World in a Word

In the public health context, "surveillance" refers to the ongoing and systematic collection, analysis, and interpretation of data on infectious diseases to enable appropriate and timely responses for the prevention of illness (Disease Control Priorities Project, 2008). More recently, this term has been used to describe the routine use of developmental monitoring and screening to identify children who may need extra support for optimal development. As such, the concept of surveillance was central to the *Early identification and screening studies* in the CHILD Project and was discussed positively and, initially, uncritically in the larger interdisciplinary CHILD group. For instance, Scandinavian government-funded early childhood surveillance programs with frequent monitoring, screening, and diagnostic assessments of young children were often presented as enviable examples of caring governments' commitment to supporting young children's optimal development. However, ICP and AHDP participants raised several concerns about the meaning and practice of "universal surveillance" for Indigenous Peoples living in the shadows of devastating colonial interventions.

In discussions with the larger CHILD Project group, the term "surveillance" evoked a strong negative response on the part of the first Indigenous coordinator of the ICP, as did the idea of introducing a universal school readiness assessment tool in First Nations communities. This coordinator ultimately resigned from the study, finding that several different foci and objectives of the overall CHILD Project failed to resonate with the historical experiences or current needs and goals of Indigenous communities. Given the history of government invasions into the lives of Indigenous children and families, such responses are unsurprising. Many ICP and AHDP participants reported being negatively affected by screening and assessment, as well as by school-based monitoring of "school readiness." Parents and practitioners expressed concerns that developmental "testing" or "monitoring" situates Indigenous children, families, and communities within a deficit framework. Some ECE/D program managers saw current calls for routine universal developmental monitoring—for example, through the Early Development Instrument (Janus & Offord, 2007; Kershaw, Irwin, Trafford, & Hertzman, 2005)—as motivated by the needs of governments and researchers, more so than by a true desire to understand children and families holistically. Participants noted that this kind of surveillance does not necessarily entail any follow-up services, leading them to question the purpose and utility of such initiatives for children, families, and communities. Thus, the discussion of surveillance as an example of "words of power and the power of words" had the effect of forcing others in the broader CHILD network to seriously reflect on what until that point had been considered a neutral or descriptive term.

Respondents also expressed the fear that surveillance could provide "ammunition" to remove children from families and communities. In this regard, the term seemed to evoke the sense of police surveillance—that is, the close observation of a person or group under suspicion. Again, this fear must be understood within a historical context: generations of Indigenous children have been removed from their families to be raised in residential schools and/or the foster care system. This issue remains a genuine concern for Indigenous families in Canada. For example, in British Columbia, where the CHILD Project took place, Indigenous children comprise 7 percent of all children, but close to 50 percent of all children within the foster care system (Joint Special Report by the Representative for Children and Youth and the Office of the Provincial Health Officer, 2007). Indeed, AHDP Home Visitors reported that when inviting parents to participate in the HIPPY program, one of the first questions families asked was whether it was associated with the Ministry of Children and Family Development, the ministry responsible for child protection. Families were often reluctant to allow surveillance and monitoring of their children and their parenting, out of fear that their children might be taken from them.

On the other hand, many parents and most practitioners in Indigenous communities expressed a desire to know if a child could benefit from extra supports. Despite indicating that they perceived developmental screening, and diagnostic assessments as culturally challenging, most parents and practitioners felt these methods could be useful if practiced "respectfully." Most agreed that it is highly desirable to identify a serious developmental disability, delay, or challenge so that early interventions can be introduced. Similarly, in the AHDP, parents welcomed the opportunity to engage with their children in community-based, family-paced, nonjudgmental, and growth-oriented programs. In this kind of family-centered program, parents were receptive to further information on child assessment and other potentially supportive services.

The ICP and AHDP highlight the need to develop respectful and empowering early identification processes that lead to accurate identification of children who need extra supports, while avoiding "one-size-fits-all" assumptions that portray Indigenous children and families as deficient. Early identification processes must be clearly linked to the provision of supportive services, rather than being used simply to document developmental patterns in Indigenous populations. Appropriate collaborations with Indigenous peoples might lead to the co-construction of approaches that empower parents and early childhood educators, while avoiding the unwitting perpetuation or reproduction of expert-subject dichotomies, dependencies, and oppressive child welfare practices—just some of the fears expressed among ICP and AHDP participants about universal surveillance.

The Pivotal Role of Relationships

ICP and AHDP participants repeatedly stressed the foundational role of positive interpersonal relationships in conducting research with Indigenous partners and in the practices of screening, assessment, and intervention with Indigenous children. Around the time the CHILD Project began, some frameworks for ethical research involving Indigenous peoples and Indigenous knowledge were emerging (e.g., Cole, 2002; Interagency Advisory Panel on Research EthICP, 2003; Schnarch, 2004; Smith, 2002). However, to date, there remain no formal points of reference or guidelines for working in and with Indigenous communities. Relationship-building was key to this process. In this ongoing learning process, the openness, patience, and generosity of our community partners, our shared commitment to social justice, and our willingness to depart from mainstream research training and practice were all essential. In developing our sensitivity to the importance of relationship-building, we relied on our Indigenous colleagues, community partners, and the current literature on Indigenous research methods (e.g., Schnarch, 2004; Smith, 2002). Along the way, we learned a great deal through trial and error, self-reflection, and dialogue with Indigenous team members, some of which we discuss below.

Non-Indigenous university-based researchers need to acknowledge their positions of power as members of the dominant society and of prestigious academic institutions. Otherwise, research can unwittingly serve as an instrument to oppress Indigenous peoples, perpetuating a history of exploitation. One significant issue that arose within the AHDP concerned the title of the research study. Relatively early in the study, we announced to our Indigenous partners that we had changed the name of the study from "Aboriginal HIPPY" to "HIPPY in Aboriginal Communities." The reason for the name change was well intended. At that time, the aim of the study was to evaluate the effectiveness of HIPPY, an imported program, in Indigenous communities. We felt it was presumptuous to call the program "Aboriginal" HIPPY when it had originated in Israel and was as yet "untested" for Indigenous children and families. The Indigenous Home Visitors strongly objected both to the name change and to its having been made without consultation with them. To the Home Visitors, the name change conveyed that the program and the research study no longer belonged to them and their communities, an important loss reminiscent of other losses incurred by Indigenous peoples at the hands of those in power. This example illustrates the need for researchers (1) to be aware of, and sensitive to, the sociopolitical history and lasting impact of colonial relationships between Indigenous and non-Indigenous people; (2) to explicitly acknowledge differences in power; (3) to establish and maintain an egalitarian research relationship; and (4) to be vigilant about the importance of language and terminology, particularly in settings where power differences are at play.

Drawing on these principles, the Aboriginal Home Visitors and the university-based team in the AHDP came to a deeper knowledge and trust of each other by individually and collectively exploring the colonial history of Indigenous childhood. These explorations culminated in a retreat, supported with funds from the research study, in which the full study team traveled to the Chehalis reserve in southwestern British Columbia to participate in a two-day cultural workshop including drum-making, storytelling, singing, dancing, eating, and a tour of sacred sites. This is an example of but one activity that built trust and understanding within our university-Indigenous community research partnership.

In both the ICP and AHDP, relationship-building took considerable time, which put us "out-of-step" with the timelines established for the larger CHILD Project. While other studies were moving into data collection and analysis, we were still trying to establish who our community partners really were in practice. At the point of applying for the research grant to support the CHILD Project, the national offices of HIPPY Canada and Aboriginal Head Start served as the nominal partners of the AHDP and ICP, respectively. However, as the studies began to unfold, it became clear that the Indigenous community members who were actively implementing and contributing to the studies and with whom we were building relationships were our working partners. Moreover, there was a strong desire on their parts to "take ownership" of the research as well as of the substantive topic or program. In both studies, the identification of the national offices as partners became somewhat problematic, potentially reproducing the perceived interference of agencies and governing authorities in community and personal decision making. In some instances, Indigenous community partners felt awkward and even potentially threatened by the national partners, perhaps fearing that as funders, these authorities might be privy to, and try to influence, what was being discovered about the internal workings of programs and screening processes. This predicament harkens back to the theme of surveillance discussed earlier.

In addition to providing the foundation for research between Indigenous and non-Indigenous partners, within the ICP and AHDP trusting relationships between Indigenous families and providers of ECE/D interventions were essential to maximize the benefits of those programs to children and families. The ICP and AHDP highlighted two common ways in which ECE/D professionals enter into relationships with Indigenous children: (1) through developmental screening and assessment; and (2) in the context of early education programs.

Developmental screening and assessment processes tend to focus on the individual child, ignoring parents, extended family, or community. Parents in both the ICP and AHDP reported their displeasure with this approach, associating it with "surveillance," the continued marginalization of Indigenous families' knowledge and role in supporting children's development, and the associated transfer of power from families to specialists. Rather than using screening and assessment as the portal for engagement with Indigenous families, community leaders and practitioners repeatedly underscored the priority of rebuilding parents' confidence in their own capacity to understand and respond appropriately to their children, even when specialists or others are needed to provide extra support.

ECE/D programs, such as Aboriginal HIPPY and Aboriginal Head Start, are a second common starting point in building relationships with Indigenous children and families (Indian and Northern Affairs Canada, 2008). In contrast to screening and assessment programs, in which the links between "testing" and the provision of supportive services are not always clear, ECD/D programs such as these offer immediate benefits to children and families. These family-based interventions share several characteristics, in that they

- regard families with dignity and respect;
- provide families with information to support decision making, including about intervention options;
- apply individualized, flexible, and responsive practices;
- foster parent–professional collaboration and partnerships; and
- provide and mobilize resources and supports necessary for families to care for their children in ways that produce optimal child, parent, and family outcomes (Ingber & Dromi, 2010).

The relational competencies of ECE/D professionals in these programs must include knowledge of the sociohistorical context of Indigenous childhood, along with empathy, respect, a nonjudgmental approach, and positive beliefs about parenting capabilities. This approach to relationships differs considerably from that found in developmental assessment and screening programs, and was overwhelmingly preferred by participants in both the ICP and AHDP. Provision of specialist support in the form of screening, assessment, and targeted early intervention for individual children, can be offered after these important foundational steps have been taken.

The Primacy of Process

ICP and AHDP participants noted that once a door to engagement has been opened in a relationship, the ensuing interpersonal processes are more important than the content of any tools or programs provided. For example, a key ICP finding was that the ways in which developmental monitoring, screening, and assessment were introduced, conducted, reported, and acted upon were of greater concern than the specific tools used. Similarly, in the AHDP, community members were concerned about who decides what ECE program(s) are available in communities and who staffs the program(s), as these issues were seen as closely tied to how the program would be run.

Most Indigenous parents and ECE/D practitioners saw the screening and assessment of Indigenous children as perpetuating of the colonial imposition of policies, procedures, criteria, and performance demands that has produced the social exclusion of Indigenous children, parents, and caregivers. Similarly, formal education programs have notoriously required that parents leave their children at the door and return only when asked to meet with school staff or to serve as an audience for children. In general, meaningful parental inclusion has never been a strong feature of formal education, and this has been particularly true for Indigenous families,

In both studies, parents expressed grave dissatisfaction with professionals' perceived lack of respect for parents' own knowledge of their children; and, in the ICP, with professionals' failure to inform parents of the assessment and its nature, to obtain their consent, and to provide feedback about assessment results. This dissatisfaction extended to the Early Development Instrument (Janus & Offord, 2007), used in public schools to gauge school readiness and to other school-based monitoring and assessment practices. In the AHDP, participants expressed frustration with the perceived failure of educators in off-reserve preschools and public schools to solicit information from parents about their children or to listen to parents when information was offered.

In the ICP most parents demonstrated little knowledge about the assessment tools that were used in their community, the content of those tools, and the purposes of assessment. Few parents or community-based practitioners generated substantial recommendations for Indigenous content. The distinctiveness of the cultures, language issues and preferences, practices and developmental goals for young children that exists between First Nations and between communities on reserves and in more urban centers off reserves was emphasized; underscoring the monumental difficulty of creating any tools that would be fitting across a range of Indigenous populations even within the province of British Colubmia. While community members' testimonies rarely distinguished explicitly between the process and content of assessment, nearly all concerns expressed by respondents pertained to *how* assessment was done, rather than to the specific tools used.

A salient theme in ICP respondents' testimonies pertained to who decides that assessment will take place. For example, many participants experienced federal and provincial funding and advisory bodies as authoritarian rather than consultative in their demands for particular kinds of assessment. Respondents often considered these bodies to be unreasonable in their expectations of unprepared, overworked frontline practitioners, and inattentive to feedback from community-based agencies. Most frontline practitioners reported feeling excluded from decision making about developmental assessment. Moreover, community-based practitioners repeatedly commented on a perceived failure of ECE/D program funders and early intervention specialists to recognize their knowledge of the children and families with whom they worked as possibly providing the richest and most valid source of information necessary to monitor development and to identify the need for diagnostic observation or early intervention services.

A prominent theme in AHDP respondents' testimonies concerned who delivers early education programs and where they are located. Participants strongly preferred ECE/D programs to be locally delivered by community members, as this approach was seen to promote culturally appropriate programs that are responsive to families. One feature of the HIPPY program that respondents viewed positively was its delivery by community members. Their belief that this feature would result in greater responsiveness to families' needs was confirmed. Over time, the Home Visitors became increasingly sensitive to the need to include and support culturally based teaching and learning opportunities. Equally importantly, all Home Visitors were willing and able to adapt the program to meet the needs of individual families by recognizing and supporting their desire to teach their children within the constraints of multiple burdens and responsibilities. Sometimes this meant adjusting the pace of the program, the timing of home visits, or who would be working with the child. This responsiveness not only helped to build trusting and positive relationships between Home Visitors and families, but also helped ensure that children and families experienced success.

In both studies, participants cited the importance of involving parents. For instance, in the ICP, participants suggested that professionals should consult with primary caregivers (whether fathers, mothers, grandparents, or aunties), and reinforce their existing skills in observing and supporting children's development, rather than making them feel that professionals always know more or know best. AHDP participants valued the HIPPY program, despite its "outside" origins, because it emphasized supporting parents' role in their children's development and education. Indigenous participants noted the importance of parental involvement in supporting their children's education, but also spoke of barriers to meaningful engagement in their children's education once the children were in public school. Respondents identified racism, a lack of respect for parents, and the tendency to view Indigenous children from a deficit perspective as factors that negatively affected school-community relationships and parental involvement in education. Although public school teachers reported wanting greater Indigenous parental involvement, they also described methods of soliciting parent involvement that have not proven successful with Indigenous families (e.g., posting volunteer sign-up sheets in their classrooms). Further, kindergarten teachers reported knowing little about the ECE/D programs Indigenous children had participated in prior to school entry, a situation that could be remedied through direct communication with families.

ICP participants noted that formal tools had sometimes worked well to identify the source of a problem that had mystified a parent, or to establish a child's eligibility for a desperately needed therapy program. However, parents in all communities noted that referrals often created false expectations that services would be delivered, when in fact, long waitlists and geographic inaccessibility of services sometimes resulted in a lack of follow-up. Participants also told stories about a perceived misuse of formal tools—cases where tools were used as "ammunition against the parent to prove that their child had a delay" or taken out of context, as in the use of an English vocabulary test on a non-English child, resulting in a possibly inappropriate diagnosis of language delay.

Regarding assessment, some ICP participants expressed concerns about privacy, confidentiality, and social exclusion. Respondents also raised concerns about the overwhelming focus in BC on assessments of school readiness, overlooking common Indigenous values and concepts relating to children's developing spirituality, cultural knowledge, Indigenous language proficiency, subsistence skills, and relationships with Elders and other clan members. Similar concerns were raised by participants in the AHDP, who saw educators' tendencies to overlook Indigenous values and developmental concepts as significant contributors to the alienation that Indigenous children and their parents often feel in school contexts. In both studies, parents and practitioners alike voiced dismay about media reports of surveys

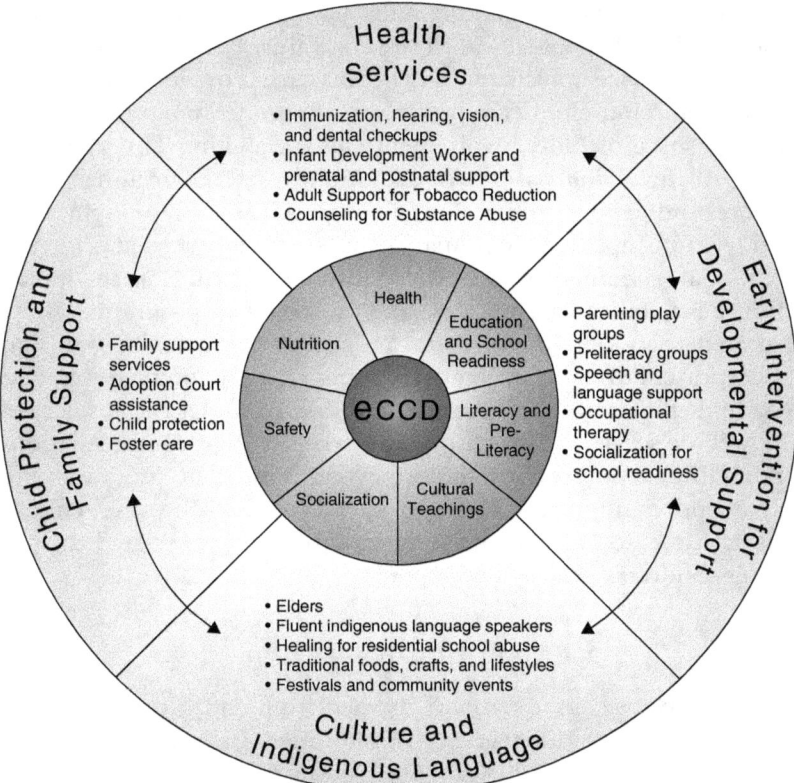

Figure 5.1 The Hook and Hub Model in Indigenous Communities

of health, development, or school readiness that often negatively compare Indigenous children with non-Indigenous children, without providing historical or political analysis to contextualize the results, and without surveying strengths or resiliencies of Indigenous children in the face of overwhelming environmental challenges. Community participants disparaged the perpetuation of negative stereotypes of Indigenous children and families in Canada that they perceived as an all-too-frequent outcome of surveillance and survey research.

The values and care practices emphasized by community participants in both projects generally supported the holistic model of caring for young Indigenous children demonstrated by a number of First Nations in an earlier study reported by Ball (2004). The elaboration of multiservice hubs designed and operated by communities to serve local Indigenous children and families has come to be known as the "Hook an Hub" approach, illustrated in figure 5.1. An incremental approach to service implementation begins with provision of baby clinics and infant and child care programs, alongside community kitchens and a space of Elder involvement and socializing. This approach starts with involving parents in a culturally safe environment that promotes Indigenous culture and values as well as the development of social relationships that are primarily supportive rather than primarily educational or framed as early intervention. Over time, as the model in figure 5.1 indicates, child care and development programs can be integrated or co-located with social and health services, screening and services for children requiring extra support, early intervention, and even child and family support programs offered under the auspices of child welfare services. This model supports AHDP recommendations of providing resources for families beyond immediate programming such as opportunities for adults to interact with each other, enrichment activities for adults, and information on topics related to supporting children's healthy development.

Embedded Research

In this section we share what we learned from engaging in research partnerships with Indigenous communities within a collaborative context in which the dominant paradigm was not informed by Indigenous concerns. First, several months after the studies began, community members echoed our questions, described earlier, about who their partners in the studies really were. Although all community partners had received copious written and verbal information about the location of the ICP and AHDP within the CHILD Project, confusion—and ultimately, alarm—arose when the realities of being embedded within a larger project began to sink in. The extent and form of collaboration among the 10 CHILD studies were unclear from the outset, a factor that became problematic for the ICP and AHDP. As the CHILD Project progressed, interstudy collaboration gained greater priority. Community and university partners in each study were invited to participate in meetings of all 10 studies, where they were expected to share data, disseminate early findings, disclose experiences of the research process, and consider community site visits from other project teams. As requests for greater collaboration emerged, ICP and AHDP team members grew increasingly uncomfortable. They saw themselves as primarily accountable to their own communities to explain and seek approval of study activities, especially those that involved non-Indigenous, university-based investigators, with whom they had no relationship.

Second, concerns arose about data sharing. In the past decade, a number of frameworks to guide ethical decision making in Canadian research involving Indigenous peoples have emerged that specify active roles for Indigenous partners in all phases of a research study (Canadian Institutes of Health Research, 2007; Castellano, 2004; National Aboriginal Health Organization, 2002; Schnarch, 2004; Ten Fingers, 2005). Many of these requirements raise new ethical concerns—for example, how to protect confidentiality when data is retained by a community, and how to extend opportunities for individuals to participate in research when an invitation is declined at the community level. They also raise practical concerns, such as the added time necessary to build relationships and negotiate community-level agreements, uncertainty about whether academic partners will be able to disseminate results, and whether community partners will achieve the outputs they hoped for. When studies are part of larger research collaborations, these concerns are magnified—especially when the larger networks include non-Indigenous partners who are unaware of or unsympathetic to research ethics involving Indigenous partners, as was the case in the ICP and AHDP.

Third, the sheer size of the CHILD Project was not conducive to the development of trusting social relationships among the Indigenous community representatives and team members. As described in a foregoing section, both the ICP and AHDP were founded on the ongoing development of trusting relationships between university- and community-based research team members. Making trusting relationships the basis for ethical engagement in research is easy to endorse, but difficult to enact. Trusting relationships require geographic proximity, time, personal risks, funding, open communication, flexible programs of activity, and other accommodations. These challenges compete with other realities of collaborative or networked investigations. The CHILD Project involved over 50 investigative team members, including a large rotation of graduate students.

Fourth, early in the ICP and AHDP studies, Indigenous team members had experiences of being the lone Indigenous person at meetings of the 10 CHILD studies, which were located in unfamiliar territory in an underground university campus in an urban centre far from their home communities. Indigenous team members reported feeling intimidated, challenged about their values and concerns, and unprepared to participate meaningfully in dialogues that were dominated by university faculty and graduate students whom they didn't know. As the CHILD Project progressed, meetings with teams in the larger collaborative fell outside of what could reasonably be expected of community-based team members, even with financial support for travel and time.

The experiences of Indigenous team members in the larger CHILD study evoke the concept of "cultural safety" discussed by scholars working in Aotearoa/New Zealand with Maori nurses (Kearns & Dyck, 1996; Papps & Ramsden, 1996), in Aboriginal nursing (Reimer et al., 2002) and in child and youth care in Canada (Ball, 2007). Cultural safety emerges from interactions in which individuals, who may be service recipients, or participants in a project or program, experience their cultural identity and way of being as respected—or, at least, not challenged or harmed. Respectful, equitable partnerships in which all parties have the right to influence the terms of engagement are essential to creating cultural safety.

Given the general receptivity and, indeed, expressed eagerness on the part of many Indigenous community members to engage young Indigenous children in ECE/D programs and to identify and meet children's needs for special supports before they start school, it is worthwhile to consider what accounts for a lack of cultural safety and what steps can be taken to promote it. To grasp the extent of the challenge, we need to step back in time to understand the historical background that undermines cultural integrity. With that historical picture in mind, we need to step back and gain a perspective on how the contemporary focus on rising "standardization," "universal surveillance," and "one-size-fits-all" approaches to parent education, child development curricula, and evaluation of school readiness are likely to be experienced by Indigenous children, families, and communities.

Conclusion

"Be prepared for the unexpected" can be a difficult stance when pitching a project to federal research funding agencies or when working within a larger research network. Indeed, the outcomes of our studies may have been disappointing to those who had hoped for the creation of a developmental monitoring or screening tool for Indigenous children, the original intention of the ICP, or a child-based evaluation of the Aboriginal HIPPY program, the original aim of the AHDP. Yet, this is the reality—and the potential—of building secure and productive Indigenous community-university partnerships. When relationship-building and good process are given priority over predetermined research agendas, methodologies, and output commitments, the potential for new knowledge, learning opportunities, and collaborative partnerships opens up. Our experiences in the ICP and AHDP studies show that university-community partnerships can teach us valuable lessons about ourselves, our preparedness, and our competence to engage in collaborative research with Indigenous Peoples.

"Do it in a good way" is advice that we often heard from Elders and other Indigenous community partners when we were struggling to address emerging concerns and goals for our work together. This statement doesn't prescribe a set of principles or steps to move forward. Rather, it calls upon us to be forthright, reliable, and responsive in our engagement with community members and to be mindful of the relative importance and potential impacts of our research within the broader context of the healing journey of Indigenous Peoples in Canada and the overwhelming drive for self-determination. While it is not possible to offer a prescription for a "good way" in all Indigenous communities, our learnings in the ICP and AHDP concerning the importance of cultural safety, relationships, and process provide guidelines for future endeavors.

Just as there is no prescription for how to engage in community-university research with Indigenous Peoples, there are no "best practices" for developmental screening and assessment or early learning programs that will be acceptable, useful, or timely for use with all Indigenous children, families, or communities. An emphasis on cultural safety and family-based practice is important. However, given the lack of published research in Canada on the impacts of various early childhood tools and programs on Indigenous children's development, federal investment in community-engaged research is necessary to explore new and existing approaches to promoting child development in diverse community settings and to document promising practices.

Notes

1. This chapter has been reviewed and approved by the Indigenous coordinator of the AHDP, Tammy Harkey, and of the ICP, Pauline Janyst. The authors acknowledge significant contributions to the projects reported in this chapter made by project coordinators Michelle Beatch and Pauline Janyst. The authors thank the Indigenous parents and practitioners who participated in the research and the community partners who made the studies possible.

2. The terms Indigenous and Aboriginal are used almost synonymously at this time in Canada to refer to people who identify themselves as descendents of the original inhabitants of the land now called Canada. Section 35 of the Canadian Constitution recognizes First Nations, Inuit, and Métis as Aboriginal people of Canada. The term Aboriginal was coined in the 1980s by the Canadian colonial government. The term Indigenous (as used here) is inclusive of First Peoples internationally. Many prefer the term Indigenous as a resistance against imposed colonial naming and because the term Indigenous is more widely used in global advocacy movements and donor agencies to promote Indigenous Peoples' rights, development, and equity.

CHAPTER 6

What We Learned about Early Identification and Screening

Hillel Goelman, Laurie Ford, Mari Pighini, Susan Dahinten, Anne Synnes, Lillian Tse, Jessica Ball, and Virginia E. Hayes

This chapter focuses on *The Developmental Pathways, Infant Neuromotor, Community-Based Screening,* and *The Indigenous Child* studies.[1] We have chosen to focus on these four studies for two particular reasons. First, issues around early identification and screening have been identified as priority areas in those disciplines represented in the CHILD Project. These include paediatrics (AAP, 2001; Drotar, Stancin, & Dworkin, 2008; Sand et al., 2007; Synnes, Lisonkova, Houbé, Klassen, & Lee, 2004; Synnes et al., 2006); rehabilitation sciences (Lee & Harris, 2006); nursing (Pinto-Martin, Dunkle, Earls, Fliedner, & Landes, 2005); school psychology (Carlton & Winsler, 1999; Pianta & McCoy, 1997); and First Nations Studies (Ball, 2004; Panagiotopoulos, Rozmus, Gagnon, & Macnab, 2007). Second, precisely because each of these studies arises from particular disciplinary contexts, they present different but complementary perspectives on efforts to determine the health and developmental status of young children. This chapter briefly provides the context, content, and main findings of each of these studies. It also discusses the ways in which these studies both contributed to and were informed by the other studies in CHILD, and the implications for early intervention practice and for further research.

All four of these studies arose out of the recognition that in any population there are children who need extra support. The research has shown that the early identification of these children and their subsequent participation in high-quality early intervention programs can have positive developmental outcomes. All four studies discussed in this chapter, in different ways, speak to the importance of the two-part strategy presented by Coleman, Buysse, and Neitzel (2006) of *recognizing* young children with special needs with accuracy, sensitivity, and cultural fairness and *responding* to these children and their families with appropriate services. In the following section we provide some background on the history and current practices related to the recognition of and response to the early identification of young children who need extra support.

A Brief Overview of Screening and Early Identification in Early Childhood

The terms "assessment," "screening," and "early identification" can have a variety of meanings to those in different disciplines or professions and for this reason we define the meanings we are using in this chapter. We have adopted Meisels' and Atkins-Burnett's definition of *assessment* as the broadest of these possible terms in that, "the goal of early childhood assessment is to acquire information and understanding that will facilitate the child's development and functional abilities within the family and community" (2001, p. 232). The assessment process can provide insights into a child's developmental strengths and limitations and can identify children who may be at risk for developmental challenges and who may need extra support. *Early identification* could include the process of *screening* a population of children to uncover preliminary concerns about a child's development and/or subsequent diagnostic procedures designed to provide more detailed information about a specific developmental disorder or delay.

For some, the term *assessment* is synonymous with "formal, standardized testing" and for others, it it includes a wide range of formal and informal, quantitative and qualitative techniques, which draw on, for example, observations of children's play; descriptions and observations of children's art, music, and puzzle play; developmental checklists; and children's participation in formal, standardized testing. At their core, all such efforts are interested in assessment as a systematic process for understanding child development, and as part of this systematic process, those collecting assessment data must ask themselves four key questions:

1. What do we want to know about this child?
2. Why do we want to know this?

3. How will we gather the necessary information?
4. What will we do with this information once we gather it?

Brofenbrenner's (1977) observation on the limitations of experimental procedures with young children can apply to screening and early identification procedures as well: "The science of strange behavior of children in strange situations with strange adults for the briefest possible period of time" (p. 513). As Meisels and Atkins-Burnett (2000) have acknowledged, "early childhood assessment is a field in transition" (p. 231), and the psychometric view is no longer as dominant. This transition continues with new approaches, techniques, measures, and tools uniquely suited to the developmental needs of children in the early years from different disciplinary perspectives. With changes in policies, procedures, and in some cases laws, the need for a wide range of assessment procedures that address the unique needs of children in early childhood continues.

Major national organizations in the United States and Canada including the Council on Children with Disabilities (CCD; 2006), the American Academy of Pediatrics (AAP; 2001) and the Canadian Paediatric Society (CPS; 2010) have all endorsed screening procedures for young children as matters of public policy. The CPS has stated two major objectives for their policy

1. To identify populations that are at risk, and to obtain important ecological and epidemiological data on their circumstances; and
2. To evaluate the success of public health interventions by tracking their effectiveness (CPS, 2010).

The expansion of early childhood special education programs, school readiness initiatives, and other early intervention programs has contributed to the growth and need for reliable, valid, and culturally fair assessment of children in early childhood. The expansion of programs, policies, and procedures has also been accompanied by the articulation of basic principles that should guide the early screening and identification of young children in need of extra support. Meisels and Atkins-Burnett (2000) have proposed that the assessment of young children be based on a number of key principles including the following: assessment should be a collaborative process drawing on parents, family members, and professionals; assessment should draw upon parental information and feedback; assessment should draw on multiple sources of information; assessment should address children's current levels of strength as well as anticipated growth areas in the future; assessment should be seen as a step in the process of intervention and continued feedback; and the assessment process should be nonthreatening, safe, and nonjudgemental for children and parents.

Assessment, screening, and early identification processes are not without their critics (e.g., Bloch, 1990; Canella, 1997). Dahlberg, Moss, and Pence (1999), for example, have criticized the historical hegemony of developmental psychology in the field of early childhood. They have also rightly pointed out that developmental psychology has long argued for a universal approach to the understanding of the ages and stages of child development and how this view has influenced curricula, programs, and the assessment of young children. Scholars writing from a reconceptualist orientation have identified the ways in which this traditional hegemony has been used as means to marginalize, control, and oppress specific populations of young children and their families. Their appeals for more holistic and culturally fair screening and assessment procedures have invited a number of constructive additions to the growing repertoire of such procedures. New Zealand's integrated curriculum framework known as *Te Wharike* includes approaches and techniques, which allow classroom teachers in early childhood classrooms to understand the learning and development of children (Carr, Hatherly, Lee, & Ramsey, 2003). These include the systematic collection of portfolios, which document the children's development through photographs, the children's art, and emergent writing. Perhaps most exciting is their creation of "learning stories" that generate narratives around the ways in which young children discover, build, and organize their learning experiences in the classroom. Similar approaches have been developed in the Reggio Emilia learning centers in Italy (Edwards, 1993) where portfolios, anecdotal record keeping, and ongoing parent-teacher conferences form the basis for ongoing consultations on the children's progress. Both the Reggio Emilia and *Te Wharike* programs, it should be pointed out, are approaches used with all of the children in the classrooms and are not designed specifically to identify children with developmental challenges. The other encouraging news about these approaches is that they demonstrate the potential for collecting information on children's health and development in ways that are multidisciplinary and respectful of the children, their parents, and families.

In summary, all of these formal and informal approaches to monitoring children's growth and development should be consistent with the principles articulated by Meisels and Atkins-Burnett (2000) and to help determine the kinds of information which are needed and the ways in which the information will be obtained.

Overview of Early Screening and Identification Programs in British Columbia

Screening and early identification practices in British Columbia include a combination of universal and targeted approaches for children of different ages, for different purposes, with different instruments and conducted by different medical, health, educational, and social service professionals. As indicated in table 6.1, some procedures are routine and nearly universal; others are intended for all children but parents are not mandated to participate; and others are recommended for children who appear to be at risk for developmental challenges.

All children receive Apgar scores at birth and although this is not actually a screening measure per se, the Apgar score assists the medical staff in attending to the vital aspects of the newborn child. Recently, British Columbia has also instituted newborn hearing screening. Most infants are discharged directly from the hospital to their homes, but at-risk infants are instead transferred to a Neonatal Intensive Care Unit (NICU) where they are given a detailed medical assessment. Upon their discharge from the hospital, these infants who had been treated in the NICU undergo a systematic assessment process. The most vulnerable babies, including those with birth weights under 800 grams, have their development monitored through the hospital's Neonatal Follow-Up Program (NFUP).

Table 6.1 Current (2010) Early Childhood Screening and Early Identification Procedures in British Columbia: Who Gets Assessed, By Whom, When, and Why?

1. Universal (routine): All infants after birth, Apgar screening
2. Universal (routine): All infants after birth, newborn hearing
3. At-risk infants, up to 72 hours after birth—more detailed medical diagnoses
4. Universal (routine): All infants, birth to one year, public health nurse visits, general screen
5. Vision screening at three years (Not yet universal although this is being planned.)
6. Family physicians and pediatric visits, birth to five years general screen (as needed, requested, referred)
7. Suspected deficits, diagnostic testing, birth to five years (as needed, requested, referred)
8. Universal vision screening at kindergarten

After discharge from the hospital both NICU and non-NICU infants usually receive at least one follow-up home visit by a Public Health Nurse that includes an overall health check-up. Should specific concerns arise following the administration of any of the checklists used by the PHNs, such as the Ages and Stages Questionnaire (Bricker, Squires, & Mounts, 1999), follow-up assessment and early intervention, support referrals are generally in place. Throughout their preschool years, children may participate in the voluntary screening and early identification programs that are offered to the entire population. The population-based newborn hearing screening occurs soon after birth (prior to hospital discharge). It is not only a screening program but is a coordinated Early Hearing Detection and Intervention program (BC Early Hearing Program) with services across multidisciplinary service providers and involves multiple ministries. There is a dental (caries) risk assessment conducted by public health staff, which typically occurs when the child is 12 months old. The caries risk assessment is not an in-the-mouth assessment; public health staff pose questions to parents and assign a risk level. Vision screening is also not yet available province-wide (although universal three-year-old vision screening is the goal). These regularly scheduled voluntary screening and early identification programs may or may not result in referrals for more diagnostic testing and/or intervention programs.

There are many different assessment and intervention pathways, which may be used in the zero-to-five age period. Children with identified or suspected developmental challenges may be assessed at any point in the early years as a result of parent concerns and/or professional referrals. Some children are referred by family physicians, nurses, Infant Development Consultants, or Aboriginal Infant Development Consultants. They may be referred to medical subspecialists such as pediatricians or to other health care professionals such as optometrists, audiologists, psychologists, or physical or occupational therapists. In some cases, children may be referred directly by their parents. Developmental assessment practices will in many cases be linked to recommendations (by these various professionals) to parents to enrol their children in early intervention programs. This support may be provided through home-based or in-center consultation and/or therapy services for babies and young children with "suspected" risks, as in the case of those identified during the Public Health Nurse's home visit (BC Centre for Ability, 2010). Assessment and intervention may be provided by the same agency or may be conducted through different auspices. There is no one systematized pattern to these various services, referrals, assessments, and interventions. There is no one entry point or exit point and parents must be their children's best advocates in order to best negotiate these multiple options.

Despite the existence of these various pieces of the early identification puzzle, there is no one, integrated universal program for the screening of children's developmental status in all domains throughout the early years for all children from birth to school entry. For the most part, the efforts to provide screening, identification, and intervention in British Columbia try to meet the needs for those children who are most medically and developmentally fragile. As a result, it is the children in the "grey area" who are frequently missed by established screening and early identification processes. They may be in the "grey area" because their developmental difficulties are so subtle or because the assessment devices are not sensitive enough to identify their particular condition. Alternatively, a child may not be identified with a specific diagnosis because he or she has fallen through the cracks of the system for routine monitoring, screening, and assessment. This can happen for a number of reasons. For example, the child and her family perhaps do not speak English; may change address frequently; or may have a lapse in insurance coverage. Another reason is that the child may be in foster care. Assessment and intervention services may be limited in remote and isolated communities, and/or the child's caregiver(s) may choose not to have their child monitored, screened, or assessed by developmental health personnel. The identification of children with diagnoses as well as children in the grey area continues to be an ongoing issue across the medical, educational, and social service sectors in the province. One essential element in all of British Columbia's developmental screening practices is the close connection between the assessment/identification process and the funding provided for services for children assigned to specific labelled categories. Assignment to these categories is strictly dependent on a medical or developmental diagnosis (Pighini, 2008; Pivik, 2008). This labelling/funding process is also used to provide educational support for children ages five and older as they enter the school system (British Columbia Ministry of Education, 2000b). However, for children without labelled diagnoses, funding is discontinued once they enter the school system (Committee on Children with Disabilities, 2005; Pighini, 2008). Only through "special needs" labelling will these children have access to more individualized resources and program adaptations outlined in their Individualized Educational Programs (British Columbia Ministry of Education, 2000a; Learning Assistance Teaching Association of British Columbia, 2002).

Brief Summary of the Design and Findings of the Four Studies in the CHILD Project

The four studies we discuss in the chapter offer a range of different approaches and methodologies. As shown in table 6.2, which was constructed on the basis of the studies' respective CHILD*Talk* papers (see Chapter 3), each of the studies identified the information they needed, their reasons for needing that information, and the very different methodologies each one used. On the fourth question—what the information they collected would be used for—there was much greater similarity than difference in their responses. All of the studies wanted to use their data to help improve the system of screening, identification, and early intervention in the province.

The lead academic researchers in *The Developmental Pathways Study* were a neonatologist and a developmental paediatrician and their community partner was a provincial early intervention program, the Infant Development Program of British Columbia. *The Developmental Pathways Study* examined the mortality, morbidity, development, and hospital utilization rates of children who were treated in NICUs at birth (Schiariti et al., 2008; Synnes et al., 2004, 2006). One analysis revealed that infant mortality rates among extremely low-birth weight NICU-treated infants from 1983 to 2002 decreased significantly compared to previous years. However, the disability rates for these children during the same time period were unchanged. A second analysis examined the medical and social determinants of hospital utilization rates of NICU infants born in 1996–1997 with a broader range of birth weights. The medical factors that were statistically associated with the rates of hospital utilization were congenital anomaly, gestational age, severity of illness, and health status; the social determinants were the larger number of children in the family, lower levels of family income, and the involvement of early intervention services. Based on their years of doing assessments on at-risk infants, the team members concluded that the classification system that was used was reliable in identifying moderate to severe disabilities but was not sensitive enough to pick up "softer" or "milder" forms of disabilities of children in the so-called grey area.

During the life of the CHILD Project two important spin-off programs of research were developed. In one, a population health study was initiated by using Ministry of Health administrative databases to collect (anonymized) data on over 70,000 children of whom approximately 10 percent had been treated in NICUs for at least 24 hours. The administrative set allowed the researchers to develop full medical

Table 6.2 Four Questions about Screening in the Four Studies[2]

	What do we want to know?	Why do we want to know this?	How will we gather information?	What will we do with the information?
The Developmental Pathways Study	The objectives of these studies are to define the incidence of various aspects of developmental delay in various groups of at-risk neonates.	The results of this study will help us target and triage at-risk newborns referred to the Infant Development Program by classifying the degree of risk.	This is a cohort study measuring the long-term medical and psychological outcome of NICU survivors.	The role of the IDP in this research project will be to disseminate the results amongst leaders within the IDP and participate in discussions of the policy implications of the results.
The Infant Neuromotor Study	To determine whether or not early screening for at-risk and healthy infants for motor development has positive outcomes for infants and their families by age three, and to compare two methods of training child professionals to use two different assessment measures.	Very little research has been directed to examining the effects of early diagnosis of generalized motor or cognitive delays, even though early referral and management are associated with better long-term developmental, educational, social, and family outcomes.	Typically developing and babies at risk for neuromotor delays will be assessed on the HINT and the AIMS. Professionals will take part in face-to-face and online training sessions for the AIMS.	Increase the number of qualified trainers in the province; increase the number of babies assessed, and increase the number of babies identified at risk for neuromotor delay and follow-up.
The Community-based Screening Study	To help the CHILD Project, the local community, and the broader community to understand the effectiveness of screening young children with the Nipissing District Developmental Screen.	Will increase Public Health and Ministry of Children and Family Development Screening Task Group's knowledge of the impact that screening has had for the children, families, care givers and professionals in our community.	Parent questionnaires and direct assessment of children; case studies, individual interviews, focus groups, and document review. Parent completion of the NDDS.	Will help to guide future community screening practices. May influence policy-makers to make budgeting decisions that will allocate additional resources to promote school readiness, that is, address service waitlists.

Continued

Table 6.2 Continued

	What do we want to know?	Why do we want to know this?	How will we gather information?	What will we do with the information?
The Indigenous Child Project	The overall goal of the project is to explore new approaches for gathering information and designing assessment strategies that ensure the cultural and community relevance, or ecocultural validity, of procedures used for determining service needs and impacts in early childhood learning and development.	It is important to hear from community members about "assessment"— what it means to them, whether or how it has been be useful to them, how it might be made useful—within the broad agenda of Aboriginal peoples' recovery from the Residential School era and a desire for postcolonial / antioppressive relations with non-Aboriginal peoples and agencies.	Interviews in communities, conducted by community-based team primarily with parents about goals for children's development, cultural practices, desired and actual supports for young children and views about assessment. Transcription, content and quantitative analyses, feedback.	To identify local requirements for research, possible research strategies, data collection opportunities, and interpretations of the context and meanings of data obtained.

histories for these at-risk children from birth to age nine. Permission has been requested to link these medical files to the children's files in the Ministry of Education in order to examine the children's developmental and educational outcomes (Goelman, 2008). The second study also addressed questions of developmental trajectories of at-risk children but did so through a multiple case-study approach. Using qualitative methods including interviews and focus groups, this study examined families' experiences and their perspectives on the assessment and intervention processes that they lived through (Pighini, 2008).

The Infant Neuromotor Study was led by an interdisciplinary team of academic researchers from nursing, occupational and physical therapy, and community partners from two provincial early intervention programs, the IDP, and the British Columbia Centre for Ability. *The Infant Neuromotor Study* set out to determine the concurrent validity of two specific tools designed to identify infants under one year of age with neuromotor difficulties: the *Alberta Infant Motor Scales*

(AIMS) (Tse et al., 2008) and the *Harris Infant Motor Test* (HINT) (Mayson, Hayes, Harris, & Backman, 2009). The AIMS was designed for children from birth to 18 months while the HINT was designed for children from 2.5 to 12.5 months of age. There was a high level of convergent validity between the two measures at Time 1 (4–6.5 months) and at Time 2 (10–12.5 months) with a sample of 72 children who were referred to the study because of suspected neuromotor delays/disorders and 49 children where neuromotor delays/disorders were not suspected. The study also established the predictive validity of the HINT by using the *Bayley Scales of Infant Development II* at 24 months and the *Bayley Scales of Infant and Toddler Development* at 36 months (Bayley, 1993, 2006).

In order to expand the training opportunities for interdisciplinary early child development professionals in both urban and rural settings to reliably screen for neuromotor delays/disorders, *The Infant Neuromotor Study* team developed and piloted both face-to-face and online formats to deliver course material to learn to administer the AIMS. The online version was used and tested with professionals mostly in remote communities, thereby offering them and their clientele services that would otherwise not have been possible due to a lack of training opportunities. In addition to occupational and physical therapists, the courses also enrolled nurses, early childhood educators, and other early interventionists. The researchers concluded that both course delivery formats could help in early screening and detection of infants with delays and, therefore, lead to increased early referral to intervention services.

The Community-Based Screening Study evaluated a population-based developmental surveillance program that had been implemented in the community 18 months prior. The two previously discussed studies dealt with diagnostic assessment conducted by professionals, while *The Community-Based Screening Study* explored the use of a parent-completed measure—the *Nipissing District Developmental Screen* (NDDS)—to screen a nonrisk population for children who might require subsequent diagnostic assessment and perhaps intervention. The children in this study included infants, toddlers, preschoolers, and kindergarten students. Although the children were initially recruited through nonrandom sampling, an effort was made to obtain a sample that was representative of the diversity in the general population. Recruitment of the younger children was conducted at a public health immunization clinic, a family support center, child health fairs, and through advertising in the community (e.g., newspapers, posters). Recruitment of kindergarten students took place through selected classrooms within selected schools. The study also made use of the Bayley Scales of Infant Development for the 193 children aged 4, 18, and 24 months and of the Stanford-Binet for the 90 36-month-old children and 89 kindergarten students.

The Community-Based Developmental Screening Study found that the NDDS was able to correctly identify children with major developmental concerns or with no major developmental concerns (i.e., high test specificity for major concerns). However, the measure was much less reliable in its ability to identify children with mild or moderate disabilities. The screening program also yielded a number of positive benefits at the family and community levels. The screening provided a framework for public health nurses to discuss child growth and development with parents and other community professionals from the health, medical, social service, and education sectors (Ball, 2005; Canam, Dahinten, & Ford, 2007; Dahinten, Ford, & Lapointe, 2004; Dahinten, Ford, Canam, Lapointe, & Merkel, 2007). In fact, this study was launched as part of the CHILD Project at the initiative of the community public health nurses who were interested in exploring the effectiveness and usefulness of a program of community-based developmental screening (Anstett, 2003; Dahinten et al., 2004).

As discussed in Chapter 5, *The Indigenous Child Project* addressed the perceptions of and beliefs about child development among parents, professionals, and Elders in Indigenous communities. In particular, this study examined the participants' experiences with previous early childhood assessment practices in their communities and their recommendations for assessment practices in the future. Through focus groups and interviews, the participants described their personal experiences with previous child assessments as depersonalized and "high-handed" due to a number of factors. Parents were often not asked to give informed consent to the assessments, which were frequently conducted by professionals behind closed doors. Typically, these assessments were conducted with no or little input from parents or others who knew the children well. Further, parents received little in the way of feedback, discussion, or consultation based on the assessments, and written copies of reports were rarely provided to the parents. Parents felt that many of the measures were not culturally fair or sensitive to Indigenous children and did not acknowledge or respect local knowledge, history, custom, and language. Parents reported situations in which assessment results were often used to place children into remedial educational streams from which it was extremely difficult to have them removed.

To remedy these problems, the communities recommended that all assessments be guided by respect for Indigenous peoples and their culture and traditions—a perspective that is being reported increasingly in research on screening in Indigenous communities (e.g., Panagiotopoulos et al., 2007). The process of conducting child assessments must be built upon meaningful relationships with the members of the Indigenous communities; these relationships must be expressed through reciprocity between the professional assessors and the child, the child's family, the child's community, and the community Elders. Parents expressed interest in learning more about standardized assessment instruments in order to determine whether there were ways in which these instruments could be modified or customized to be used with First Nations communities. Overall, community participants were in favor of activities that could help parents, teachers, and other professionals to gain a better understanding of their children's development and to use the results of different forms of assessments to continue to develop programs that could respond to the unique needs of each child.

The Benefits and Challenges of Interdisciplinary Research in Early Identification and Screening

The benefits and challenges of conducting these four complementary studies under one project umbrella fall into three general categories: shared and complementary methodologies; implications for complementary levels of practice; the uses, misuses, and possible abuses of language in the assessment and diagnosis of young children.

Shared and Complementary Methodologies

The sharing of research methodologies, instruments, and training procedures can save time and money and can certainly facilitate cross-disciplinary discourse. *The Developmental Pathways Study* (at 18 months), *The Infant Neuromotor Study* (24 and 36 months), and *The Community-Based Screening Study* (4, 18, and 36 months) all used the Bayley Scales of Infant Development, resulting in cost-savings to the CHILD Project as a whole. Further, the school psychologist involved in *The Community-Based Screening Study* also trained the research assistants in *The Infant Neuromotor Study*. The CHILD Project provided a shared context for discussing the advantages and disadvantages of developmental assessment measures across these four studies.

The success of the interdisciplinary training program for use of the HINT in *The Infant Neuromotor Study* reveals the potential and importance of shared preservice and in-service training for health and early intervention professionals and how this kind of training can serve as a basis for further collaboration and interaction across existing professional boundaries. With a broader range of professionals (e.g., nurses, child care workers, IDP consultants) trained to administer a broader range of assessment measures, a province-wide system of early screening and identification would be much more flexible and responsive (see also Browning & Solomon, 2005; Strelnick, Bateman, & Jones, 1988).

The four studies demonstrated that what is often presented as a dichotomy—universal versus targeted approaches in early identification—can actually be viewed as a continuum of complementary and mutually reinforcing approaches to both research and practice. The inclusion of all four studies allowed the CHILD Project as a whole to explore issues relating to broad community-based universal screening practices at one end of the continuum and to the use of diagnostic assessments to identify individual children with specific atypical developmental profiles at the other end of the continuum (figure 6.1). A major contribution of *The Indigenous Child Project* was the emphasis placed on the child's culture and history and on the importance of respectful and ongoing communication with the child's parents. We recommend including these concerns as integral to assessment procedures across the entire continuum.

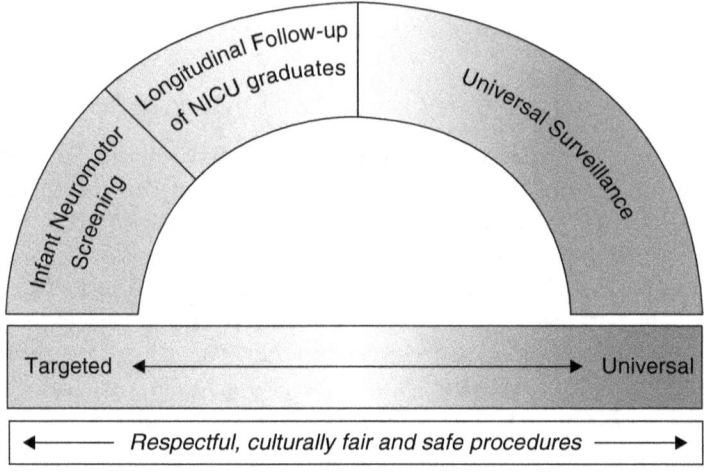

Figure 6.1 Continuum of Screening Models in the CHILD Project

Implications for Complementary Levels of Practice

The complementarity of the four studies also lends itself to possibilities for bridging the gaps in the province's current approach to screening and early identification. In table 6.3 we have built upon the current suite of processes and procedures and have suggested where the assessment techniques described in this chapter might best fit in. Jointly, the four studies provide a framework of complementary approaches to early screening and identification programs in the province. Guiding this framework are the basic assessment principles proposed by Meisels and Atkins-Burnett (2000) as essential in this

Table 6.3 Current and Proposed Early Screening and Identification Procedures in British Columbia

Respectful, culturally fair and safe procedures				
Screening of all children, routine administration	Screening available to all children, voluntary	Screening for children with suspected or diagnosed conditions		Diagnostic follow-up for children with suspected or diagnosed conditions
All infants right after birth, routine medical screening All infants, universal newborn hearing soon after birth		At-risk infants, referral to NICU Suspected deficits, identified disabilities		Continued follow-up for most vulnerable infants (<800 grams) through early and middle childhood referral for intervention
As needed between zero–five years	Consultations with, assessments, and referrals by • Parents; • Public health nurses; • Pediatricians; • Infant Development consultants; • Occupational, physical therapists; • Elders.	*Neuromotor screening with HINT at six months.* Suspected deficits, identified disabilities		• Referral to early intervention program. • Continued follow-up and monitoring. • Continued consultation, involvement with parents.
Scheduled 18 months, 36 months, 54 months	Universal, comprehensive screening, all aspects of health and development	*Suspected deficits, identified disabilities;*		

complementary model: assessment based upon parent involvement and collaboration; assessment based upon the use of multiple sources of information; an assessment of child strengths and challenges. To these principles we would add those recommended by *The Indigenous Child Project*: That all assessment be conducted with dignity and respect; and that all assessments be conducted in ways that are culturally fair and culturally safe. The framework is intended to address the needs of children from birth to age five across the entire spectrum of typically and atypically developing children and is based in part on similar models developed by Miller and McNulty (1997), Guralnick (2004), and Goelman et al. (2004).

At the broadest level, the framework recognizes the need for screening procedures that are delivered almost universally and are performed routinely at specific times and places (e.g., at birth, at kindergarten entry). The next level would be screening programs, which are offered universally to all children and families who are strongly encouraged to participate but not mandated to participate. In this category we are proposing neuromotor screening (HINT) at 6 months

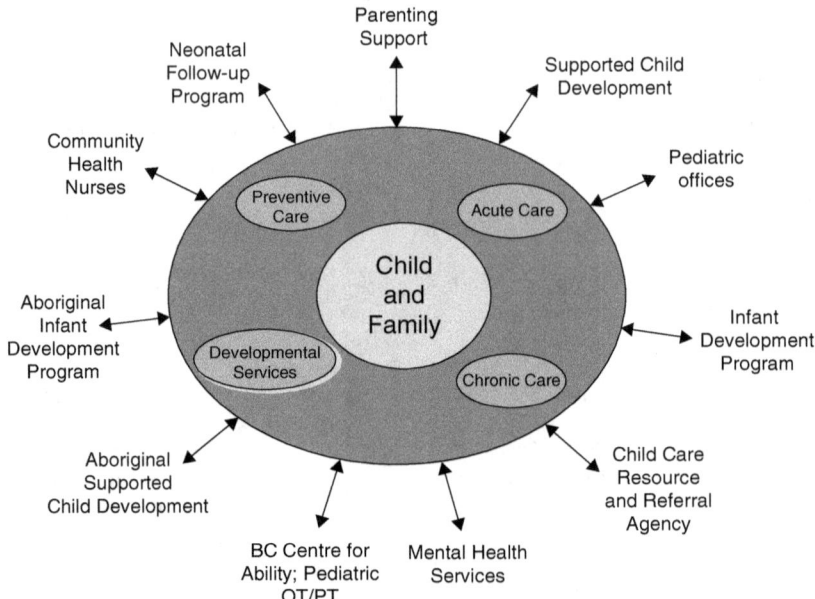

Figure 6.2 Proposed Integration of Screening and Intervention Services in British Columbia Based on the CHILD Project

Source: Adapted from N. Halfon, 2004.

and a complete developmental assessment at 18, 36, and 54 months across all domains with a valid screening tool. If the results indicate the presence of a developmental concern, further referrals for diagnostic assessment would be recommended.

At a more targeted and specific level, children cared for in the NICU at very high risk of neurodevelopmental disabilities would continue to be monitored through Neonatal Follow-up Programs. Woven throughout these timelines for regular developmental assessment would be numerous opportunities for parents to initiate assessments of their children through, for example, home visits by community nurses, Infant Development Consultants, or during visits to pediatric offices. The framework would allow for multiple points of entry and would strongly encourage a high degree of information sharing and collaboration among parents and various health, educational, and social service professionals. Figure 6.2 provides an overview of the various offices and agencies, which would be expected to play a role to facilitate this essential coordination.

Language: The power of words and words of power

The CHILD Project included qualitative and quantitative researchers from the health and social sciences and community professionals from different professions. In some ways, and at certain times, the members of the CHILD Project found themselves speaking different dialects of the same language and sometimes even different languages. As one of the principal investigators on *The Income Assistance Study* put it, child development research has used "the power of words" to describe how professionals describe the children they have assessed. Conversely, "words of power" have been used to label, diagnose, or to control children and their families. We have learned from our experiences that the languages of assessment can have both positive and negative effects.

One such issue discussed at length in Chapter 5 on the Indigenous studies was the use of the terms "screening" and "surveillance" that were used by *The Community-Based Screening Study*, *The Developmental Pathways Study*, and *The Infant Neuromotor Study* to describe an approach to monitoring children's health and development in a universal, consistent, and systematic fashion. Developmental surveillance is a technique more commonly used by health professionals including physicians and public health nurses. One of the more widely cited definitions of surveillance is put forth by Dworkin (1993) who defined developmental surveillance as "a flexible, continuous process in which knowledgeable professionals perform skilled observations of children during the provision of health care" (p. 531). In its most basic form it is the process undertaken by a health care provider in their day-to-day work with young children, observing their development. It includes the provider's attendance to the concerns of the parents, coupled with their obtaining relevant developmental history. Checklists are often completed to help track milestones. Many view surveillance and screening, particularly universal screening, as similar processes. "Screening" is a brief procedure with the goal of working to determine those in need of more in-depth follow-up for possible diagnosis. The spirit of both is to identify those in need of further follow up or monitoring. While surveillance is thought to be a longitudinal process occurring as a part of effective day-to-day practice (Dworkin & Glascoe, 2005), screening, in contrast, involves a more summative snap shot of the child at a given point in time. Its purpose is to identify those children in need of further in-depth assessment. Screening is often considered a part of effective developmental surveillance or ongoing systematic review of the child's development.

The term "surveillance," however, carried ominous overtones in particular to some members of other study teams within the CHILD Project. For researchers and community partners in *The Indigenous Child Project*, the term "surveillance" had connotations of the kinds of governmental control and manipulation of First Nations people for centuries. Similarly, *The Income Assistance Study* of families living in poverty also had strongly negative reactions to "surveillance." Many of the families living in poverty who participated in interviews and focus groups reported that the governmental regulations that framed and monitored their eligibility to receive income assistance relied upon different forms of government reporting and "surveillance" of, for example, their incomes, expenditures, family status, and marital status.

The research community itself is apparently beginning to recognize the problematic status of the word "surveillance" and has begun to advocate for stronger parent voices and control in programs of developmental surveillance (Glascoe, 1999, 2006).

The "power of words" was also found to be an issue in the kinds of diagnoses that were distributed to children based on their ethnic or Indigenous identity. One of the researchers on *The Income Assistance Study* quoted from one of the interviewees: "How come when my kid acts up they call it Fetal Alcohol Syndrome but when my white neighbour's kid acts up they call it Learning Disability?" Thus, while terms like developmental surveillance, Fetal Alcohol Syndrome, and learning disability may be intended to be used as objective, diagnostic, and value-free words, we learned that depending on the context, they can each carry powerful negative implications for people on the receiving end of the diagnosis.

The terms "delay," "disorder," and "disability"—especially when coupled with the adjectives "mild," "moderate," and "severe"—all create meanings that do not always travel well beyond the boundaries of one discipline or even beyond the definitions of a specific assessment measure. This issue of the language of diagnosis also arose in discussions of how best to describe children for whom there were developmental concerns but who did not fall into any universally agreed upon definition of disability. In the pediatrics literature, Glascoe, Foster, and Wolraich (1997) described the problem in this way: "Unfortunately, many disabilities are difficult to recognize; they are often subtle, rarely associated with dysmorphology or other obvious characteristics, or incompletely manifested during pediatric encounters" (p. 830).

The CHILD Project studies reviewed in this chapter reported the relative ease of identifying children with "severe" conditions but the great difficulty they had in assigning diagnoses to children with "soft" or "mild" conditions. The prevalence of these hard-to-diagnose children was in fact predicted and confirmed by the community partners on the respective research teams and led some in the CHILD Project to refer to these undiagnosed children as being in the "grey area." These were children who appeared to perform within the normal range on developmental assessments but for whom there remained concerns caused by some combination of trauma at birth, social behaviors in early childhood, or parental reports of something being "off" or "not right," which was found in observations and experiences. In other words, the precise language of diagnosis and disability was often found to be inadequate; instead of forcing children into an inappropriate diagnostic category the research teams acknowledged the complexity of the developmental profile of these children and in response, created new language to more accurately reflect that complexity (Goelman et al., 2007).

Conclusions

The CHILD Project represents one attempt to better understand the process, content, and study of child development, especially for children who present with developmental concerns. By bringing together researchers from different disciplinary and professional perspectives the CHILD Project created the opportunity for these researchers to articulate and share the meanings of "children," "childhood" and "disability" that had guided their research to date and to invite them to engage in the process of extending and co-constructing new meanings through collaborative discourse, problem-finding, and problem-solving. Similarly, the collaboration of community professionals and university researchers allowed for an ongoing exploration on how the worlds of professional practice and academic research construct meaning and knowledge regarding the conditions, policies, and programs that best support children and their families. The design and implementation of the CHILD Project generated information on the practical needs of parents and health care professionals and real-life applications of the CHILD Project's findings.

Taken together, the studies reviewed in this chapter can be understood to recommend different types of parent involvement in the screening and early identification process. There are at least two specific recommendations that emerge from an ethic of parental respect. First, it is important even for so-called universal screening programs to obtain informed consent from all parents for data to be collected on their children. The second is that participation rates will increase when there are parent involvement and education programs, which explain the value and importance of early screening and identification programs.

The screening and early identification studies in the CHILD Project have provided valuable information on the health and social development of typical and atypical young children, and have also begun to teach us about both the benefits and challenges of collaborative, interdisciplinary work. As noted throughout the chapter, the screening and identification practices in the province are fragmented with few coherent guidelines. In recent years, however, the new BC Early Hearing Program involving universal early hearing detection and intervention has done a great deal of work to try to address issues of fragmentation. They've developed provincial standards and protocols for professionals across sites and disciplines through a coordinated, cross-ministerial approach. Different medical, health, educational, and social service agencies—and different government departments and ministries—are involved with different mandates, protocols, and funding procedures. The research studies have reported data that demonstrate the "best practices" within their own specific disciplines and professions. Taken together, the four studies discussed in this chapter provide guidance for substantive programmatic revision in the area of screening and early identification.

NOTES

1. See chapter 5 for a full discussion of the findings of the two studies on child development in First Nations communities.
2. Developmental Pathways CHILD*Talk* Paper, May 19, 2004; Infant Neuromotor CHILD*Talk* Paper, May 19, 2004; Community Community-Based Developmental Screening CHILD*Talk* Paper, May 19, 2004; Indigenous CHILD CHILD*Talk* Paper, September 28, 2004

CHAPTER 7

Nurturant Environments for Children's Social, Emotional, and Physical Well-Being

Jayne Pivik, Susan Herrington, and Michaela Gummerum

Where, after all, do universal human rights begin? In small places, close to home—so close and so small that they cannot be seen on any maps of the world ... Such are the places where every man, woman and child seeks equal justice, equal opportunity, equal dignity without discrimination. Unless these rights have meaning there, they have little meaning anywhere.

Eleanor Roosevelt

This chapter describes the results from *The Outdoor Criteria Study* mentioned previously and conducted by Susan Herrington and two new studies within the CHILD Project that were conducted by the Postdoctoral Fellows in the third year of the project. Michaela Gummerum, a developmental psychologist interested in social behavior, collaborated with Susan Herrington and Kim Schonert-Reichl of the *Safe Spaces Study*, to explore the influence of playground design on the social behavior of children in her *Playground Study*. Jayne Pivik, a community psychologist with a background in child development and environmental influences, conducted a community evaluation of features important for children and youth in her *Child and Youth Well-being Study*. This chapter presents the theory associated with nurturant environments, briefly describes each study, and then presents the results of each study that apply to environments that support children's physical, emotional, and social development, the importance of play and safety, and the environmental features that children and youth identify as important.

Theories associated with children, development, and the environment cross many disciplines, have different foci, and use a multitude of ways to test their ideas. Such a complex subject has caught the attention of developmental psychologists, urban and community planners, environmental and community psychologists, designers, and social and cognitive psychologists. Most relevant to this discussion of nurturant environments for children are *transactional theories* (Altman, 1987; Altman & Rogoff, 1987). Transactional approaches stress a bidirectional influence where the child can have an impact on the environment and the environment on the child, with neither agent holding a deterministic role. According to Altman (1987), transactional approaches assume that psychological phenomena are holistic events composed of inseparable and mutually defined psychological processes and physical and social environments. As such, understanding these phenomena requires participant involvement and usually occurs in natural settings.

A broad-based transactional theory that covers many domains of child-environment engagement is Bronfenbrenner's *Ecological Systems Theory* (Bronfenbrenner, 1979) and later, the *Bioecological Theory of Human Development* (Bronfenbrenner & Morris, 2006). As mentioned in Chapter 2, this theory focuses on a series of five nested environmental contexts with bidirectional influences within and between the systems, where any or a combination of them may influence child development. Each system (microsystem, mesosystem, exosystem, macrosystem, and chronosystem) contains roles, norms, and rules that can powerfully shape development. Examples related to nurturant environments may include how neighbors react to the child; the child's selective sensitivity to the physical and social environment; the desire of the child to reshape his/her environment; and the child's guiding beliefs about their place within the environment. The beauty and challenge of this theory is its expansive interactional and complex potentialities of proximal and distal influences on development. For example, children living with a single parent on a very limited income in a resource poor and potentially dangerous neighborhood should theoretically be at a disadvantage for school readiness (Hertzman, MacLean, Kohen, Dunn, & Evans, 2002; Kershaw, Irwin, Tafford, & Hertzman, 2005) or psychosocial adjustment (Brooks-Gunn, Duncan, Klebanov, & Sealand, 1993; Chase-

Lansdale & Gordon, 1996; Duncan, Brooks-Gunn, & Klebanov, 1994) but may instead be highly resilient and doing well because of the support of peers, mentors, or supportive social policies and programs (Bradley & Corwyn, 2002). This theoretical model posits that development is transactional and potentially influenced by many factors such as familial, economic, social, institutional, cultural, and political influences.

The work by ecological psychologists Gibson (1979) and Barker (1968) are also transactional approaches, stressing the importance of jointly studying the person and environment from functional and systemic perspectives. Gibson's use of affordances in his *Theory of Ecological Perception* (1979) links behavior to environmental opportunities for action and movement. Affordances are understood as interrelated to both the child (developmental stage, context, bodily qualities, functional demands of current actions and intentions) and the material, social, and cultural environment (Kyttä, 2004). For example, a tree may provide an opportunity for a child to climb, make a tree fort, practice physical skills, sit under and reflect, or challenge themselves. Recent research has compared the presence and absence of child-friendly affordances for outdoor environments (Heft, 1988), mobility and independence (Kyttä, 2004), and social environments (Gaver, 1996).

In some ways, Barker's behavior settings in his theory of *Ecological Psychology* (1968) are much like a cluster of affordances that provide a social context for collective human-environment interactions. Behavior settings describe the functional rules associated with a context. For example, a school playground as a behavior setting forms systems of physical or social activity according to certain norms, rules, and practices. For students, recess at the playground might mean playing whereas for teachers it might mean supervising students. A defining feature of this theory is the collective shared understanding of behavior settings by groups based on common experiences within those settings. Both Barker's and Gibson's theories are grounded in human-environment interactions that are studied in real world settings.

Another group of theories applicable to nurturant environments for children are associated with person-environment congruence. Person-environment congruence is generally defined as the degree of fit between an individual's needs, capabilities, and aspirations and the resources, demands, and opportunities provided by the environment (Coulton, 1979; Kaplan, 1983; Lewin, 1951; Stokols, 1977). Stephen Kaplan (1983) proposed *The Model of Person-Environment Compatibility* that features purposive action as an integral component.

In his study of preferences for natural environments, he found that certain environmental characteristics (e.g., distractibility or noise) negatively influenced an individual's perception and potential ability for carrying out their goals and/or plans. Rachael Kaplan extended the theory to include one's beliefs, values, needs, and desires, which in turn influences feelings of control, mastery, and an understanding of the world (Kaplan, 1991).

The past decade has seen a worldwide movement to research, build, and evaluate environments that promote child-environment congruence (UNICEF Innocenti Research Centre, 2004, 2007). This movement was launched in 1996 based on the resolution passed during the second UN Conference on Human Settlements (www.unhabit.org) to make cities livable places for all, particularly children. Three defining features intrinsic to this movement and associated research are as follows: (1) that children and youth are involved in planning and decision-making in compliance with the United Nation's Convention on the Rights of the Child (1989); (2) a focus on positive environmental features; and (3) consideration of sociocultural differences of children in the natural and built environment (Chawla & Heft, 2002).

Environmental Child-friendliness is the term given by leading researchers studying child-environment congruence (Björklid & Nordström, 2007; Chawla, 2002; Horelli, 2007; Kyttä, 2004; Haikkola, Pacilli, Horelli, & Prezza, 2007). According to Horelli (1998),

> Environmental child-friendliness is a community product developed from local structures beyond the individual level. It comprises a network of places with meaningful activities, where young and old can experience a sense of belonging whether individually or collectively. The participation of children and youth in the shaping of their settings plays a central role in the creation of child friendly environments. (p. 225)

Horelli (2007) provides a framework for environmental child-friendliness that includes 10 normative dimensions complimented by both person-environment fit and collective-environment fit criteria. Based on a content analysis of research on child involvement with their environments and studies exploring youth feedback, she identified the following dimensions as critical for good environments for children and youth: (1) housing and dwellings that are flexible and secure; (2) the availability of basic services, for example, health, education, and transportation that facilitate everyday life; (3) opportunities for children to participate in planning and development within their environments; (4) feelings of physical and psychological safety and security; (5) opportunities for close social relationships with family, kin, peers, and community; (6) environments that are functional, aesthetic, and cultural that provide a variety of interesting affordances and arenas for activities; (7) resource provision and distribution and poverty reduction; (8) elements of nature and sustainable development; (9) a sense of belonging and continuity; and (10) good governance that includes and acts on youth decision making about their environments.

Added to these dimensions are the need to ensure that the environment provides support or perceived support for one's goals and needs (person-environment fit; see Kaplan, 1983; Lewin, 1948; Stokols, 1979) and community supports (collective-environment fit) such as social networks (Rissotto & Tonucci, 2002) and supportive collective infrastructures (Barker, 1968; Horelli, 2002). Tied to all of these criteria are the need to ensure that children and youth are legitimately involved in the planning and evaluation of these environments in a culturally sensitive manner.

The following section explores the characteristics of community and neighborhood environments that support children and families. Results of research from *The Outdoor Criteria Study, The Playground Study,* and *The Child and Youth Well-Being Study* provide insight into the programmatic and environmental contexts that promote children's positive physical, social, and emotional development. Specifically, we present features that promote social-emotional development; features that promote physical development; and features that promote a sense of safety. Also, we discuss the importance of play in development and how children and youth define good communities. This chapter is a summative review of these three studies. After describing each study, the goals above are addressed with a brief description of the current literature and our results.

The Outdoor Criteria Study

The outdoor play environment can contribute in incommensurable ways to children's cognitive, social, physical, and emotional development (Moore & Young, 1978; Moore, 1986; Moore, Goltsman, & Iacofano, 1992; Moore, 1993; Moore & Wong, 1997; Rivkin, 1995; Herrington, 1997; Herrington & Studtmann, 1998; Herrington & Lesmeister, 2006; Olds, 2000; Kylin, 2003). Building upon this research, *The Outdoor Criteria Study* was a five-year investigation that examined the developmental contributions and shortcomings of outdoor play environments in 17 licensed child care centers in the city of Vancouver, British Columbia, Canada. Approximately 216 children aged three–five were studied in relationship to their center's outdoor play space. In addition, researchers interviewed 78 early childhood educators (ECE) working at these child care centers.

Seventeen centers were selected from eleven different neighborhoods. These neighborhoods exhibited varying degrees of social and economic support as indicated by a Human Early Learning Partnership (HELP) map analysis of Vancouver in comparison with rates of children's vulnerability (Kershaw, Irwin, Trafford, & Hertzman, 2005). Centers were also selected for their architectural configuration (at grade, below grade, roof top), and their willingness to participate. Children three–five years old were selected as subjects because this age group is increasingly involved with the physical environment as a medium for play and development (Moore, 1986). At this age, they also experience important developmental milestones such as increased physical ability, curiosity, imagination, memory, language, imitative play, and more complex cooperative play. Moreover, three–five years is also the age when parents are most likely to register their children in licensed child care (Goelman, Doherty, Lero, LaGrange, & Tougas, 2000).

The Outdoor Criteria Study was based on an action research model. This methodology combines different ways of undertaking a research problem and involves collaboration between different groups of individuals for the purpose of bringing about change in concrete situations (Stringer, 1996). Specifically, a review of the literature, field observations, focused group interviews, center-wide workshops, and videotaping of children using the play spaces were used (Herrington, 2008).

The review of the literature helped identify other studies that have linked the design of outdoor play spaces with child development and provided a set of criteria for the field observations. These criteria are called the Seven Cs (Herrington & Lesmeister, 2006; Herrington, Lesmeister, Nicholls, & Stefiuk, 2007) and include the following: (1) *Character* indicates the overall feel of outdoor play spaces; (2) *Context* involves how the play space interacts with its surroundings; (3) *Connectivity* indicates the physical and visual connectedness of the play space through a hierarchy of paths and the link between indoors and outdoors; (4) *Change* refers to the range of differently sized spaces and how these spaces change over time. Living things can signal change in the seasons and growth and elements for play; (5) *Chance* provides an opportunity for children to create, manipulate, and leave an impression on their outdoor play space; (6) *Clarity* integrates physical and perceptual legibility. Play spaces should promote spontaneous exploration, but not confusion; and (7) *Challenge* refers to the available challenges (physical and cognitive) that a play space provides.

Field observations and scaled plan-view drawings of each outdoor play space were conducted. Drawings identified materials and equipment in the play space. Photographs were also taken of these spaces at an adult's height and a child's height. Play spaces were evaluated with regard to the Seven Cs using these drawings and photographs. Videotaping of the children playing in the spaces at different times of the year allowed researchers to gain further insight into the life of the outdoor play spaces. Computerized random sampling of all tapes of all centers revealed how these play spaces were being used by the children; thus how the detailed aspects of the physical environment were helping or hindering children's development and play.

Focused interviews with the participating centers' early childhood educators (ECEs) and two center-wide workshops with ECEs filled in gaps not captured on video. Interview notes were analyzed by comparing the responses of ECEs at different centers. Positive and negative comments were counted and compared with (1) the location of the center; (2) the layout of the play space; and (3) the presence of plant material in their center's play space. Positive versus negative observations were identified by the adjectives and phrasing used. The presence of material in or near the play space was accounted for as well. Specifically, plant material included trees, shrubs, grass, and ground cover, but did not include empty boxes, empty pots, or temporary displays of flowers. Large shade trees that bordered the play space and brought in dappled light and mediated the play environment were also counted as plant material.

In order to ascertain what future changes the ECEs thought were needed in their outdoor play spaces, we analyzed key words and phrases from the interview notes. After matching, coding, and counting words and phrases across centers, we categorized them in terms of themes and specific suggestions. Remarks made within focus group sessions that directly contradicted each other were not counted nor were casual remarks that were not duplicated elsewhere. Few contradicting remarks were made, so this was not an important facet of the study.

The Playground Study

The question of how the physical environment influences humans' perceptions, cognitions, and actions has been a reoccurring topic in the history of psychology (e.g., Bronfenbrenner, 2005; Gibson, 1977; Skinner, 1971). However, as Evans (2006) points out, psychological studies have mainly focused on the features of a child's psychosocial environment (e.g., family context, peer relations, types of schools, cultural context) and have mostly ignored the physical contexts of development. *The Playground Study* examined how the design of preschool children's play spaces in their day care centers affects their social play and other social behaviors with peers. The study was based on the theory that the physical environment presents action possibilities or affordances to an actor, as suggested by Gibson (1977, 1979). That is, affordances represent certain qualities of an environment that allow an individual to perform an action, depending on their capabilities. In relation to playground design and children's play, Pellegrini (1995) stated that certain features of the playground can facilitate or constrain strategies children use in their play. For example, playgrounds with zones for individual, small-group, and large-group activities provide opportunities for different kinds of interactions between children, their peers, and teachers, thus assisting the development of competencies necessary for those different relationships.

In *The Playground Study*, the analysis of the physical playground environment was based on Susan Herrington and colleagues' Seven Cs, mentioned above (Herrington & Lesmeister, 2006; Herrington et al., 2007). Previous research suggests that four of the Seven Cs might be particularly influential for the development of children's social play. Hart and Sheehan (1986) proposed that the *character* of a playground, that is, the overall feel and design intent of the play space might affect preschool children's social play. In their study, two- to three-year-old children showed more unoccupied behavior on a contemporary versus a traditional playground. The traditional playground was less structured and contained more movable equipment, more open spaces, and features, such as a sandbox, swings, and slides. In contrast, the contemporary playground featured less open spaces and less equipment that could be rearranged.

Previous studies have also found higher levels of play in outdoor play spaces that present children with flexible materials, graduated challenges, and enclosed areas that foster small group play (Brown & Burger, 1984; Campbell & Frost, 1985; Johnson, Christie, & Yawkey, 1999; Weilbacher, 1981). These features correspond to the Cs *change, chance*, and *challenge* in Herrington and colleagues' system. Trancik and Evans (1995) point out that these features are important for promoting competency in preschool children, that is, the ability to interact effectively with one's physical and social environment. Specifically, the creation of differently sized subspaces (change) allows children to experience interactions in dyadic or small groups and to get away from large groups. Being able to manipulate one's physical environment (chance) gives children the opportunity to gain control of the physical environment and be active in their development. Different levels of challenge prevent frustration in children as they might either be too overwhelmed by the difficulty of a new task or lose interest in it if it is not challenging enough.

To investigate how preschool children's social play styles and behaviors differ in relation to the design of the outdoor play space in their day care center, the videotapes collected in *The Outdoor Criteria Study* were reanalyzed. The videos of three of the original 17 day care centers were excluded from the present analysis as they mainly served toddlers whose social play has been shown to differ from older preschool children (e.g., Parten, 1932). To obtain a comparable age range in each of the day care centers, we limited the analysis to centers serving children from three to five years of age. In each of the day care centers, children's play activities were videotaped on two rainy and two sunny days for about one hour each. Two types of coding were conducted: (1) coding of the design elements of the outdoor play space (7Cs); and (2) coding children's social (play) behavior following a manual by Ladd, Price, and Hart (1988) using an event-coding technique (Hoch, Pellegrini, & Symons, 2004).

Social behavior coding. In classifying a particular action, the coder has to determine whether behavior was interactive (i.e., with other people) or noninteractive. Noninteractive behaviors were coded into the following categories: unoccupied, onlooking, solitary play, parallel play, or aggressive. If a behavior was classified as interactive, then the person the child was interacting with and the type of interaction was recorded. Interactive behaviors between children and teachers were coded as either a teacher-initiated or child-initiated interaction. Interactions between children were coded as social conversation, argument, unilateral bids, cooperative play, rough and tumble play, object possessiveness, aggression, or friendly touch. Interactive behavior toward other persons (e.g., parents, nonteaching staff) was coded in a separate category. Two independent raters coded seven entire videos using the program ProcoderDV (Tapp, 2003). Agreement between coders was defined as giving the same code to the same behavioral event in the videos. Interrater agreement was 83 percent.

The Child and Youth Well-Being Study

The evidence linking child health in relation to the environment is mounting rapidly (Beauvais & Jensen, 2003; Connor, 2001; Stroick & Jensen, 1999). Health, as defined by the World Health Organization, is "a state of complete physical, mental and social well-being and not merely the absence of disease or infirmity" (2007). Different constructs have been promoted for explaining neighborhood effects on children. For example, Ellen and Turner (1997) suggest that the quality of social services, socialization by adults, peer influences, social networks, exposure to crime and violence, and physical distance and isolation influence child development. Jencks and Mayer (1990) suggest that the availability of, and competition for neighborhood resources, peers, familial, and outside adults can have an impact on child and youth outcomes. Connor and Brink (1999) also suggest social contagion, collective socialization, resources—and add competition influences—whereas Shonkoff and Phillips (2000) add environmental conditions, such as toxins and safety. The goal of the *Child and Youth Well-Being Study* was to determine which aspects of a community are important to children and youth from their perspective and why.

The community under study was a coastal island, 20 minutes away by ferry from West Vancouver, British Columbia, Canada. This semi-isolated rural island has the largest population of children under 5 years per capita adult in British Columbia according to the 2001 Canadian Census, 3,500 permanent residents and is surrounded by ocean. About 500 workers and over 200 students commute to offices and schools on the mainland every day. There are 65 km of hiking/walking trails, shops, 4 churches, a thriving arts community, 4 schools, and a park and recreational program that runs mainly out of the community school. The size, location, and rural aspect of the island provided an ideal opportunity to examine those features of the environment that might influence children and youth, such as, how the physical environment promotes or hinders well-being; physical activity; play and recreation; the effect of fewer services; the impact of social capital and community cohesion; the effect of parents working off island; and the influence of commuting by ferry.

An information letter and consent form was distributed by the principals of the four schools on the island (a public elementary school, a Montessori school, an Independent Middle school, and a Supported Learning Centre for part-time home-schoolers). In addition to getting parental consent to participate, all children provided verbal assent.

The data collection took place at the children's school. The total sample included 82 children/youth (4–15 years). Data were analyzed by 3 epoch groups: young (4–8 years, n=20); middle (9–11 years, n=25); and older (12–15 years, n=37). The primary author scored all of the data, with 30 percent scored by a second rater. Interrater agreement was 87 percent, with disagreements resolved through discussion.

A community mapping approach (Berkowitz & Wadud, 2003; Kretzmann & McKnight, 1993) was utilized, which focused on identifying the important elements of the community, in this case, from the perspective of children and youth. Using multiple methods, children were asked to participate in each of the following activities: cognitive mapping, an individual interview, community asset mapping, and a group discussion, in this order. Having each child complete all of these activities provided the opportunity to conduct a comparative analysis of the different methods and the opportunity to determine those aspects of the community that are important to children and youth at different stages of their development. All the activities were videotaped and audiotaped for educational training purposes and to ensure accuracy of the feedback. In addition to the researcher, three research assistants were required at the various stations, as the children cycled through the activities at their own pace. The following describes each method employed.

Cognitive mapping. Cognitive maps reflect mental processing of relative locations and attributes of phenomena in one's everyday or spatial environment. The maps provide a way of identifying how the child sees its environment and what is important to them. Children were asked to "draw a map of where they live." They were provided with a variety of pencils, pens, markers, and a sheet of plain paper. The cognitive maps along with the child's description of it (during the individual interview), were examined in relation to the presence and absence of a number of features: natural elements, built structures, housing/street congestion, proximity to neighbors, level of neighborhood depicted (house, street, neighborhood, town/city, world) and the sites associated with recreation (e.g., parks), programs (e.g., dance class) or resources (e.g., school, library). The number of occurrences in each category was identified along with the individual's age and gender.

Individual interviews. Individual interviews were then conducted in which the children verbally described their cognitive map and answered the following questions: (1) Why is this community good for kids? (2) Why is it not good for kids? and (3) Can you think of any solutions? Content and thematic analyses were conducted using NVivo 7.0. The data were unitized (i.e., units of data such as words, sentences, or multisentence chunks that can be analyzed for meaning were selected). The units were then coded into categories, which represented common ideas or themes. Along with the qualitative analyses, the frequency of each theme was recorded.

Asset mapping. A large map of the island was hung at eye level and each child was given four different-colored stickers. Children were asked to place a sticker on a location on the map that related to the following: (1) Their favorite place in the community; (2) Where they spend the most time with friends; (3) The place where they most often do after school activities; and (d) The place they would go if they needed help and family wasn't around. The child's age, gender, and answers to the questions were recorded. This method allowed a connection between place and activity and addressed social networking as well programs and resources. For example, where they do after school activities provided a description of the types of activities that the children are involved with and the programs and services of the community.

Group discussions. The same questions asked in the individual interviews were used for the group discussion, that is, (1) Why is this community good for kids? (2) Why is this community not good for kids? (3) Can you suggest changes or solutions? Like the interviews, content and thematic analyses were conducted.

Features That Promote Social and Emotional Development

The natural environment. Previous research has shown that children who consistently play outdoors exhibit more positive feelings about each other (Moore & Wong, 1997). Outdoor play also triggers positive social interactions among children (Bixler, Floyd, & Hammitt, 2002; Moore, 1986). A 1997 study conducted at the University of California compared infant development in a nongreen outdoor play space with a play space designed with plants and terrain. Researchers found greater social development occurring in the green play spaces (Herrington, 1997).

On a more macro level, research has identified that natural settings within neighborhoods positively affect children. Seminal work by Kaplan and Kaplan (1989) found that natural settings are more restorative, reduce cognitive fatigue, and enhance positive affect. In natural settings, children engage in more creative play (Faber Taylor, Kuo, & Sullivan, 2001; Kirby, 1989), and develop better motor skills (Fjortoft, 2001). Natural settings have also been shown to enhance attention (Wells, 2000) and reduce symptoms of attention deficit hyperactivity disorder (Kuo & Faber Taylor, 2004).

A random sampling of video sessions of all outdoor play spaces in *The Outdoor Criteria Study* found that children spent 15 percent of their time engaged with plants or other living things. Not all centers contained plants, but the ones that did enhanced social interactions. Play sessions involving plants included three children on average, who often engaged in emotionally intense verbal exchanges regarding the killing or preserving of plants, worms, and spiders. Living organisms not only promoted verbal exchanges but often led to moral debates among the children. Supporting this finding, the literature suggests that early childhood experiences with animals and plants may instill empathy for living things (Dighe, 1993; Finlay, 1988; Harvey, 1989; Russell, 1973). ECEs were impacted by plants as well. Those ECEs who worked in outdoor play spaces with plants reported significantly more positive feedback than those who worked in spaces without plants (Herrington, 2008).

Similar results were found in *The Child and Youth Well-Being Study*. In this study, positive benefits of the natural environment were identified by all 3 age groups, although especially children 9–11 years of age. Children reported that the natural environment was calming, serene, and provided wonderful opportunities to play. They appreciated the quiet and the lack of crowding, pollution, and traffic. Consistently, the beaches were identified as favorite places or places that they spent time with friends. This high importance given to the natural environment supports thinking by Evans (2006), Polivka, Lovell, and Smith (1998), Shonkoff and Phillips (2000), and the large body of work conducted by the Kaplans (Kaplan, 1983; Kaplan & Kaplan, 1989).

The built environment. The Playground Study investigated whether the design of the outdoor play spaces in preschool children's day care centers influenced their social behavior and social play styles. Based on a subsample of half of the original videotapes (one sunny day, one rainy day per day care center), two kinds of social interactions were defined; positively engaged interactions and negatively engaged interactions. Positively engaged interactions refer to social behaviors in which the child interacts in an emotionally positive way with another peer and contains the original coding categories: social conversation, cooperative play, and friendly touch. In contrast, negatively engaged interactions denote social behaviors, in which children relate in an emotionally negative way with other peers or the physical environment, including arguing, object possessiveness, aggression, and aggression to objects. The analyses indicated that on playgrounds with a modular and reuse character, children showed more negatively engaged social interactions whereas on playgrounds with an organic or metaphor character, children engaged in more positive than negative interactions. This finding indicates that the character of a play space can influence the social behaviors of preschool children who play on this space.

By using a median split procedure, play spaces were classified as either high or low in challenge or chance. The results indicated that significantly more positively engaged behavior occurred in playgrounds high in challenge compared to those low in challenge. Similarly, there was significantly more positively engaged behavior on playgrounds high in chance. However, there was no significant difference in social interactions in spaces high or low in change. This suggests that play spaces that provide children with different levels of physical challenge and those in which children can manipulate and leave an impression on their environment (e.g., malleable materials and loose parts) are associated with more emotionally positive interactions between children.

Finally, we investigated whether the overall number of 7Cs influenced the occurrence of positive or negative behavior on the playground. For each day care center, we summed the total number of 7Cs and defined playgrounds high in 7Cs and low in 7Cs using a median split. In spaces with an overall low number of Seven Cs design elements, children showed more negatively engaged interactions than in spaces with an overall high number of Seven Cs.

The social environment. Across a broader community level, children and youth from *The Child and Youth Well-Being Study* identified the social environment as very important. The important social aspects related mainly to social cohesion, that is, a caring and friendly community, its small size where most people are familiar, and the feeling that people look after each other. Social cohesion has been reported as important to children by others (Bandura, 1986; Connors &

Brinks, 1999; Ellen & Turner, 1997). In this study, most of the children reported that they would turn to their neighbors in times of need.

The older children (ages 12–15 years) also identified adult role modeling and social control as essential (Jencks & Mayers, 1990; Leventhal & Brooks-Gunn, 2000). They appreciated the support by other community members and enjoyed mixed-aged community events. The smaller population level of the community was associated with the need to get along with others and communal activities with people of different ages. However, even though the older children reported positive aspects of a close-knit community, they also felt a sense of surveillance by other adults ("where you know they are going to tell your mother on you").

Features That Promote Physical Development

Seven percent of Canadian children under the age of six are now classified as obese, and twenty percent are overweight (British Columbia Legislative Committee, 2006). According to Health Canada, obese children tend to become obese adults, facing increased health risks. In a Canadian study of child care centers, children in 36 percent of the studied centers spent less than 10 percent of their time engaged in outdoor play. Lack of space was the main reason for not engaging in outdoors activities (Maufette, Frechette, & Robertson, 1999). Children who play regularly outdoors show better motor fitness, including coordination, balance, and agility, and are sick less often (Fjortoft, 2001). Ample outdoor play spaces can also provide fundamental motor skills, such as those associated with running, biking, jumping, and throwing. A comparative study of children's caloric costs in outdoor versus indoor settings found that outdoor physical play burned more calories than indoors (Pellegrini, Horvat, & Huberty, 1998). Physical development has also been linked to bone strength in later life. In a study that examined associations between physical activity and bone measurement in 368 preschool children, researchers found that there were statistically significant associations between physical activity and optimal bone development (Janz et al., 2001).

Adequate resources. A random sampling of all video sessions in *The Outdoor Criteria Study* found that children played on the playground equipment only 13 percent of the time. When equipment was played upon, it was used as intended only 3 percent of the time. For example, the equipment was used in conjunction with loose parts (such as pouring sand down the holes of the support columns) 5 percent of the time, while children played underneath the structure 4 percent of the time and used the play structure to visually survey the area 1 percent of the time.

In addition to equipment, the provision of ample outdoor space for exercise is key to children's physical development. Research on outdoor play environments for young children indicates a need for more outdoor space per child than current standards call for in North America. For example, 6.9–9.2 m² of outdoor play space per fully enrolled child at child care centers has been a standard in North America since the 1980s (Moore, Goltsman, & Iacofano 1992). This space is equivalent to half of a parking stall. However, a spatial density study by Smith and Connolly (1980) found correlations between limited physical space and reduced gross motor activity. It was also found that 7.62 m² per child was the threshold dimension where activity was marked by aggression and a significant reduction in group play. A 1999 Canada-wide safety assessment of outdoor play spaces in child care centers recommended 13.5m² outdoor space per child in order to provide children with the diversity of experiences needed outside for their development while respecting safety standards (Maufette, Frechette, & Robertson, 1999). In *The Outdoor Criteria Study*, only 9 of the 17 centers studied conformed to the regulated child-to-space ratio and operated at maximum levels of density. This spatial deficit was clearly understood by the ECEs working in the studied centers. From the focus group interviews, 64 percent of ECEs identified the need for more space (Herrington, 2008).

All groups in *The Child and Youth Well-Being Study* identified the need for additional resources that related to play and recreation. Supporting the Neighborhood Resource Theory (Leventhal & Brooks-Gunn, 2000) and the Institutional Model (Jencks & Mayer, 1990), the children reported wanting more recreational opportunities such as a public swimming pool, a recreational center, and more organized sports. The younger and middle groups also wanted more play structures and parks. Older youth wanted more and different programs, as well as places to gather as a group, play music, or do pick-up sports.

Features That Promote a Sense of Safety

Safety has been consistently featured in the research literature on children's health and development. Regarding outdoor play environments, the most common playground injury is falling from equipment. As a result, the play equipment and the standards that regulate them have been lowered in height and are less challenging than previously designed equipment (Herrington & Nicholls, 2007). Fifty-seven percent of ECEs interviewed as part of *The Outdoor Criteria Study* wanted more challenging equipment in their outdoor play spaces (Herrington 2008). Ironically, less challenging equipment may, in fact, diminish actual safety for children playing in outdoor play spaces. A lack of challenging things to do in play spaces has been identified as a primary reason for increases in bullying (Blatchford, 1989; Rivkin, 1995).

A sense of safety was a dominant theme of a good community identified in *The Child and Youth Well-Being Study*, often combining aspects of both the physical and social environment. For the youngest group, safe communities included: no robbers, not a lot of toxic stuff, not too crowded or busy, and not too much traffic. The few negative comments identified by the younger children were concerns related to pedestrian safety and worries about drugs and alcohol. The middle group reported feeling safe because the community had no robbers, no gangs, people who steal kids, and the streets are safe to play on. The oldest group reported feelings of safety because the community is small, there is very little crime, very little traffic, and it provides an increased sense of independence and freedom. The importance of safety identified by these children has been supported by reviews of proxy data (Connors & Brinks, 1999; Ellen & Turner, 1997) and reports from other children (Chawla, 2002; Figueria-McDonough, 1998; Polivka, Lovell, & Smith, 1998). Likely unique to a small semi-isolated community, the children's sense of safety was also associated with more independent activities and less adult supervision, explaining reports of children playing unsupervised at beaches, the forest, and in fields with their friends.

The Importance of Play in Development

Developmental research has demonstrated that play benefits competency development across different domains, particularly social development in the preschool years. The preschool years can be characterized as the play years, because children of this age spend most of their waking hours at play (Frost, Wortham, & Reifel, 2001). Preschool children also start to interact with people outside their family context, particularly with same-aged peers. Thus, the foundation for later peer relationships and friendships emerge from those first social interactions in the preschool years. One of the first theoretical accounts concerning the development of social play during the preschool years comes from Parten (1932). Through observations of children's interactions, she concluded that social play develops along five developmental levels. At the first level, unoccupied behavior, the child is not interacting with others but engages in watching things happening around him or her or wanders around aimlessly. At the next level, onlooker behavior, the child is observing other children, but does not engage in play with them. This level is followed by solitary play where the child plays alone and makes no attempt to interact with other children. At the next level, parallel play, children play independently but in close proximity to each other. Even though children may engage in the same or similar activities, their play is not mutual and there is no communication between children. Finally, in cooperative play, children engage in similar activities with each other, the play is mutual, and children subordinate their individual interests to the goals of the play group.

Even though research following Parten (1932) does not interpret these levels in terms of a developmental succession, they still serve as categories for coding play interactions between children. Studies by Rubin and colleagues (1976, 1978) have shown that cooperative play increases both in frequency and intensity over the preschool years and that children increasingly play with a wider range of peers (Frost, Wortham, & Reifel, 2001). One type of cooperative play that has gained special attention because of its importance to emotional development is sociodramatic play. In sociodramatic play, children imitate people and real-life occurrences, and role-play typical events in their (social) environments (e.g., playing family, playing doctor, playing school). According to Smilansky and Shefataya (1990), sociodramatic play involves interactions with at least two players who verbally play out a theme over an extended period of time. It has been argued that through the acting out of social roles, relationships, and experiences, children live through the emotions of the person they are playing. Furthermore, sociodramatic play encourages children's role-taking abilities. Similarly, pretend or make-believe play, a component of sociodramatic play, helps children to develop their theory-of mind skills and facilitates their understanding of what other people think, desire, believe, and feel (Lillard, 2001; Taylor & Carlson, 1997).

The Playground Study investigated whether the outdoor play environment effects children's social play as defined by Parten's (1932) social play levels. The study focused particularly on differences in cooperative play and unoccupied behavior. As pointed out above, Parten (1932) regarded cooperative play as the most developmentally advanced form of play, and this type of play lays the foundation for children's subsequent cooperation with peers, perspective-taking abilities, and emotional development. If children engage in much unoccupied behavior on the play ground, they do not train their physical or social competencies. Results from *The Playground Study* showed that children engaged in more cooperative play in play spaces that are high in challenge and high in chance (opportunity for manipulation of the environment). Overall, children on play spaces that were low in challenge and chance tended to exhibit more unoccupied behaviors than children on play spaces that were high in challenge or chance.

Play was another major theme in *The Child and Youth Well-Being Study*. A number of differences were noted across the epoch groups. Underlying these differences was the desire for increased independence as the children grew older. This move toward independence was reflected in their accounts of play and socialization and was related to a sense of safety, the natural environment, the social environment, and available resources. The younger children liked the community because they could play on the street in front of their house, fly kites in the fields, go fishing, and ride on the many bike trails. When not playing in their neighborhoods, the younger children played at the playground at the community school.

More independent play was evident from the middle group and tended to focus in natural settings, such as at the beach, building forts in the forest, or playing in the fields—further afield from their neighborhoods. Quite a few children in this group reported that due to the lack of advanced play structures for their age, more imaginative play occurred; however, this may also have been the result of playing in natural settings (Faber Taylor, Wiley, Kuo, & Sullivan, 2001; Kirby, 1989). Safety concerns impacting their independence were also expressed by the younger and middle groups regarding the lack of sidewalks and lights for children to cross streets.

Play for the older group translated into the desire for opportunities and places for greater social interactions with friends. They wanted more and different recreational and arts programs as well as places to gather as a group such as cafés, shops, or drop-in centers. Their increased sense of independence was also evident in their desire for better transportation around the island and more frequent ferry service to go off island.

How Children and Youth Define Good Communities

Based on *The Child and Youth Well-Being Study*, four broad categories emerged as important for nurturant environments for children and youth. These included the physical environment, the social environment, feelings of safety, and available resources. These themes were identified across the different methods and across the different age groups. Specifically, positive benefits of the community for all of children/youth regardless of age included a sense of safety, the positive influence of the natural environment, a close-knit community, and available resources, programs, and services.

The majority of responses by the younger and middle groups reported some aspect of the physical environment as a positive element of their community. Typical responses for children aged four–eight years included "lots of nature," "lots of trees," "can play on street," "can fly kites," and "can go fishing." Responses from children aged 9–11 years also mainly focused on how the physical environment assisted in play, such as, "lots of different places and spaces to play"; swimming at the beach, safe to play on the road, great biking trails, nice and quiet, and lots of trees. The older group felt the community was good for children because it provided the chance to see lots of wild animals, had wide open spaces, where nature was very calming, and there was no pollution.

The importance of the social environment was highlighted by all groups but particularly the older youth. Overall, this community was identified as good for children because people are nice and friendly, they look out for each other, and due to the small size of the community, most people are familiar. Finally, in the category of resources, the younger children felt that the island had good schools, fun things to do, a toy store, and for some swimming at a private neighborhood pool. The older children mentioned the schools, trails, the Teen center, and the arts and recreational programs.

These results are consistent with research examining environmental child-friendliness, which also uses child and youth reports. For example, Haikkola, Pacilli, Horelli, and Preeza (2007) tested the theoretical framework of environmental child-friendliness (mentioned in the introduction) by asking children, their parents, the elderly, and professionals about those features of two different urban neighborhoods in Helsinki and Rome that were positive for children. The following describes the children's responses. The most important features of the Finish neighborhood, according to its children, were recreational services, public areas, the social environment, and a sense of safety. These 12-year-olds either preferred resources that promoted recreation (playgrounds, sports facilities, youth center) or the social environment (familiarity, social security, friendliness). Negative features of the environment related to a sense of safety in one area (junkies, alcoholics) that effectively limited their autonomy. Ideal environments from these children's' perspective would include a swimming place (pool or lake) and an amusement center. Children from Rome (11–12 years) indicated that services (e.g., stores, game center, school) were important to them and also indicated the importance of green spaces (e.g., providing clean air, doing group sports, socializing with friends). Two other factors were identified as important: proximity—ease of reaching a specific place; and spaciousness or the largeness of spaces. Negative elements included traffic, urban decay (garbage, pollution), and boredom (lack of things to do). Ideal environments would include recreational opportunities/services, less pollution, green spaces to play, less crowding, and opportunities for greater independence such as using streets for bicycles only. The overriding features of both neighborhoods from the children's perspective were the need for settings that allowed for safe play and social interactions with peers. Chawla (2002) and Horelli (1998) have also examined child-friendly environments from the perspective of children and found similarities across difference cultures. Children value independent mobility, opportunities for action, places to meet friends, green areas, basic services, safety, and continuity.

Conclusions

These three studies address typical places frequented by children and youth and describe findings that are positive or nurturant for their social, emotional, and physical development. Although child outcomes were not directly measured, through analysis of their behavior and from their own words, our research found that nurturant environments include natural elements, child- friendly built elements, feelings of safety and positive social interactions. Playgrounds that include living, natural elements promoted social interactions and discussions about the importance of nature. Neighborhoods that include natural elements such as forests, beaches, and fields also provided greater social interactions and opportunities for play. In addition, positive emotional responses were noted for natural environments such as a sense of serenity, calmness, and the opportunity to view wildlife. Conversely, environments that included crowding, pollution, and traffic were disliked by children and youth.

The built environment was also shown to influence children's social and emotional behavior. Play spaces that provide children with different levels of physical challenges and where they could manipulate the environment resulted in more positive social interactions with their peers. Also, play spaces that were low in challenge and chance tended to have children who exhibited more unoccupied behaviors than children on play spaces that were high in challenge or chance.

A supportive social environment was also found to be important to children and youth. The important social aspects identified relate mainly to social cohesion and a close-knit community. Adult role modeling and knowing that adults were looking out for them were also positively identified as important.

The availability of child-friendly resources was also shown to be central for children's physical development. Playgrounds that did not stimulate the children were not used the majority of the time. Further, playgrounds without enough space for children to move around and play were considered inadequate. Resources were also identified as important in the community study. Children reported wanting more recreational opportunities such as a public swimming pool, a recreational center, and more organized sports. The younger and middle groups also wanted more stimulating play structures and parks. Older youth wanted more and different recreational programs, as well as places to socialize.

Findings from these research studies suggest that other physical environments are worthy of study. These studies focused on playgrounds at day care centers and a rural coastal community. Places not examined include other types of communities or neighborhoods (e.g., urban, rural, suburban), community recreational centers, public parks, and school settings. Further research should endeavor to examine these settings to determine those aspects that promote positive social, emotional, and physical development in children and youth.

Even with this restricted scope, our findings supported 7 out of 10 dimensions of Horelli's *Framework for Environmental Child-Friendliness* (2007). These included (1) feelings of physical and psychological safety and security; (2) opportunities for close social relationships with family, kin, peers, and community; (3) environments that are functional, aesthetic, and cultural that provide a variety of interesting affordances and arenas for activities; (4) resource provision and distribution and poverty reduction; (5) elements of nature and sustainable development; (6) a sense of belonging and continuity; and (7) opportunities for children to participate in planning and development within their environments. Two dimensions that we would add based on our findings are environmental features that provide stimulation and the opportunity for developmentally safe risk taking in order to develop competencies; and a category related to play spaces that incorporates different developmental needs and levels of independence.

As pointed out by Bronfenbrenner (2005), the physical environment is an important contextual factor that can promote or hinder children's (positive) development. The findings from these three research studies corroborate the transactional nature of person-environment relationships, from the scale of an outdoor play space to an entire community. They also increase our knowledge about places frequented by children that are structured by institutions and agencies, such as planning boards and health agencies, whose goals rarely factor in children's development. We recommend that people working day-to-day in children's environments, such as practitioners in child development, community psychologists and social workers, as well as children themselves, be involved in decisions regarding children's environments. By drawing upon research that identifies the powerful link between person-environment relationships and child development; community-based programs can help introduce the very human needs of children into official plans, initiatives, strategies, and services.

However, this effort needs to extend beyond communities into the realm of public policy. As Gill (2008) indicates, countries that promote and support child play, activity, and freedom, such as the Netherlands and other Scandinavian countries, have the highest levels of subjective well-being and the best outcomes around family and peer relationships and child health behaviors and risks, according to an international assessment of child well-being in developed nations (UNICEF, 2007). Some may argue that a society that endorses and supports children's rights to a safe environment that promotes recreation, learning, social interaction, psychological development, cultural expression, and civic participation, as identified by UNICEF's Child-Friendly Cities Initiative, is utopian. We believe that the development of our future citizens necessitates careful consideration of how our environments influence their health and well-being and requires a concerted effort toward value-based public policies that supports them.

CHAPTER 8

What We Learned about Interdisciplinarity

Hillel Goelman and Martin Guhn

> *Interdisciplinary science has emerged as the defining feature of the scientific endeavor in the twenty-first century.*
>
> Kessel and Rosenfield (2008, p. ix)

"Neurons to neighborhoods" is the current catch phrase that refers to the importance of the confluence of biological science, social science, and policy science in research on early child development (Phillips & Shonkoff, 2000). This kind of work must by definition involve the knowledge, expertise, techniques, and insights of different disciplines, and there is now a broad consensus calling for more interdisciplinary research in this area. There is, however, no universally accepted consensus on what does and does not constitute interdisciplinary research. What precisely is the promise of interdisciplinary research and what are the challenges associated with it? It is worth beginning this chapter by recalling why the CHILD Project so strongly endorsed interdisciplinarity in the original proposal and why so much of the discourse during the five years of data collection and analysis focused on it as well. We also briefly review the literature on interdisciplinarity science to gain a broader understanding of some of the epistemological, ontological, and methodological issues that are relevant and important to this topic. We close the chapter with an exploration of the explicit and implicit lessons we learned in the CHILD Project about the theory and practice of interdisciplinary collaboration in early child development.

Expectations of Interdisciplinarity in the CHILD Project

Many of our initial assumptions about the value of collaborative interdisciplinary research grew out of our understanding of and enthusiasm for Bronfenbrenner's bioecological theory of human development (1979, 2005; Bronfenbrenner & Morris, 2006). By defining his model as "bioecological," Bronfenbrenner described the interactions within a multisystem, dynamic framework where events and activities at one systemic level influenced, and were influenced by, events and activities in other systemic levels. In drawing on this model, we saw the inherent value of bringing together a range of different disciplines with different theoretical lenses on child development and with different methodological tools with which to study child development. However, it is important to point out that for many individuals in the CHILD Project, this represented their first experience in interdisciplinary research. Further, some individuals were familiar with the bioecological perspective and others were not.

Despite the theoretical guidance provided by Bronfenbrenner, at no time did we "assign" different studies to specific ecological systems. What became clear in our continuing collaborative work was that each of the 10 studies within the CHILD Project provided information and insight into the different systemic levels. All of the studies, for example, considered the proximal processes in the various microsystems in which children participate (table 8.1). All of the studies were also alert to the influences of the exosystem; that is, the microsystems under study were contextualized within, for example, government regulations, professional training programs, or funding programs. Finally, the CHILD Project tried to understand in what ways macrosystem variables—for example, societal values, attitudes, beliefs, histories, and culture—provided philosophical envelopes, and how these macrosystem variables influenced the exosystem and in what ways the different social, educational, and health policies were enacted in the exosystem.

One of the major challenges in the CHILD Project was dealing with the conceptual and methodological disciplinary diversity within one overarching interdisciplinary framework (table 8.2). Some of the studies focused primarily on young children (e.g., *The Infant Neuromotor Study*) while others focused on families with young children (e.g., *The Parent Counselling Study*). Some were concerned with *targeted* groups of children with specific defining characteristics (e.g., *The Developmental Pathways Study*) and others had

Table 8.1 Interconnected Ecological Systems in the 10 Studies in the CHILD Project

Study in the CHILD Project	Ecological systems		
	Microsystems	Exosystem	Macrosystem
Cluster 1: Policy Studies in Early Child Development			
The Income Assistance Study	Lone mothers and their preschool children on Income Assistance	Income Assistance policies	The feminization of poverty
The Child Care Policy Study	Survey of characteristics of child care settings	Child care regulations, funding	Women in the paid labor force; government support for nonparental care
Cluster 2: Early Childhood Development in Aboriginal Communities			
The Indigenous CHILD Project	First Nations children, families, communities	Government policy toward First Nations	Historical and cultural oppression of First Nations
The Aboriginal HIPPY Documentation Project	First Nations children, families, communities	Government policy toward First Nations; School readiness policies	Historical and cultural oppression of First Nations
Cluster 3: Early Identification and Screening Studies			
The Developmental Pathways Study	Infants in NICUs	Medical policy, health priorities	Lowering mortality rates, lowering disability rates
The Infant Neuromotor Study	Children with neuromotor delays/disabilities	Early screening and intervention programs	Early identification leads to early intervention and remediation
The Community-Based Screening Study.	Preschool children at home	Capacity building for programs for young children	Population health approach to healthy child development
Cluster 4: Early Childhood Intervention Programs			
The Outdoor Criteria Study.	Children in outdoor play spaces in child care centers	Government regulations on play spaces	Value of play, safety, and security and the fear of litigation
The Parent Counselling Study.	Children perceived as at risk by child welfare authorities	Government policies and regulations on child welfare; effectiveness of training programs	Child safety, family stability
The Safe Spaces Study	Children in child care centers	Effectiveness of training programs	Importance of social, and emotional self-regulation in young children

Note: Bronfenbrenner's "mesosystem" level is not presented in this table because it is comprised of relationships among the various microsystems under study.

Table 8.2 Relative Emphases in the 10 Studies in the CHILD Project

Study in the CHILD Project	Research Focus		
	Children/Families	Targeted/Universal Program	Qualitative/ Quantitative Data
Cluster 1: Policy Studies in Early Child Development			
The Income Assistance Study	Family	Targeted	Qualitative
The Child Care Policy Study	Child	Universal	Quantitative
Cluster 2: Early Childhood Development in Aboriginal Communities			
The Indigenous CHILD Project	Family	Targeted	Qualitative
The Aboriginal HIPPY Documentation Project	Family	Targeted	Qualitative
Cluster 3: Early Identification and Screening Studies			
The Developmental Pathways Study	Child	Targeted	Quantitative
The Infant Neuromotor Study	Child	Targeted	Both
The Community-Based Screening Study	Child	Universal	Quantitative
Cluster 4: Early Childhood Intervention Programs			
The Outdoor Criteria Study	Child	Universal	Both
The Parent Counselling Study	Family	Targeted	Quantitative
The Safe Spaces Study	Child	Universal	Quantitative

more of a *universal* perspective and were concerned with normative child development (e.g., *The Outdoor Criteria*). Finally, the studies could be differentiated on whether they used quantitative methods, qualitative methods, or, in some situations, a combination of both. Further, while it is very common for interdisciplinary studies in child development to collect different kinds of data on the same group of children, the 10 studies in the CHILD Project used different methodologies to collect different kinds of data on different groups of children.

In setting up the CHILD Project, we had succeeded in recruiting a range of different disciplines with different theoretical constructs, different methodologies, and foci on different groups of children. (Much of the recruitment of the academic researchers had been conducted via the University of British Columbia Child and Family Project, a working group of professors and community activists who organized seminars and lecture series in the three years prior to the beginning of the CHILD Project.) In order to foster interdisciplinarity among the different disciplines represented in the CHILD Project, an ongoing task during the course of the CHILD Project that we had framed for ourselves was to reflect on what each of the studies was learning from the other studies and what each of the studies was contributing to the other studies. For guidance in understanding the levels and manifestations of interdisciplinarity in the CHILD Project, we now turn to a discussion of the research literature on interdisciplinarity.

Review of the Literature on Interdisciplinarity

The discourse on interdisciplinarity is based upon attempts to first define the characteristics of individual disciplines and disciplinary research. Lattuca (2001) points out that

> Disciplines are complex phenomena. They can be defined as sets of problems, methods, and research practices or as bodies of knowledge that are unified by any of these. They can also be defined as social networks of individuals interested in related problems or ideas. The first definition stresses the infrastructure of the disciplines, the second their social, cultural, and historical dimensions. (p. 23)

Becher (1989) expands on the social network notion by describing disciplines as the "tribes of academe" that are intent on preserving the primacy and exclusivity of their discipline. He claims that

> Alongside the structural features of disciplinary communities, exercising an even more powerful integrating force, are their more explicitly cultural elements: their traditions, customs and practices, transmitted knowledge, beliefs, morals and rules of conduct, as well as their linguistic and symbolic forms of communication and the meanings they share. (p. 24)

There is a general consensus among scholars that interdisciplinary research has the potential to contribute to new ideas, new perspectives, and new insights; however, there are differences of opinion in the literature over what the results of interdisciplinary research might look like. Smith (2006) claims that interdisciplinary research can bring to bear "separate, distinct disciplinary perspectives on phenomena," while Maton and colleagues advocate for a research product "in which the disciplinary perspectives of collaborators are merged, resulting in a new, integrative perspective" (2006, p. 4). In other words, does interdisciplinary generate parallel results in different fields? Is the point of interdisciplinary research to "add" results from one discipline to another? Or must all interdisciplinary research create qualitatively new kinds of knowledge?

While some scholars of interdisciplinarity have attempted to respond to these challenges with proposed frameworks and consistent language (e.g., Klein, 2006), the field has generated much discussion on the theoretical constructs that guide interdisciplinary research, the identification and definition of different types of interdisciplinary research, and methodological and practical concerns in conducting interdisciplinary research. Salter and Hearn (1996) describe categories of *instrumental* and *conceptual interdisciplinarity*, and further differentiate the latter into interdisciplinarity that uses disciplines as a starting point for research and interdisciplinarity that is an epistemological critique of disciplinary-based research itself. Similarly, Klein (1996) describes *instrumental interdisciplinarity* as building bridges between disciplines, *epistemological interdisciplinarity* as restructuring an approach to defining a discipline, and *transdisciplinarity* as a search for a unity of knowledge across all disciplines. Klein claims that *exogenous interdisciplinary research* deals with real-world problems and *endogenous interdisciplinary research* has the goal of producing an overall unity of knowledge that transcends disciplines.

Kockelmans (1979) addresses the degree of integration across disciplines in different forms of interdisciplinarity. For Kockelmans, the term *pluridisciplinarity* refers to the involvement of more than one discipline without coordination between them, while *crossdisciplinarity* refers to research that solves problems by borrowing tools or insights from multiple disciplines without trying to integrate the disciplines. Kockelmans uses the term *interdisciplinarity* to refer to research that resolves problems that require the integration of parts of disciplines into a new discipline; and *transdisciplinarity* as research that is undertaken with "an attitude oriented toward comprehending the contributions of each discipline from the perspective of man's search for meaning, which is itself supra-scientific because it is inherently human" (1979, pp. 153–1544; cited in Salter & Hearn, 1996, p. 53).

D'Amour and colleagues (D'Amour, Ferrada-Videla, Rodriguez, & Beaulieu, 2005) define a *transdisciplinary action research* approach as a deliberate exchange of knowledge, skills, and expertise that transcends traditional disciplinary boundaries. According to Stokols (2006), the outcome of this type of research approach results in the development of improved strategies for enhancing collaboration among scientists and practitioners; greater sustainability of community interventions and effectiveness of public policies; more rapid refinements of behavioral and public theories brought about by the exchange of community-based knowledge between scientists and practitioners; and the establishment of innovative educational programs for students. The transdisciplinary action research approach factors in the different groups of individuals involved in the collaboration (academics, practitioners, students, policymakers), the different disciplines or professional training associated with those involved, the systems associated with the research objectives (e.g., microsystem, mesosystem), contextual factors associated with collaboration, and both the processes and outcomes of research.

Across all of these taxonomies of interdisciplinary research, the literature in this area emphasizes four key elements for success. First, interdisciplinary research addresses complex problems, and since the study of complex and multifaceted phenomena requires multiple theoretical and methodological approaches, no one discipline can provide sufficient depth, breadth, and detail. Second, disciplines often need to "borrow" the research tools, understandings, and thinking from other disciplines (Klein, 2006). Third, interdisciplinarity is as much, if not more, about the process of conducting research than about the final research outputs produced by the collaboration. This leads us to the fourth and probably most important element, the positive relational characteristics of the individuals and the relationships among those who participate in an interdisciplinary research endeavor.

This opens up the discussion to whether certain types of researchers are better suited for interdisciplinary research than others. One prominent view is that what characterizes successful interdisciplinary research is a shared passion for and commitment to the research project. Are there other characteristics? In reviewing interdisciplinary programs of research, Klein (1990) observed that "compatible personalities, [with] common interests and a common vocabulary, were essential for successful interdisciplinary research" (p. 185). Klein goes further:

> Certain abilities have also been associated with interdisciplinary individuals; not only the general capacity to look at things from different

> perspectives but also the skills of differentiating, comparing, contrasting, relating, clarifying, reconciling and synthesizing. Since Interdisciplinarians are often put into new situations, they must also know how to learn..... We would know more about how individuals use these skills if there were more accounts of how Interdisciplinarians actually work. Unfortunately, there are very few accounts, and there is only one publication that deals directly with the issue of measuring individual participation on interdisciplinary teams. (p. 183)

Finally, numerous authors have discussed the importance of positive and responsive leadership characteristics, which provide both structure and support to diverse groups of researchers engaged in interdisciplinary research. It is vital that this respectful research process encourages the voices of all participants in discussing and articulating research questions and in the interpretation of research results. While diversity can be a challenge, it can also be a strength that can yield a process, which Klein (1990) describes as "productive complementarity," because:

> Interdisciplinarity is neither a subject matter nor a body of content. It is a process for achieving an integrative synthesis, a process that usually begins with a problem, question, topic or issue. Individuals must work to overcome problems created by differences in disciplinary language and worldview. (p. 188)

Klein also lists the kinds of activities that contribute to this process including regular meetings and presentations; shared organizing and planning; common objectives; joint presentations, publications, and papers; shared continuing education activities; common equipment, facilities, and instruments; articulating and addressing differences; and common data gathering, analysis, and interpretation.

We now turn back to the CHILD Project to explore the ways in which the CHILD Project has learned from the research literature on interdisciplinarity and what it can contribute to this literature as well.

INTERDISCIPLINARITY IN THE CHILD PROJECT

The research teams in the CHILD Project were brought together on the basis of a shared, compelling, complex question: What differences make a difference in early child development? Besides a fascination with this question, the researchers brought with them a recognition that no one discipline could provide all of the answers to this question and that each of the participating disciplines brought important pieces of, and perspectives on, the puzzle of early child development. For the vast majority of the participants in the CHILD Project, this was the first time that "neurons" and "neighborhood" researchers—and all of those in between—have maintained sustained research collaborations that demand a high level of "intellectual decentring" in order to understand what different lenses bring to a fuller understanding of early child development.

One of the first understandings identified in these discussions was that while academic disciplines may be divided into intellectual silos, the world inhabited by the community partners was far more interdisciplinary in practice than much of the academic research. In their professional lives, the community partners were continually building alliances among health, mental health, educational, and social service agencies on behalf of their child and family clients.

For these reasons, it is important to note that interdisciplinarity in the CHILD Project existed at different levels of theory and practice. For example, there was interdisciplinarity at the *level of disciplines*, as each of the participating disciplines did not represent a homogeneous body of thought and action. The argument could be made that each of the participating disciplines was, in its own way, an amalgam of previously separate disciplines. At one CHILD Learning Forum, for example, a graduate student in Landscape Architecture asserted that the field in which he was studying and obtaining a graduate degree was interdisciplinary in nature:

> It is true that Landscape Architecture is an interdisciplinary profession. The overlap with other professions is both an advantage and a disadvantage. An advantage because landscape architects are good at managing teams of different disciplines because of generalist knowledge but a disadvantage because the landscape architect is not the first person to come to mind for particular projects. For example, if a town wants an environmental assessment done or an inventory they will usually call an ecologist or a conservation biologist. If they want to alter the zoning of said green space to eventually turn it into a park they will contact the planners. If they want to install parking and infrastructure on the site they will often contact engineers. As landscape architects we are trained to do all of the above in some capacity but usually get contacted at the end of the process to install benches, paving stone, and shrubs from a catalogue. (J. Nichols, personal communication, 2010)

Other examples of interdisciplinary disciplines in the CHILD Project included Women's Studies and Gender Relations, First

Nations Studies, Community and Regional Planning, Policy Studies, and Child and Youth Care. What further enhanced the interdisciplinary process was the presence of multiple disciplines *within each study*. The exploration of common questions with shared research instruments in a climate of shared inquiry and yielding complementary findings often resulted in the crossing of disciplinary boundaries within and across the individual studies.

The interdisciplinary collaboration in the CHILD Project was enhanced by the number and quality of communication and information sharing opportunities that were built into the CHILD Project's infrastructure. These included (1) Writing the original proposal; (2) Milestone reports; (3) CHILD*Talks*; (4) Child Learning Forums; (5) Cluster Reports; (6) Annual Reports; (7) Annual retreats; (8) Midterm Report; (9) Hiring committee for the postdoctoral fellows; (10) Final conference; and (11) Writing this book. These activities reflected aspects of the processes and relationships, which created a number of key interdisciplinary research outcomes.

Examples of Interdisciplinary Outcomes in the CHILD Project

The most informative data we have on the interdisciplinary outcomes and processes in the CHILD Project come from the CHILD Learning Forums (CLFs) and the Cluster Reports. As discussed in Chapter 3, the CLFs were held every three months, and at each CLF, three or four different studies reported on their progress to date. A key part of the presentation was when each study reported what it had learned from and could contribute to the other studies in the CHILD Project. In response and in small groups, each study reflected on the presentation and what they had learned from and could contribute to the presenting study. The Cluster Reports were more intensive and focused. In Year 3 of the CHILD Project, graduate students interviewed the academic, community, and graduate student partners in each study. In effect, we were practicing what Weingart (2000) referred to as "reflexive interdisciplinarity." The researchers had now become the subjects of the study, in which it was their views, perspectives, and attitudes on the collaboration that constituted the data on interdisciplinarity in the Consortium.

On a practical level of what might be called "instrumental interdisciplinarity," some of the CHILD researchers from different studies began using the same or similar research instruments or methods. For example, two of the three screening studies used the same quantitative measures, such as the *Bayley Scales of Infant Development*, 1993, 1996 and trained their research assistants together. Similarly, the studies in the CHILD Project that collected qualitative data exchanged their expertise on the most suitable qualitative analytical software programs, how to acquire the appropriate training for the programs' use, and assisted each other in specific instances pertaining to data collection, analysis, and interpretation.

Other methodological skills or approaches that researchers felt that they could either contribute to or wished to learn from the other studies included:

1. *The Outdoor Criteria Study*, which collected all of their observational data in child care centers, wanted to learn from *The Aboriginal HIPPY Documentation Project* how to collect observational data in home settings.
2. *The Developmental Screening Study* wanted to work with the other screening studies in order to have a common approach to determining cut-off points for developmental screens for validity purposes.
3. *The Aboriginal HIPPY Documentation* Project and *Indigenous CHILD Project* were interested in sharing their approaches to working in Indigenous communities and, in particular, how to deal with the issue of ownership of data.
4. *The Safe Spaces Study* wanted to learn from the qualitative observational methods used in *The Outdoor Criteria Study*.
5. *The Aboriginal HIPPY Documentation Project* wanted to learn techniques of program evaluation and implementation from *The Safe Spaces Study*.

Instrumental interdisciplinarity could thus be seen as a form of "parallel play," in the sense that studies may use similar methodologies, but conduct their respective research without any further significant interaction among them. The processes in the CHILD Project, however, also resulted in more "associative play patterns." That is, researchers attempted to understand how the data from one study could inform, complement, or extend the work of another study. One example that was cited in the Cluster Reports pointed to the value of the policy information generated and reported by the two other studies in the Policy Cluster. Researchers and community partners in *The Income Assistance Study* and *The Child Care Policy Study* were tuned into the ongoing policy changes and implementation procedures and regularly updated the other studies about these policy changes. This information both contributed critical contextual information to the other studies and opened the door to discussions on public policy and priorities in the health, social service, and education sectors. Similarly, population health data on the number of babies treated in Neonatal intensive Care Units (NICUs)—shared by the *Developmental Pathways Study*—were seen as a helpful context for the results of the other screening studies in the CHILD Project.

We have already seen how the four CHILD Project's studies dealing with early screening and identification created a model of complementary approaches to the identification of children with developmental challenges (see Chapter 6). Two critical threads running through the early screening and identification studies are the importance of a community-based longitudinal follow-up of children who were identified at birth with specific developmental challenges and the awareness and understanding of cultural perspectives, in general, and the experiences and perceptions of Canada's First Nations peoples in particular. There was a strong consensus among the researchers in these four studies with respect to the development and articulation of this perspective; however, the studies' teams first had to overcome what Salter and Hearn (1996) refer to as a "translation problem," because words—for example, "developmental surveillance" (which is routinely used in population health research)—carried very different meanings and connotations in different disciplines, professional sectors, and communities, as discussed in Chapters 4, 5, and 6.

The landscape architects in *The Outdoor Criteria Study* and the developmental psychologists in *The Safe Spaces Study* collaborated on their common interest on children's social play and the physical environment. This interdisciplinary collaboration explored how the "Seven C's" of playground design (character, context, connectivity, change, chance, clarity, and challenge) influenced the positive interactions (social conversation, cooperative play, friendly touch), negative interactions (quarrelling, aggressive play, object possessiveness, aggression), and noninteractions (unoccupied, on-looking, solitary play, parallel play, aggression against objects) in play areas in child care centers. The results (see Chapter 7) showed that playground design facilitates certain social behaviors. The data showed that more positive behaviors were found in spaces with a high number of the Seven Cs. Further, more positive behaviors and higher levels of social play were observed in spaces that gave children the opportunity to explore their environment, to find challenging activities, and to create and manipulate features of the play space (Gummerum, Herrington, Schonert-Reichl, & Lesmeister, 2007).

This specific collaboration also opened up a discussion pertaining to the "translation problem," regarding the words "safe" and "safety." In *The Safe Spaces Study*, safety meant the absence of bullying, and a psychological and physical zone that is comfortable for children. In contrast, the term "safety" in *The Outdoor Criteria Study* conjured up images of play environments that are sterile, boring, unchallenging, and, as one of our colleagues put it, descriptive of "a place that will not invite law suits."

Researchers in the CHILD Project also organized two symposia, which were presented at the 2007 Biennial Conference of the Society for Research in Child Development. One symposium was entitled *Urie Bronfenbrenner, Interdisciplinarity and the CHILD Project*, and included three papers (Forer, Goelman, & Kershaw, 2007; Goelman, 2007; Gummerum et al., 2007). The second symposium, *The Ecology of Early Screening and Follow-up Programs*, also included three interdisciplinary presentations (Dahinten, Ford, Canam, Lapointe, & Merkel, 2007; Scher, Tse, Harris, Hayes, & Tardif, 2007; Synnes, Houbé, & Klassen, 2007). For most of the nonpsychologists in the CHILD Project (neonatologists, epidemiologists, policy analysts, statisticians, nurses, occupational and physical therapists), it was their first time presentation at what was essentially a Developmental Psychology conference. Crafting and organizing the two symposia required the various presenters to focus on the commonalities that characterized their collective work under the umbrella of the CHILD Project.

Examples of the Interdisciplinary Process

It was not uncommon in group discussions and presentations for researchers in the CHILD Project to have an "aha" moment, when they would suddenly see a link between their own study and one of the other CHILD Project studies. For example, when the developmental psychologists and policy analysts in *The Child Care Policy Study* reported on the "hidden fragility" and the lack of quality, affordable, and accessible child care spaces, the medical researchers in *The Developmental Pathways Study* understood why so many of the developmentally delayed children on their caseloads were unable to access child care programs that would support their cognitive, language, social, and emotional development. While this understanding did not result from or create a new research collaboration per se, it is an example of how the CHILD Project created a conceptual space where research findings from one study provided insight and/or context for another study.

Another key process issue to address is how the university researchers, community researchers, and graduate students were able to sustain an interdisciplinary research project over five years. It would be a simplistic argument to state that the CHILD Project was fortunate to recruit a cohort of dedicated "interdisciplinarians" to conduct the 10 studies (Klein, 1990). While we can see the value of the research partners being compatible and sharing a passion for the project, we do not believe that these kinds of personal characteristics tell the whole story. For one thing, the world cannot be divided into "interdisciplinarians" and "noninterdisciplinarians." Further, the necessary collaborative interpersonal interactions were embedded within different contextual factors, akin to a *person-process-context-time* (PPCT) model (see Chapter 2; Bronfenbrenner & Morris, 2006). That is, we argue that successful interdisciplinarity research does not hinge on individual factors, but on a good match between (1) the given research objectives, researchers' personal characteristics (e.g., overlapping interests, shared passion for the research question, complementary knowledge); (2) research process characteristics (e.g., regular, accessible meetings, which provide opportunities for exchange); (3) the research context characteristics (e.g., incentive structures in which young academics' career obligations do not conflict with the demands of interdisciplinary research project); and (4) the time (chronosystem) characteristics (e.g., the current state of the involved disciplines allow for cross-fertilization). In short, we believe that in conducting successful interdisciplinary research, "main effects are likely to be found in the interactions" (Bronfenbrenner & Morris, 2006, p. 802) between these various characteristics.

These multiple interactions are based on the critical shared premise that no one discipline or perspective (level, or system) can suffice in building knowledge; there is always something we cannot see due to the limitations of our own disciplinary lenses. What sustained the CHILD Project was thus, to a large extent, the fact that we deliberately and frequently created opportunities for confronting the limitations of our own disciplinary knowledges and for acquiring alternative or conflicting epistemologies—and these opportunities, in turn, set the stage for the CHILD Project to (co-)create new knowledge.

CHAPTER 9

Lessons in University-Community Collaboration

Jayne Pivik and Hillel Goelman

Individually, we are one drop. Together, we are an ocean.

Ryunosuke Satoro

In the third year of the CHILD Project, Jayne Pivik, a Postdoctoral Fellow, joined the CHILD Central Team. One of her studies was an evaluation of the collaborative efforts between the academic and community-based research partners, which took place in the fourth year of the CHILD Project. From the beginning, the CHILD Project strove to achieve high levels of collaboration and cooperation. The original grant proposal was written in collaboration with First Call, a province-wide child and youth advocacy organization that consisted of approximately 90 different agencies. Community partners also participated on the CHILD Executive Committee and in all report-writing (i.e., Milestone Reports, CHILD*Talk* Reports, Cluster Reports), presentations (CHILD Learning Forums), and on the CHILD Executive Committee.

This chapter describes the models associated with community-based participatory research (CBPR), contextual factors identified as important considerations in CBPR, and the summative results of her process evaluation. Specifically, this chapter presents the academics' and community-based service providers' responses on the importance of community involvement in different stages of the research; relational factors; factors supporting community access;

issues associated with supporting partnerships; the provision of educational, informational, and training support; methodological process issues; and methods for fostering collaboration. Also, both groups provided information on the impact and benefit of the collaboration, facilitators supporting the collaboration, barriers, the importance of a partnership agreement, and recommendations for future CBPR efforts.

Collaborative research is a term that describes many different types of research initiatives depending on the participants involved, the level and type of involvement, and who initiates the project. For example, community-based participatory research, action research, and interdisciplinary research are all forms of collaborative research. The defining features of collaborative research are that different groups work together toward a common goal. In the case of the CHILD Project, the actual studies were community-based participatory research projects between academics and community service providers, although each study also had an interdisciplinary component, as indicated in Chapter 8.

Community-based participatory research (CBPR) is a collaborative approach to addressing real world problems using both systematic inquiry and experiential knowledge. Principles of this research approach include equitable participation by both researchers and community members; a willingness to learn from each other; system development and capacity building; a focus on empowerment; participatory strategies; and concrete action (Israel et al., 2006). Essentially, CBPR involves different groups equitably working together toward a common goal to address concrete issues and problems (Currie et al., 2005; Minkler, 2005). Although the CHILD project included academics and community service partners focused on child health and development, as table 1.1 indicates, there was a wide diversity of organizations, goals, disciplines, and objectives. The purpose of this chapter is to describe the lessons learned about facilitating CBPR across these different contexts.

CBPR and Contextual Factors

Models describing the key factors of CBPR have been developed for many different contexts. Typically, these are multidimensional, developmental, and interactive (e.g., Currie et al., 2005; Fawcett et al., 1995; Suarez-Balcazar, Harper, & Lewis, 2005). That is, CBPR is influenced and impacted by a multitude of interrelated factors that develop over time. Intrinsic to most of the models for CBPR is a focus on process and relational factors. For example, Suarez-Balcazar, Harper, and Lewis (2005) developed the *Empowerment Model of Collaboration* that addresses the challenges of gaining entry into the community, the potential barriers impacting collaboration, and the benefits and outcomes of the project. All of these activities are dependent on trust and mutual respect, adequate communication, respect for diversity, developing a culture of learning, the development of an action agenda, and respecting the culture of the setting.

Fawcett et al. (1995) developed the *Contextual-Behavioral Model of Empowerment* to address the personal and environmental factors that affect behaviors and outcomes associated with individual and community empowerment related to CBPR. Their model is based on a transactional approach, where one's level of empowerment is postulated to influence both person or group factors and environmental features. Person or group factors influencing empowerment include knowledge and critical consciousness, skills, history of empowerment, values and beliefs, and physical/biological capacity. Specific strategies and tactics to address the person or group factors include: (1) increasing the knowledge about issues, the causes of problems, and the possibilities of change; (2) facilitating skill acquisition (e.g., goal setting, problem solving, and communication); (3) early involvement of community partners in the process; and (4) assuming values and beliefs that are consistent with the empowerment goal. Environmental factors influencing empowerment include stressors and barriers, information access, and positive reinforcement (financial and material resources and policies and laws).

The presence of differing organizational cultures has also been identified as an important contextual consideration for CBPR. For example, Stokols (2006) points out a number of possible barriers to community-university collaborations including differing worldviews, perceived status differences, and the logistical considerations faced by the respective partners. He suggests the following factors that can help smooth the path for positive working relationships: the clarity of shared goals; regular communication; active representation by key community stakeholders; and continuity of participation from the inception to the completion of the CBPR project. Similarly, Shonkoff (2000) describes the three often competing "cultures" of research, public policy, and community practice that must be acknowledged in CBPR. Shonkoff points out that these three cultures differ in their respective rules of evidence, with researchers relying heavily on empirical evidence, community practitioners drawing on personal and professional experience and expertise, and public policy officials considering political and governmental agendas. Time can also be a point of difference between the three perspectives, with community professionals desiring practice-relevant results quickly; researchers taking time to analyze data and planning their next research project; and public policy officials more interested in the most recent set of findings rather than identifying research questions for future consideration.

Along with organizational culture, other contextual factors must be considered. For example, research in inner-city communities has shown that effective collaborations require the acknowledgment of the community's contribution, respect, recruitment, and training of local participants; clear communication; power sharing strategies; and valuing diversity (Kone et al., 2000). Thompson, Story, and Butler (2003) also recommend the importance of communication, trust, and local representation as well as using an asset-based needs assessment to increase motivation, broaden perspectives, and inspire collective will. Reed, Schumaker, and Woods (2000), in their study of urban revitalization, recommend that successful collaborations include a history of collaboration, good personal relationships, trust, simple organizational structure, informality and flexibility, clear and frequent communication, a shared vision, visibility of the university partners, and integration of university resources. Collaborations centered on health promotion require honesty, transparency, and equity (Community-Campus Partnerships for Health, 2006).

Less is known about the important elements of partnerships and the processes that facilitate CBPR with community service providers. King, Currie, Smith, Servais, and McDougall (2008) describe four interdisciplinary research models used at their pediatric rehabilitation center that promote the co-creation of knowledge between researchers and clinicians; provide clinicians with research support, education, and training; and facilitate knowledge sharing, program/treatment evaluations, and dissemination. Their review suggests that the processes facilitating collaboration include time, resource support, and immersion within a research-focused center. Shoultz et al. (2006) describe a CBPR consortium between academic nurses and four community health centers focused on intimate partner violence in multicultural and multilingual communities. Factors facilitating collaboration in this CBPR project included: (1) a stable research team; (2) shared decision making; (3) available time; (4) accessible meeting places; (5) a communication strategy; (6) shared activity on the research design, data analysis, and oral dissemination; (7) meetings to ensure consistency in procedures across settings; (8) training in research ethics and

CBPR methods; (9) developing a mission statement to identify core values, common goals, and principles; (10) respect; (11) trust; (12) release time for academics; (13) payment for community researchers; (14) rotation for first place in publications; and (15) a memorandum of understanding that details principles and expectations. Although the Shoultz et al. (2006) study provides excellent recommendations for facilitating collaboration between academics and community service providers for a CBPR consortium, they focused on a single project across four sites that dealt with adults, not children. Alternately, the Currie et al. (2005) paper describes many different research projects that address child health using different methods but used a local and centralized research team. Furthermore, both papers present their findings based on the researchers' perspective.

This study attempts to add to the CBPR literature by (1) directly evaluating the processes, benefits, barriers, and facilitators to collaboration; (2) gaining the perspective of both academic and community partners; (3) exploring a large number of different contexts, that is, eight distinct but related studies; and (4) providing recommendations for facilitating CBPR at the individual study, consortium, and institutional levels. This evaluation provided a unique opportunity to explore collaborative research from the perspective of community service providers and university researchers working in a multitude of different contexts due to varied organizational mandates, the type of clients being served, the specific experiences and goals of participants, systematic issues such as funding and available support, and different study objectives. Of particular interest was identifying whether there were key factors important for collaboration in CBPR across all contexts or if different contexts influenced the collaborative partnership experience.

Study Participants

Of the 10 studies in the CHILD Project, 8 studies are represented in this evaluation (2 studies were unable to participate due to time constraints). From these eight studies, two had multiple components headed up by different principal academic investigators and one study had two different community partners represented. Six of the eight studies had representation from both academic and community partners. In total, 10 academic researchers and 9 community researchers participated in this evaluation. Table 9.1 lists the eight studies represented in this sample, descriptions of the discipline or community organization of the participants, objectives of the study, and the

Table 9.1 The Studies, Academic Disciplines, Community Partners, and Methods Represented from the CHILD Project

The Studies and Their Main Objectives	Academic Discipline	Community Partners	Research Methods
The Income Assistance Study. To assess the impact of changes in income assistance policy on lone-parent families with young children.	Women's Studies	Social Planning and Research Council of BC; Canadian Centre for Policy Alternatives	Qualitative analyses of multiple interviews and focus groups with lone mothers on income assistance with preschool children. Also, documentary and econometric analyses of income assistance policies.
The Child Care Policy Study. To investigate the impact of child care policy changes on communities, child care facilities, families, and children.	Early Childhood Education; Policy Analysis	Westcoast Child Care Resource and Referral	Analyses of government policies and programs on child care use patterns and the accessibility, affordability, and quality of child care services.
The Chilliwack Developmental Screening Study. To determine the effectiveness of a universal, community-based, developmental screening program.	Child Development	Public Health Nursing	Administration and analyses of a battery of child development screening measures for all children in one municipality at ages 6, 12, 24, 36, 48, and 60 months.
The Developmental Pathways Study. To follow the long-term development of highly at-risk infants.	Neonatology	Infant Development Program of BC	Analyses of child development status of survivors of neonatal intensive care units using standardized child development outcome measures at 6, 12, 24, 36, 48, 60 months.
The Infant Neuromotor Screening Study. To explore the effectiveness of two types of training models for the early identification of children with neuromotor delays.	Nursing	BC Centre for Ability	Screening infants, toddlers and preschoolers for neuromotor delays/disorders using two different screening measures at 6, 12, 24, 36, 48, 60 months. Also, an evaluation of two methods of training staff to administer these measures.
Aboriginal HIPPY Documentation Project. To explore the "Home Instruction for Parents of Preschool Youngsters" program as implemented in Aboriginal communities.	Early Childhood Education	HIPPY Canada	Interviews and focus groups with Aboriginal parents, child care professionals, elders in on-reserve Aboriginal communities on the impact of the HIPPY program in their communities. The administration of child development outcome measures to assess children's school readiness upon completion of the program.

Continued

Table 9.1 Continued

The Studies and Their Main Objectives	Academic Discipline	Community Partners	Research Methods
The Parent Counseling Study. To assess the impact of counseling on parents whose children are at risk for apprehension by child protection authorities.	Social Work and Family Studies	Family Services of Vancouver	Interviews and focus groups with parents participating in a mandatory parent counseling program to prevent child abuse/neglect.
The Safe Spaces Study. To examine the short- and long-term effectiveness of a preschool antibullying program.	PI not available for this study	Westcoast Child Care Resource and Referral	Observing and evaluating children's levels of social and emotional development before, during and after completing the Safe Spaces training program.

methodology employed. Please note that while the academic research teams were interdisciplinary, only the affiliation of the primary investigator is presented. As table 9.1 shows, the participants represented a heterogeneous sample from different backgrounds, experiences, and expertise, with the only common element being a focus on promoting child health and well-being using CBPR.

Measures

This evaluation used a mixed methods approach that included both a quantitative assessment of factors associated with CBPR and a qualitative open-ended interview. This approach was chosen in order to explore the importance of factors identified with collaboration in CBPR studies as well as to tap into participants' perspectives in depth (Creswell, 2003; Johnson & Onwuegbuzie, 2004). As Yoshikawa, Weisner, Kalil, and Way (2008) explain, "examining behavior and belief systems requires both quantitative and qualitative approaches to research: quantitative methods to understand the prevalence of particular practices, behaviors, and beliefs, and qualitative methods to understand meanings, functions, goals and intentions" (p. 346).

Community-Based Participatory Research Rating Scale. Developed for this evaluation, the *Community-Based Participatory Rating Scale* was based on previous process research (Pivik, 1997, 2006); surveys of CBPR participants (Pivik & Weaver, 1997; Weaver &

Pivik, 1997a, 1997b); a survey of health consumers (Pivik, Rode, & Wade, 2004) and extensive reviews of the CBPR literature (Pivik, 2004a, 2004b). Thirty-three factors were identified as potentially impacting CBPR and included the following main categories: level of community involvement; relational issues; community access factors; mobilizing partnerships; education, information and training; methods of conducting CBPR; and fostering collaboration. All participants were asked to rate the importance of each factor on a 10-grade Likert scale ranging from 1 (not at all important) to 10 (extremely important). They were asked to consider the importance of these factors to their current CBPR study and not from a hypothetical viewpoint. Along with these ratings, participants' comments were recorded.

Semistructured interview. Open-ended questions followed the rating scale, which asked both community and academic researchers to discuss benefits, facilitators, barriers and recommendations for facilitating collaboration within their study, at their place of employment and within the consortium. Also, participants were asked about the importance of a partnership agreement or memorandum of understanding for conducting CBPR and whether they would become involved in another CBPR project in the future.

Coding and Plan of Analyses

The quantitative data were analyzed using SPSSX version 10. Due to the 10-point format of the rating scale, the data were treated as continuous, with corresponding descriptive statistics performed (Göb, McCollin, & Fernada Ramalhoto, 2007). Descriptive statistics (means and standard deviations) were computed for the 33 rating factors and grouped as academic or community researcher. Factors were then compared between groups using the Mann-Whitney U test. Although theoretically, the samples were related in that an academic and community researcher were evaluating the same study, the more stringent test for independent samples was employed since only 6 of the 8 studies met this condition. The Mann-Whitney U test is a nonparametric test for assessing whether two independent samples of observations come from the same distribution and was chosen because the sample sizes were less than 30.

The qualitative data were transcribed verbatim and then coded and analyzed using the qualitative software, NVivo7. Using content analysis, the data were coded into categories, which represented common ideas, trends, and patterns based on each interview question (Haney, Russell, Gulek, & Fierros, 1998; Stemler, 2001). The primary author and a colleague developed a checklist of categories using emergent coding, which allowed themes or patterns to emerge from the data. The data were then independently coded by both raters, resulting in a .82 Cohen's kappa score. Discrepancies between raters were resolved through discussion. Finally, the number of occurrences identified for each theme was examined across and between the academic and community researchers.

Procedure

The primary academic and community researcher from each study was contacted to participate in the interview. Participants were contacted by e-mail and/or telephone for a total of three contacts. The majority of the interviews were conducted in person; however, 6 of 19 participants opted for a telephone interview. The interview guide was emailed to the participant in advance and both in-person and telephone interviews lasted between 1 and 1.5 hours. All interviews were audiotaped with permission. The telephone interviews were audiotaped through a speaker phone system. The rating scale was completed at the time of the interview and verified with the transcripts. All transcripts were sent back to the participants to ensure accuracy. Two participants added additional information to their responses. This evaluation received ethical clearance from the *Behavioral Research Ethics Committee* of the University of British Columbia. The following results are a summary of the data. Details about the data can be found in Pivik and Goelman (in press).

Key Factors Important for Facilitating CBPR within Studies

Level of community involvement. Level of involvement refers to how important is it to have community members involved in defining the objectives of the study, developing the proposal, budget discussions, data collection, data analyses, interpretation of the data, and information dissemination. Both community members and academics reported that it was very important for community members to be involved in the interpretation of the data and dissemination of the research results. A comment by a community member reflects the majority of responses: "Because if we want to make change, then the community partners are the ones who are going to integrate this into practice, disseminate knowledge to other practitioners, saying we should be doing this, folks." The lowest importance score reported by both groups was community members' involvement in data analyses. According to one community member: "It would be a wonderful training opportunity to be able to participate in some of that but that's a research skill." However, when qualitative analyses were being conducted, having the community researcher's perspective was considered "crucial" and "very important" by both groups. Community members also reported a lower importance for being involved in budget discussions.

Relational factors. Relational factors include trust, a mutual respect for the knowledge and skills of each partner, a clear acknowledgment that no one person has superior or privileged status over others and a shared commitment between partners. Overall, relational factors had the highest mean scores compared to all other categories for both academic and community researchers. Trust and mutual respect were identified as extremely important by both groups. Valuing and explicitly acknowledging the experiential knowledge and skills of the community partner by the academic partner has been cited by many (e.g., Shonkoff, 2000; Stokols, 2006) as essential for facilitating CBPR. This mutual recognition is seen as a key aspect of "power sharing" among the partners. The higher mean importance score given by the academic partners (mean=9.0) than the community partner (mean=8.1) is the one major discrepancy in this section, and suggests somewhat different perspectives. One telling comment by a community member—"Actions are the telling part about power relations"—suggests while the academic partners may have felt that they assigned a high importance to power sharing, their community partners did not feel that sense of power sharing in practice.

> *There's the trust; you know the person, you know their history, you know they're not going to go down the garden path, any time you put into it will be well worth it. You want to do this work— you know it's going to be successful. You know you're working with people who are committed and knowledgeable.*
>
> —Community partner

Community access factors. This category includes remuneration for participation, flexible timelines and meeting places, reimbursement for expenses such as parking and travel, and access to technical assistance. In this case, remuneration refers to the issue of "Release-Time Stipends" from the funding agency that allowed the university researchers to pay a substitute instructor for one of their scheduled courses. The same amount of money was included in the budget for community agencies.

While researchers and community partners tended to assign community access issues (remuneration for participation, flexible timelines and meeting places, reimbursement for expenses such as parking and travel, and access to technical assistance) at the same general level of importance (in either the middle or lower third of their respective lists), there are a number of discrepancies in the actual rating scores generated by the two groups. The academic researchers reported higher ratings than community researchers on all items except for "access to technical assistance" in which the one-point differential was higher for community partners than for academic partners (A=5.9, C=7.1). Flexible timelines were ranked higher by academics than by community members. Interestingly, categories related to money—reimbursement (A=8.0, C=5.0) and remuneration (A=8.1, C=5.2)—showed statistically significant differences between community and academic members in relation to importance. Specifically, community members rated remuneration and reimbursement as less important than the academic researchers. This may be due to the fact that the researchers were in fact the grant holders and were legally and administratively responsible for the research funds spent by both the academic and the community partners. It may also be due to the fact that the release-time stipend made little practical sense to the community agencies. While university instructors could calculate the replacement cost for one course (25 percent of one's teaching load) it was impossible to calculate 25 percent of an agency director's time and to then hire someone for that time. In the end, the funds were given to the agency to defray administrative costs. As noted, this may have been a university-level administrative detail that had little relevance to the community partners. As one academic partner suggested, "this process and the imbalance in financial responsibilities – and dealing with university bureaucracies may have been too onerous and daunting for the community partners." This point was reinforced by a community researcher: "I had to send in an itemized invoice for hours and days and activities, but it doesn't work like that. It's very difficult. We found a way to do it, but it's just that it's not that easy, you know we can't just hire somebody to go and teach a class for you like the academics."

Mobilizing partnerships. The mobilizing partnerships category included identification and discussion about available resources; having clearly identified roles and responsibilities; establishing ground rules for collaboration; having a common definition of the research objectives or problem; and developing a strategic plan of collaborative action. Community partners and academics rated mobilizing the collaborative partnerships as moderately important. Community members did rate having a strategic plan higher than the academic partners and also rated discussions about resources slightly higher than did their academic partners. Regarding resources, one community member stated, "It's important, and I think the definition of what we mean by resources is really important too. Because what the community might put in the category of resources and what the university might put there might be different."

Academic researchers, on the other hand, rated detailing clear roles and responsibilities and establishing ground rules as more important than the community researchers. Although clearly identified roles and responsibilities were recognized as very important for most projects in the CHILD Project, these evolved over time or were informally defined. For establishing ground rules, an academic researcher gives a representative response, "It's pretty important as protection. I think it's more important for establishing trust and so whatever it takes to establish a relationship of trust, that's what the guidelines contributed to—whether or not you need to formalize that in a memorandum of understanding, yeah probably. It's probably the safest thing to do." Once again though, most of the respondents reported that there needed to be flexibility over time in relation to ground rules.

Education, information and training. Education and training of community partners for CBPR was not rated as highly important by either community or academic researchers. According to an academic researcher, "I don't think that having educational materials was particularly important because I think they already had the educational materials that they needed." With the exception of a few projects whose purpose involved training community members in a new method, training was not typically identified by either community or academic partners as essential. As one academic researcher cautions, "a community researcher doesn't need to do the same things as an academic researcher. And we need to be able to get our heads around that and still think of people as equal partners."

Having clear communication received very high importance ratings by both groups. Continuous information sharing was rated as very important by the academic researchers but included conditions. The general consensus was that information sharing should be considered and moderated according to the needs of the partners. Most participants felt overwhelmed by the number of e-mails sent out by the Consortium Coordinator. As a community member reported, "I don't like continuous information sharing, because we're already overwhelmed. So it would be more strategic information sharing—that I would give a 10, but not continuous." Clearly, the amount and method of information sharing should be discussed.

Methods of conducting CBPR. Methodological process factors include the importance of regular meetings, the use of consensus building and conflict resolution strategies, and regular assessment of partner satisfaction. Regular meetings were valued as very important by both academic and community researchers, providing a "deadline" to complete tasks, an opportunity to keep connected, and a method to facilitate communication and momentum. The importance of consensus building and conflict resolution strategies was rated higher by the community partners than the academic researchers. Most of the academic researchers indicated that the use of these types of strategies were not necessary for their team because "they came quite naturally." One academic reported that "anything that uses the term 'strategies' gives me a headache. I mean it's important we have consensus, but I'd rather just have that evolve out of trust I guess." Also, disagreements were not viewed by some academics as necessarily a bad thing—if it promoted a deeper understanding of another's perspective or position. Similarly, having a regular assessment of partner satisfaction was not something that was consciously done but was considered important.

Fostering collaboration. Fostering collaboration includes shared decision making, shared goals, public acknowledgment of the community members' involvement, and common values. Shared decision making and goals were rated as "very to extremely important" for both groups. A significant difference between community partners and academic researchers was found for public acknowledgment of the community partners' involvement (A=9.4, C=6.2). Academics felt that public acknowledgment provided support for the study within the communities, legitimacy, and ecological validity within the university. Community members were concerned only when their organization's name was incorrectly advertised or incorrect information was publicized on the Web site.

While the rating scale data provided a useful framework for understanding some of the major themes and issues regarding university and community partners' perspectives, the interviews explored in greater depth the nuances and complexity associated with each study's individual context. The open-ended questions gave participants the opportunity to discuss benefits, facilitators, barriers, the value of a partnership agreement, and recommendations.

Impact and benefits. Participants were asked to identify the potential impact and benefits to collaboration from a personal perspective and for their study. Seven of the ten academic partners identified the relationships that resulted from the collaboration as an important personal benefit, closely followed by a sense of increased knowledge and enhanced networking opportunities. Reported benefits to the study were that the collaboration added an important perspective, provided a vehicle for information dissemination, ensured relevancy, provided credibility within communities, and opportunities for students.

> *Collaboration keeps us grounded in reality and attached to practice.*
>
> —Academic partner

> *I don't have a graduate degree and I've not been involved in formal research but I have been involved in the practice on a community level and certainly in program development. I think that to be able to sit at the table and talk the research language and realize that I do know what they're talking about—whether they know I do or not—and that I can actually contribute to their thinking about what it is we're going to be doing has provided validation for me.*
>
> —Community Partner

The greatest personal benefits to collaboration identified by community partners were increased knowledge and networking. Most of the benefits identified by the community members were associated with their organization, such as an increased profile for the community organization, the provision of greater resources to the public and greater credibility to obtain further funding.

Facilitators. When asked to identify the factors facilitating collaboration, relational issues were predominantly mentioned. Having a positive relationship with their research partner was mentioned most often. One academic reported, "Basically the willingness of the partner, their attitude, their responsiveness and them being so positive all the way along, working around barriers and just trying to make a go of it. They've been great."

A community member summed up why they had such a positive relationship with their researcher, "I would have to say what's worked most is the flexibility, the openness of our own researcher, her willingness to just put her cards on the table and say this is what I know and I know nothing about that and then hand the cards to me and say you take it from here, because I don't know. She was so open to say what she didn't know and to give me the responsibility to step in when it was my turn."

Similarly, a personal relationship that existed or was developed with their research partner was identified by both academics and community members and typically identified trust and respect as key features. The other reported facilitators were nicely summed up by an academic researcher: "Facilitators included CHILD learning forums, personal contacts and networks and the personalities and professionalism of our team. Community members provide a quality to the knowledge and richness to our discussions."

Barriers. By far the most often reported barrier to collaboration within the research studies was the lack of time. As most community members indicated, due to their priority to service provision, the research was often done off the side of their desks, "well I mean, common to everyone, time. I don't have the time to commit to the degree that I would like to and I don't have people that I can delegate these responsibilities to." The following quote from an academic partner typifies many academic perspectives on why CBPR takes more time, "the success is in establishing a relationship which requires time—with community partners and respecting the way in which they're prepared to be involved in the collaboration means a spectrum of things and that you will have community partners who are collaborating but that doesn't mean that it all looks the same. And that it doesn't need to be the same, and to respect that."

Availability issues were also identified as barriers, including having researchers and community members not physically located together, lack of availability to one's partner due to busy schedules, trying to organize meeting times to address all schedules, career interruptions, two–three hours traveling to attend meetings, and long distances between partners. To address the last few points, most of the research meetings were conducted in the community, often at the community partners' organization.

Systemic issues were also identified as barriers, especially the discontinuation or restriction of funding to community organizations by the government resulting in concern for their survival, reduced staff, and even less time to devote to research. Financial issues served as barriers to collaboration in other areas as well. In the original design and budget of the Consortium, funds were allocated to serve as "release time" for both academic and community partners. As mentioned earlier, for the academics, these funds were used to hire substitute instructors who would carry part of the normal academic teaching load (usually one course). The same amount of money was initially allocated to each participating community agency to free up a certain amount of time of the community partner. Instead the funds were used to pay for administrative costs.

Some of the arrangements intended to facilitate collaboration across the Consortium, such as CHILD's Learning Forums (CLFs), where all participants convened to present findings and discuss similarities across studies, presented challenges. The most frequently reported challenge regarding the Consortium was the focus on identifying similarities across very different studies. As one academic researcher noted, "in the big picture, when I think back to the first couple of forums, it was a challenge to take people with such different backgrounds and discover that we're not all talking the same language. So we had to work on bridging those areas." Although the CLFs were considered extremely useful by both academic and community members in the long run, it did take time for individuals to feel comfortable and understand discipline-specific terminology, concepts, and similarities across studies.

Partnership agreement. Eight of the ten academic researchers and all nine of the community researchers agreed that it would have been helpful to develop a partnership agreement at the beginning of the research process, with the proviso that it not be "set in stone." As an academic researcher noted, "I think you can lay it out as sort of a framework or a statement of intention, but to be monitoring it and figuring out if it's working, if it's not working and what do you need to change to make it work." Benefits reported for a partnership agreement included the opportunity to prospectively discuss such factors as roles and responsibilities, the goals and objectives of the study, communication strategies, decision-making strategies, modes for information dissemination, budgets, and timelines. As a community researcher indicated, "Obviously discussions about those definitions—like, What does collaboration mean?, Who's going to do what?, and, What benefit will come out of it? Going through that whole process of discussing each and every thing beforehand helps so that everybody is clear where they're going and what they're going to be doing."

Most telling about the value of CBPR was whether participants would take part in future CBPR studies. All 10 academic partners indicated "yes" (if they weren't planning to retire, n=2). Eight of the nine community partners also indicated that they would be interested in participating in another CBPR study. The remaining community partner would become involved in the future if it was more participatory in nature.

Recommendations. Participants were asked to provide recommendations for facilitating CBPR research within their studies, within their organizations, and for consortiums. The recommendations by community partners specific to their research studies focused on communication, shared decision making, education, and modes of dissemination. Academic researchers' recommendations for studies also focused on communication and dissemination activities. Specifically, these included providing opportunities for more and regular dialogue and showcasing the study in the community organization's annual report. Also, academic partners recommended that the benefits of research be made more explicit and that research involvement become a part of an agency's mandate. Within organizations, both groups recommended support for conducting CBPR—be it more time, recognition for professional requirements (academics), and resource support such as training and information (community researchers). Recommendations for consortiums for both groups included a memorandum of agreement or a focused research plan, and increased time, learning, and funding support. Academics also suggested spaces for community partners to lead dialogue, and community researchers recommended that consortiums address issues associated with information dissemination, acknowledgment, and partnership assessments.

The Impact of Context on CBPR in the CHILD Project

This study supports the premise that context plays a role in influencing CBPR. The participants' professional focus and corresponding support regarding time and money are noteworthy examples. In the CHILD Project, the community partners represented members of service agencies dedicated to improving the lives of children and families. All saw the importance of participating in research to provide further insights and evidence-based practice; however, their first priority was service provision. This was evident in their desire to participate in data interpretation and information dissemination, suggesting an interest in the role of advisors or consultants as opposed to a more participatory action role, with the exception of one study that was initiated by the community where they did assume a more active role in research decision making and activities. This focus on clients also explains the identification of time as a major barrier, the interest in clear but strategic communication and the lack of interest in personal acknowledgement of their participation (however, proper acknowledgment of their agency was considered important). In addition, the interest in having a partnership agreement, clearly defined roles and responsibilities, shared decision-making strategies, and an understanding of how to respond to conflict also reflects their focus, time constraints, and their participation in a research process that was not completely familiar to most. A similar focus was reported by King, Currie, Smith, Servais, and McDougall (2008) in their "clinician-researcher skills development model." Although the community service providers were not able to be involved in all aspects of the research project due to their clinical load, they and their academic partners felt that their contribution was important and valuable. These data suggest that the definition of CBPR be broadened to include participation in the research process at whatever level is feasible to the participants instead of the blanket statement dictating that community members must be involved in all aspects of the study.

Time was understood and experienced very differently by the community and university partners. The researchers spent more time and a larger proportion of their working hours on the research projects than their community partners because as university professors they are expected to apply for and receive grants, conduct research, and publish in their pursuit of tenure and promotion. For the vast majority of the community partners, research was not considered a priority and the time that was required of them to collaborate on this work directly competed with the demands they faced from their administrative, clinical, and program responsibilities.

Not only did the university partners spend more time involved in research, they were also able to spend more continuous time on the study while the community partners were involved in a more intermittent or episodic flow of time. While the researchers felt the need for frequent and regular meetings of the research team, the community professionals had difficulty in attending many such meetings, especially those that were called on short notice. There were also different perspectives on the pace and progress of the research. Many of the community partners felt the need for faster turnaround on results and findings that they could present to their sponsoring agencies. Researchers tended to work at a much more deliberate pace in order to ensure the empirical rigor of the project. Academic researchers were oriented toward writing their next research paper, proposal, and study while the community professionals placed a greater emphasis on the current results in order to implement those findings (cf. Shonkoff, 2000).

The collaborative process provided a framework within which the researchers and community members were able to adjust their expectations to their partners' time demands and constraints. These adjustments included setting regular meeting dates far in advance, meeting in the community instead of at university settings and holding meetings at times that were convenient for the community partners. Dinner was often provided for evening meetings and child care costs were reimbursed. While these efforts could not completely erase the different experiences of time, they did represent a sincere and continuing effort to acknowledge and respect the different time demands placed on both university and community partners.

There were also inherent differences in the control and access to research funds which influenced the roles and responsibilities of the university and community partners. The funds provided by the research council were administered through the researchers' respective universities. The result was that only the researcher partners had spending authority over those funds. Despite these structural differences, attempts were made to share the resources with the community partners in as equitable way as possible and appropriate. Community partners, for example, were reimbursed for any specific operational costs they incurred related to the research study (e.g., materials, postage, courier, telephones, mileage and parking costs, and room and equipment rental). As mentioned earlier, "release time stipends" (RTS) for the community professionals was an ineffective strategy. In the university context, the RTS is a fairly common mechanism that is used to hire sessional instructors in order to release the researchers from some of their teaching responsibilities. An attempt was made to provide comparable and equitable support to the community partners within each study by giving the same financial value of the university RTS to the community agency. However, the concept of "release time" in the university sense was totally foreign and impossible to implement in the community context. Community professionals could not easily remove themselves from one specific aspect of their jobs and hire another temporary person to fill in for them for a limited time. After much discussion, the idea of a comparable RTS to community partners was dropped and in its place arrangements were made to provide honoraria for the research-related expenses community partners incurred.

Money also played an important role in contextualizing the CHILD Project in broader governmental spending priorities. At the very time when the researchers on the CHILD Project received its generous research grant from the Canadian federal government, the community partners were subjected to serious cutbacks from the provincial government of British Columbia. Thus, while the research partners were becoming empowered to engage in programs of empirical research, the community partners were forced to downsize and cut back on their community-based programming, knowing that that these cuts would negatively impact the provision of services. Given the different mandates of the provincial and federal governments and the different foci of research and community practice, real financial equity among the partners was impossible to achieve. Recognizing this inequity, however, heightened the researchers' awareness of the tremendous contributions the community partners were making to the CHILD Project in spite of financial cutbacks.

Key Factors Important for CBPR Regardless of Context

Even though contextual differences were identified between the academic and community partners, in large part due to their focus, organizational mandate, and particular expertise, there were some striking commonalities. Both community and academic partners reported the following as very important for positive collaborations: trust and mutual respect; adequate time; shared commitment, decision making, and goals; a memorandum of understanding or partnership agreement; clear communication; involvement of community partners in the interpretation of the data and information dissemination; and regular meetings.

The data indicated that trust, respect, and previous relationships were extremely important for these collaborations. Trust and respect were key to developing and continuing the partnerships and had the greatest impact on the facilitation and the benefits associated with the collaborations, a finding also noted by many others (Baker, Homan Schonhoff, & Kreuter, 1999; Kone et al., 2000; Lindsey & McGuiness, 1998; Parker et al., 2003; Plowfield, Wheeler, & Raymond, 2005). For example, Myrick, Lemelle, Aoki, Truax, and Lemp (2005) identified trust as a major factor for the development of community-university partnerships resulting in the opportunity to establish equality amongst partners and facilitate communication. Clear communication and time—key factors also identified in this study—have been shown to influence positive personal relations and effective emotional connections between partners, paving the way for developing trust (Gajda, 2004; Suarez-Balcazar, Harper, & Lewis, 2005).

Trust and respect have also been tied to shared collaborative values (Suarez-Balcazar, Harper, & Lewis, 2005; Pivik, 1997). The majority of participants in this study identified the importance of a shared commitment, shared decision-making, and shared goals for facilitating collaboration. According to Suarez-Balcazar, Harper, and Lewis (2005), these collaborative values are influenced by articulating clear objectives, goals, roles, expectations, and a vision. Further, respect for the knowledge, skills, capacities, and experiences of the partners have been reported to enhance trust and collaboration (Pivik, 1997; Suarez-Balcazar, Harper, & Lewis, 2005).

The process factors agreed upon by most of the participants included clear communication; developing an information dissemination strategy; involvement of community partners in the interpretation of the data; and developing a partnership agreement or memorandum of understanding. The majority of participants indicated that clear but strategic communication was essential for collaboration. As Suarez-Balcazar, Harper, and Lewis (2005) recommend, it is important to learn about your partners' preferred style of communication (i.e., how and when it is wanted). Another process issue that was identified as important was having regular meetings. Having regular meeting dates provided the opportunity for participants to organize their time, facilitated communication between partners, and eventually provided opportunities to develop trust with partners. As mentioned earlier, involvement in the final stages of the research project (i.e., data interpretation and information dissemination) was supported by both groups as a major role of the community partners and reflected their time constraints, agency mandate, and areas of expertise.

Many of the key factors identified above could be prospectively addressed through discussions at the initial stages of the collaboration.

A partnership agreement or memorandum of understanding provides a medium for these discussions and was recommended by over 80 percent of the participants in this study, with the proviso that it was a "living" document that could evolve over time. Criteria that may be considered for developing an agreement was identified by Pivik (1997) in *The Community-Researcher Collaborative Framework*. This framework recommends that partnership agreements include: a description of methods that address full participation and accessibility; an identification of participants' strengths and constraints; a definition of participants' roles and responsibilities; decision making and conflict resolution strategies; the benefits to participation; and appropriate time lines and budget considerations that support community participation.

COMPARING THE CHILD PROJECT TO CURRENT MODELS AND FRAMEWORKS OF COLLABORATION

A comparison of these results to the recommendations of current models and frameworks for collaboration indicates both concordance and discordance. Concordance in that these results were multidimensional, developmental, and interactive (Currie et al., 2005; Fawcett et al., 1995; Suarez-Balcazar, Harper, & Lewis, 2005). For example, time-influenced feelings of trust and respect that in turn impacted on the degree and type of communication, the benefits associated with collaboration and collaborative values, such as a shared decision making. Also, key facilitators identified by both academics and community professionals (respect, trust, shared commitment, shared decision making, shared goals, and clear communication) are evident in most of the models and frameworks. For example, trust and respect were identified by all of the models/frameworks reviewed as essential (Community-Campus Partnerships for Health, 2006; Kone et al., 2000; Pivik, 1997; Reed, Schumaker, & Woods, 2000; Suarez-Balcazar, Harper, & Lewis, 2005; Thompson, Story, & Butler, 2003). Clear communication was also identified in five of the six models reviewed (Kone et al., 2000; Pivik, 1997; Reed, Schumaker, & Woods, 2000; Suarez-Balcazar, Harper, & Lewis, 2005; Thompson, Story, & Butler, 2003). These results suggest that respect, trust, shared commitment, shared decision making, shared goals, and clear communication are vital to any type of community-university collaboration regardless of the context of the research or the individuals involved.

The unique recommendations identified by this study and different from the models suggest that attention must also be paid to the purpose of the study, the groups involved, and context of the collaboration. For example, collaborations focused on work with underserved populations require respect for the cultural setting and diversity (Kone et al., 2000; Pivik, 1997; Suarez-Balcazar, Harper, & Lewis, 2005), attention to power sharing (Kone et al., 2000), and utilizing local expertise and knowledge (Kone, Sullivan et al., 2000; Reed, Schumaker, & Woods, 2000; Suarez-Balcazar, Harper, & Lewis, 2005; Thompson, Story, & Butler, 2003). As mentioned earlier, collaborations centered on health promotion include the need for honesty, transparency, and equity (Community-Campus Partnerships for Health, 2006). As this study indicated, facilitators for collaborations between academic researchers and community service agencies require not only the key factors indicated above but also consideration of their time constraints, their primary focus on serving clients, and organizational factors associated with the agency. Awareness of these considerations and discussions between partners about the "realities" they face (for both community and academic groups) should facilitate future community-university collaborations.

CHAPTER 10

Graduate Student Experiences in the CHILD Project: The Invaluable Contribution of Interdisciplinary, Collaborative Research to Young Academics and Professionals

Martin Guhn, Suretha Swart, Mari Pighini, and Silvia Vilches

This chapter features four graduate students' stories of their experience of concurrently pursuing doctoral studies in a discipline related to child development and working within the interdisciplinary CHILD Project as research assistants. The stories highlight the insights that the students' participation in the interdisciplinary, collaborative CHILD Project provided. Collectively, the stories present a strong argument in favor of complementing and enriching graduate programs in human development, applied developmental science, or any other discipline related to child development, with interdisciplinary and collaborative research experiences. Particularly, the stories illustrate how the process of intertwining interdisciplinary research experience with theoretical studies and professional training can significantly contribute to the process of meaning making and in-depth knowledge about human development. Even more importantly, the students' stories touch upon the transformative impact that the collaborative, interdisciplinary experiences have had for their respective career paths, professional motivations, current research themes, and the hopes and aspirations for their practical work with children in family, school, and community settings, and for their contributions to child development research. Each story stands on its own; however, reading the stories together illustrates in what ways biography and research themes are intricately intertwined and how they shape each other.

Interdisciplinarity and In-Depth Meaning Making in Human Development

Martin Guhn

In 2003, I started my doctorate in Human Development at the University of British Columbia. My doctoral supervisor was also the director of the CHILD Project, and under his mentorship, I became a research assistant in CHILD Central (see Chapter 3) for the years 2004–2008, and have been involved in the writing and editing of this book since. My dissertation did not draw empirical data from the CHILD Project, but the interdisciplinary experiences, readings, and learnings from the CHILD Project were one of the primary theoretical and conceptual influences on my dissertation. In my dissertation, I related Bronfenbrenner's bioecological theory on human development to a population-level measure of children's early development as reflected in their school readiness (Guhn & Goelman, in press). In the following, I share how Bronfenbrenner's bioecological theory has come to life through my participation in the CHILD Project.

Kurt Lewin, Urie Bronfenbrenner's first academic mentor in graduate school, has been repeatedly cited by Bronfenbrenner with his quote: "There is nothing as practical as a good theory." During the greater part of my (under)graduate studies in psychology and education, a concern of mine—shared by many of my fellow students—has been that many of the theories one learns might not be useful, applicable, or *"practical."* In other words, for me, with an aspiration to eventually pass on useful knowledge to others (students, teachers, parents, or educators), the question of whether the things I have learned can eventually be applied to raise children, help students learn, prepare teachers, support schools and communities, and so on, has been on my mind for several years.

A theory that has held a strong appeal for me ever since I was introduced to it was Bronfenbrenner's *Bioecological Theory of Human Development* (1979, 2005; Bronfenbrenner & Morris, 2006). The theory lays out how human development is shaped by interacting, repeatedly occurring processes between a developing person and the multiple contexts in which the person is growing up. Stated differently, human development is seen as the joint product of person factors, context factors, and process factors that interact over time (cf. Chapter 2).

In my experience, this theory typically has an intuitive appeal to those who are introduced to it. However, I also have commonly noted that the theory is disregarded as "stating the obvious," implying that it is superfluous and, therefore, maybe *not practical*, useful, or applicable. It is this latter implication that I would like to rebut by sharing insights gained from the CHILD Project. I would like to discuss how the bioecological theory has increasingly proven its usefulness to me, allowing me to concur with Kurt Lewin that there is, after all, "nothing as practical as a good theory."

The following story from the CHILD Project shows how Bronfenbrenner's framework facilitated the integration of initially segregated pieces of information on depression, and how the theory thus exponentially expanded our understanding of the etiology and entrenchment of depression.

An Interdisciplinary Understanding of Depression

In psychology, a frequently taught phenomenon is that of learned helplessness (Seligman, 1972). The concept of learned helplessness was coined after experiments with dogs: after having received electric shocks, for an extended period of time, in a cage from which they could not escape, these dogs consecutively failed to avoid electric shocks in situations in which they could have avoided the shock by moving to another cage. In other words, the dog's forced helplessness became, over time, a generalized habit, even in situations in which alternative solutions were available.

Another concept, also taught in psychology—though less frequently, and not in the context of learned helplessness—is that of dendritic growth occurring in brain cells to establish neural connections. Here, the basic idea is that the formation of synaptic connections can be facilitated and strengthened by reinforcing emotional experiences that coincide with the eliciting event. As a consequence, if those neural pathways are consecutively engaged when a person is carrying out behaviors that had originally established those pathways, the behavior might elicit emotional memories that had been experienced during the formation of the neural pathway. Those emotions, in turn, might motivate subsequent behavior (Panksepp, 1998; Schore, 1994).

The connection of these two findings to the CHILD Project and the role of Bronfenbrenner's bioecological theory are as follows: during one of the CHILD Learning Forums, one of the research groups presented findings on the experiences of lone mothers and their children living in poverty in remote rural areas. Notably, the incidence of depression among these mothers was quite high, and the description of their daily life struggles seemingly resembled the experience of the dogs that Seligman had exposed to those inescapable fear- and anxiety-creating situations. These mothers were stuck in dilemmas across multiple situations. In one case, the issues of transportation for themselves (to work) and their children (to child care) posed an unsolvable problem/insurmountable barrier, due to irreconcilable timing, great distances, and lack of public transportation. According to the interviews with these mothers, such experiences had repeatedly caused them great stress. In addition, these mothers described those experiences as continuously discouraging and inescapable—causing them to feel helpless. In the discussion that followed the researchers' presentation, the practitioners and researchers in the audience added their insights and knowledge to these stories. What became apparent was that the conditions under which these mothers were living were aggravated by numerous factors at different ecological levels: the family service experts mentioned the limited availability of child and family services in rural areas; the policy experts highlighted the limitations of current policies (e.g., income assistance and child care policies) with regard to this scenario; and those with expertise in local, cultural, and indigenous knowledges elaborated on the social and cultural dynamics that presented additional barriers for these mothers.

In combination, the theoretical background knowledge from psychology and these stories provided a coherent, comprehensive systems' view of how depression plays out, over time, at different levels—namely, at the brain level, at the personal experience level, at the family level, and at the community level—and how these processes at different ecological levels may be affected by the policy level. Neural processes in the brain, emotional experiences, individual behaviors, the effects on children, the unavailability of community support, and the lack of public policy to provide systemic support all played out jointly in the cases of the learned helplessness of these mothers. The meaningful integration of these stories about depression is, however, not the main point here. More important are the general conceptual and practical implications that arise from this example. If one wishes to support these mothers in their situations, solutions at just one level are unlikely to be effective. Medications to affect brain processes will not solve transportation issues, and solely providing bus service might not reverse learned helplessness into proactive optimism. Using Bronfenbrenner's theory to combine the stories of processes at multiple ecological levels with respect to a phenomenon of interest—in this case, depression (or learned helplessness)—thus not only serves as a successful approach to understanding aspects of human development; but the theory also provides a framework that allows one to conceptualize and design comprehensive solutions for complex issues.

Conclusion

Currently, I am a postdoctoral research fellow at the College for Interdisciplinary Studies at the University of British Columbia. The theme of my postdoctoral research has been to "investigate the joint effects of social, cultural, demographic, and socioeconomic factors on children's developmental health and education trajectories." The one common thread that runs through the multiple research projects in which I am involved is that they all draw strongly from bioecological theories of human development, with regard to my approach to research design, data analysis, conceptualization of development and childhood, and my interpretation of validity and validation in the realm of empirical child development research. I conclude by again invoking Kurt Lewin's adage that "nothing is as practical as a good theory": the experiences in the CHILD Project have essentially contributed to my own meaning making and integration of theories on human development, and for my current research nothing has been as practical (and influential) as these integrated interdisciplinary, bioecological theories on human development.

REFLECTIONS ON MY INVOLVEMENT AS A GRADUATE STUDENT WITH THE CHILD PROJECT

Suretha Swart

As I am reflecting on my involvement with the CHILD Project over the past three years, I am struck by both the uniqueness of the project and the opportunities it provided for development as a graduate student. Not only was I able to connect with academic researchers, community professionals, and graduate students from a wide array of disciplines, but as a research assistant I was able to benefit from unique opportunities to enhance my knowledge of early child development and academic-community research partnerships. Most importantly, the longitudinal nature of the project made it possible to develop a deeper understanding of the ecology of child development over time, providing opportunities for being involved at both the practical level (e.g., data collection in the field) and for reflection (e.g., participation at CHILD Learning Forums and workshops sponsored by the Human Early Learning Partnership). Although my involvement fluctuated from intense involvement to little involvement over the past three years, I felt a sense of belonging to a community where the overarching goal was to improve early child health and development and where the student voice was valued.

In this chapter, I provide some descriptive background of my academic/working life prior to applying to the School Psychology program, briefly describe my roles within the CHILD Project, and highlight what I learned by being involved with the CHILD Project.

Life Prior to Applying to the School Psychology program at UBC

My involvement with the larger CHILD Project started early in 2005. At that point, I was working as a volunteer research assistant in the Families, Children, and Communities lab at UBC, collecting data for the Kids First Project (the *Community-Based Screening Study*). Although my work as a family and child therapist in mental health in Vancouver prior to returning to graduate studies had provided me with opportunities to support (especially at-risk) families and children, I wanted to engage in further training in order to widen the lens through which I viewed the families I engaged with on a day-to-day basis. Seeing children in play therapy or working with parents in the context of a mental health clinic often made me feel that I was missing pieces of the puzzle. In addition, I was interested in exploring theories that would help me understand why many of my clients, despite experiencing adversity (e.g., health conditions or exposure to trauma), survived and even flourished. Moreover, being able to examine and better understand the role of protective factors contributing to resilience for high-risk children was an important goal that I set for myself before I applied for further graduate studies. Finally, I was hoping to find a way to better understand the interactions of genetic and biological vulnerabilities, psychiatric disorders, different pharmacological responses, psychological vulnerability, parental and peer influences, life events, and other sociocultural and environmental factors affecting the families with whom I spend most of my working day. I decided to volunteer at an early childhood lab at UBC as a first step in fulfilling my goals toward further learning.

In retrospect, I realized that my initial interest in applying to volunteer at the Families, Children, and Communities lab at UBC stemmed from the possibility of being involved in "community research." Having worked as a clinical psychologist in a community setting in South Africa prior to moving to Canada, I missed the sense of belonging that came from being part of a broader community of people connecting and working toward the same goal.

The research assistant position at the lab provided me with weekly opportunities to engage and connect with students, researchers, and professionals in the field of early childhood and specifically in the communities of Chilliwack and the Sunshine Coast. Through my involvement with the lab, I developed an interest in researching the topic of school readiness and the implementation and evaluation of systems-level initiatives targeting school readiness. Motivated by my experience as a research assistant with the Kids First Project, I decided to apply to the School Psychology program at UBC (Fall, 2005), as I felt that the program placed a strong emphasis on evidence-based prevention, intervention, and systems-level change, and, similar to my experience in the Kids First Project, provided opportunities to be involved in efforts to improve the educational and psychological well-being of very young children in high-risk contexts.

My Roles within the CHILD Project

As mentioned, I volunteered as a research assistant for the Kids First Project in 2004. In January of 2005, I moved into a paid research assistant position with the Kids First (*the Community-Based Screening Study*) Project, where my work was jointly supervised by a professor from Educational Psychology and a professor from the UBC School of Nursing. My responsibilities included data collection (assessment of preschool age children) in Chilliwack and in a mid-size coastal school district in southwestern British Columbia; data scoring and entry; and second-level data checking (for data accuracy and quality). In the spring of 2005, I took on a role as a student writer with CHILD Central (see Chapter 3), focussing on the Early Screening Interventions studies (*the Developmental Pathways Study, the Community-Based Screening Study,* and *the Infant Neuromotor Study*) within the CHILD Project.

What I Learned/Contributed Being Involved with the CHILD Project

My involvement with the CHILD Project provided me with a unique opportunity to be connected to a broader community of students, community professionals, and researchers studying early childhood development. I want to highlight some of the learning that took place while working on the Kids First Project and within the larger CHILD Project.

Enhanced Clinical Skills. Having worked as a clinical psychologist in South Africa 10 years prior to my involvement with the CHILD Project, I had some experience with administering and interpreting cognitive tests; however, the research assistant work in Chilliwack provided me with an opportunity to learn and practice my skills administering a range of cognitive tests. While I believe that my clinical skills contributed to the quality of data gathered throughout my involvement with the project, the opportunities for further learning were exceptional. As part of the training phase, I was exposed to methods of psychoeducational assessment that were grounded in contemporary research and current cognitive theories. Moreover, the exposure to contemporary cognitive theories and a battery of tests tapping school readiness greatly enhanced my skills as a school psychologist and complemented my training at later stages in my graduate program. Furthermore, I obtained unique experience assessing and interviewing very young children (from birth through the early years) and their families over a relative long period of time. The assessment of preschool age children is often pointed out as a neglected area for school psychologists in graduate programs; therefore, I believe that the experience I obtained while working on the Kids First Project was a unique opportunity. Data scoring and entry using computer-based programs, while not new to many of the graduate students in my department, was certainly new to me. Now, having just finished my comprehensive exams in school psychology, I appreciate that the level of comfort using these programs to score and interpret my exam data was a direct consequence of hours of entry and scoring I had completed while working on the project.

Surprising Moments

All of the CHILD Project studies influenced my understanding of how domains such as physical well-being, social competence, emotional maturity, and language and cognitive development could be jointly affected by ecological factors along the "neurons and neighborhoods" continuum. However, I would like to highlight two surprising moments that especially contributed to my understanding of childhood development from an ecological perspective.

The Policy Context Studies. A surprising or "Aha" moment" happened during a presentation of the *Child Care Policy Study.* The discussion revolved around the limited number of licensed child care spaces and the effects of this shortfall on families. During this discussion, I reflected on my less than positive feelings toward a mother in Chilliwack who repeatedly failed to show up for a 9 a.m. appointment with her oldest son. When we eventually connected, she explained that she had to take a bus to get to the appointment, bringing her two younger children with her. She mentioned her struggles with finding affordable day care and finding a way to afford participating in the workforce. At the time I did not understand how returning to the workforce could be an unaffordable goal. The presentation of the *Child Care Policy Study* certainly widened the lens through which I viewed the research participants in the *Community-Based Screening Study* and in the longer term, how I reviewed the families I interact with during subsequent practicum and specialty placement rotations. Along these lines, discussions that took place during a CHILD Learning Forum with researchers in *the Income Assistance Study* deepened my understanding of the environments in which families with young children live when they receive income assistance. I feel I am entering my role as a school psychologist equipped with a wider angle lens, appreciating that in addition to school and family environments, the community and economic-sociopolitical environment in which children live, not only matter, but significantly interact with (i.e., mediate and moderate) the effects of family and school factors on children's development.

The Outdoor Criteria Study. A second surprising moment took place during a HELP-sponsored presentation of the Outdoor Criteria Study. As a family therapist in my life before graduate studies, my focus had mainly been on family systems and facilitating change within family systems. Especially in a mental health context, taking a family systems perspective was seen as a "broad view." Being confronted with how the design of outdoor play environments hinder or enhance the development of young children was especially powerful, not only because as a school psychologist I am especially interested in the physical learning environment, but also because it shifted my interest as a clinician and researcher from the impact of the elementary school years to the impact of the preschool years on long-term outcomes for students.

Long-Term Impact of the CHILD Project on Further Graduate Studies

Informed by my experiences in the CHILD Project, my research goal has shifted from a focus on school-age students with Fetal Alcohol Spectrum Disorder (FASD), to an interest in explaining how primary caregivers of elementary school-aged children with FASD in British Columbia manage their children's schooling. It is acknowledged in qualitative research that the researcher brings certain background experiences associated with, for example, education and training to the research. Embarking on the new phase in my graduate program, I anticipate that my formulation of research questions, concepts, and the structural conditions within which parents process their main concerns will be strongly colored by my experiences with the CHILD Project.

My Journey into the CHILD Project and the Evolution of an Interdisciplinary Dissertation Topic

Mari Pighini

My journey into the CHILD Project began as I started my doctoral program, after being away from graduate school for 10 years. As I evoke the first stepping stones of this journey, I gain a deep sense of awareness of how separating cognitive-based experiences from their biographical context can be done only artificially. This is why both "CHILD student" and personal timelines interweave in this account of personal and academic growth where I describe developmental stages and shifts between zones.

Preoperational CHILD Play and Discovery

I was introduced to the CHILD Project's 10 individual studies through the CHILD *Talk* Papers (see Chapter 3), and was intrigued by the fact that "community partners" were participating in each study. Although I had "heard" about academic and community partnerships, this was the first time I came in contact with one. Next, I recall our first "playgroup" meeting, the Child Learning Forum (CLF; see Chapter 3), as a place where one was allowed to open Lego tubs and spread out all of the pieces. The individual themes of studies unfolded with representatives from each team discussing methodological issues and obstacles encountered so far. I began to understand how each team of researchers had their own motivations, and that their connections were rooted in both their proximity within their own working agencies and in their affinity in their research interests. While I could grasp the connections and commonalities that existed between graduate students and their academic supervisors, I was puzzled by the different languages that researchers (from different disciplinary backgrounds) and community member partners (from different professional backgrounds) used.

I soon discovered I was not the only one struggling to attach the different pieces. The project director had identified the need to help researchers and their students, and the community members to voice out and then translate their different views through concurrent guided discussion sessions. These were multiparty dialogues, and they became an essential component of the CLFs. The sessions were democratically conceived in that they allowed for all its participants to express themselves, to question, and to clarify issues pertaining to individual projects that were brought up to the collective CHILD participants at the end of the day. These sessions became for me a role model for mediated learning experiences.

As the interdisciplinary collaboration in the CHILD Project became more complex, new forms of interaction became necessary (cf. Chapters 4, 8, and 9). Dr. Goelman took on the role of a mediator not only for himself, as an individual, but also for the CHILD Project as a collective. He invited all the project or team leaders to "move" away from their disciplinary, unistructural silos, and help launch, instead, a project conceptualized within the linkage of the diverse topics and methodologies among the 10 studies (cf. Chapter 3). This was an unsettling moment for me, because I was being asked to expand my cognitive schemata and to move into another zone of proximal development at a time when I was intently working on narrowing down my area of research and dissertation topic. During this stage of the CHILD Project, I observed and experienced how challenging it was for researchers from different disciplines to find a common academic/ community language, and to realize fundamental differences in each other's methodologies and epistemologies. Also, it became obvious how demanding it was to cross the academic and community lines, to ignore the unspoken hierarchy between academics and community members; and to integrate the different approaches to research problems coming from such diverse backgrounds.

The most intricate level of collaboration that I was a part of was the series of discussions between the three teams joined within the "Screening Cluster" (see Chapter 6). Guided by the CHILD

Project's Director, those affiliated with this cluster collaborated to write a paper that would both describe the different methodological approaches and early academic findings of their studies, and be accessible to a wide academic and professional audience. The challenge of this activity revolved around the researchers' and community practitioners' determination to reveal the commonalities in their goals and recommendations while acknowledging their diverse lenses in early identification and intervention for developmentally "at-risk" children. These included the following: a longitudinal study in a hospital-based setting; a screening and intervention program set within a community; and the evaluation of a screening tool that also utilized a training component on the administration of this tool. From a graduate student's point of view, the key word that characterizes this paper (Goelman and the CHILD Collaborative, 2008) is "complementary." The fact that the different studies' teams used complementary approaches made it possible to draw from each other's strengths and to establish connections between the different methodologies. In this way, each team member was a mediator of learning activities for the rest of the members.

Two aspects were instrumental in the success of this Screening Paper. One was the drive of the participating principal and coinvestigators to find a common ground for the concept of universal screening and early identification of developmentally at-risk children; the other one was the determination of the community representatives to ensure that the paper would highlight the practical recommendations of their respective studies. As a result, the paper now represents a wonderful example of both collaboration and inclusion, leading to insights that are greater than the sum of its individual parts.

Stories are meant to have a beginning and an end. Sometimes, however, a story unfolds within another story that, in turn, was inspired in another tale. One story that started at the time I began my graduate studies crossed paths with the CHILD Project, because it involved many of the same investigators. Out of these two stories, a new, more complex, "higher" function story evolved: one major research quest for Dr. Goelman and the investigators in the Screening Cluster was to better understand the developmental paths followed up by children who, as newborns, had been admitted to Neonatal Intensive Care Units (NICUs). What were the health and developmental patterns and trends of these children, and how did they compare to their nonrisk, or non-NICU counterparts, not only in their health and development, but also in their educational activities? Did they need additional educational and/or behavioral assistance during their elementary school years?

During the early stages of the CHILD Project, it became, for the first time in BC, possible to conduct data linkages between different databases containing indicators of children's development (e.g., hospitalization records, doctor visits; see Chamberlayne, Green, Barer, Hertzman, Lawrence, & Sheps, 1998). At the same time, the preliminary findings coming from the longitudinal data from the CHILD Project's *Developmental Pathways Study* demonstrated the importance and the need to examine these pathways at a population-based level in order to obtain sample sizes large enough to allow for generalizable conclusions. Based on these developments, a proposal for a population-based study, entitled "An Interdisciplinary Study of the Trajectories of At-Risk Infants and Children" (referred to in the following as the *NICU Study*) was articulated, with some members from the CHILD Screening Cluster research team serving as coinvestigators. This project then became a component of a major project funded by Social Development Canada (Social Development Partnerships Project) between 2004 and 2008, entitled, "The Social Inclusion Project." Thus, the *NICU Study* unfolded, to a large extent, side by side with the CHILD Project, with myself as Project Coordinator.

To date, findings from the *NICU Study* enhance and extend the findings of the *Developmental Pathways Study* in the areas of health access and utilization patterns of at-risk children. The findings suggest that these access and utilization patterns are associated with children's and families' geographical location of residence in BC (e.g., urban versus rural; BC Interior versus Lower Mainland). In particular, the *NICU Study* has allowed researchers to unpack the many dimensions of pre-, peri-, and/or postnatal risk factors in light of the child and family's residential context, and mediated by personal or familiar factors, including gender, socioeconomic status, mother's marital status, number of births (siblings), and others. Ultimately, the *NICU Study* will thus be positioned to identify recommendations for addressing the specific health and developmental needs of at-risk children in BC.

The point is that the biographical paths of the researchers as well as the paths on which the different research projects have crossed and been mediated are inevitably connected, and only through these connections, mediations, and pathways can higher functions evolve. The CHILD Project was already in existence when I became part of it as a student; likewise, the seed for the *NICU Study* had been already planted years before they came into existence. Together, the *NICU Study* and the CHILD Project shaped the emergence of my dissertation topic: A Multiple Case Study of the Children and Families of the Infant Development Program of BC (Pighini, 2008). The dissertation did not draw from data from the CHILD Project or the *NICU Study*, but from a database of family case stories of the BC Infant Development Program (IDP), an organization for which I had worked as a consultant, and which was one of the community partners in the CHILD Project. The questions I explored and the quantitative and qualitative methods I employed in my dissertation, however, had grown (1) out of my involvement with the CHILD Project and the *NICU Study*, and (2) out of discussions with Dr. Goelman (CHILD Director) and Dr. Dana Brynelsen (IDP Provincial Advisor)—who had both been mentoring and collaborating with me in the CHILD Project, the *NICU Study*, throughout my involvement in the IDP, and during my dissertation.

This story has focused on the transforming influence that my involvement in the interdisciplinary and collaborative CHILD Project has had on my perspectives on child development, and how this transformation has been intricately intertwined with my life experiences throughout the process. Individual pathways have branched out to new ones; and an "I" tale has become a collective "we" narrative. The CHILD Project's mediating and nurturing learning environment provided me with the strategies to align the stepping stones that took me to graduation. It also provided our research team with the platform to integrate the findings from two research studies (NICU and IDP) that were interwoven with the CHILD Project.

This integration allowed us to interpret data from the *NICU study* and the IDP case studies in new ways, thus drawing attention from researchers, practitioners, administrators, and policymakers. The new findings have, in fact, demonstrated that there is the need for a long-term, systematic, continuous structure in place that allows one to follow-up support at-risk children and their families in a culturally and geographically contextualized manner. I would thus like to conclude by reiterating the perception that my involvement in the interdisciplinary, collaborative CHILD Project transformed my own perspectives and interpretative abilities that could not have happened within traditional disciplinary boundaries, and I am looking forward to the transformative experiences that are to come, spurred by the crossing and connecting of our interconnected stories and pathways.

Interdisciplinarity Refracted through Multiple Roles

Silvia Vilches

My understanding of the purpose of the CHILD Project was to see if multiple approaches to early childhood research could create and sustain an interdisciplinary dialogue in an ecological framework. My graduate student journey gave me an opportunity to see this process from multiple perspectives and enhanced my learning about research processes in complex settings.

Watching the interdisciplinary CHILD Project allowed me to experience the tensions of working across disciplines, as people worked through the mundane tasks of research; an insightful experience for a beginning researcher. This was also valuable to me as person in an interdisciplinary profession—social planning—because I was able to see how disciplines, like sociology or psychology, may be drawn on to feed interdisciplinary research. I could see the limits and benefits of that process, which helps me think about the planning and preparation that are required, not just to do good research, but to position that research as a foundation for effective interdisciplinary communication. Also, I could observe the CHILD Project as an experiment in creating an interdisciplinary plan. I walked away with the content of that experiment focussed on early childhood issues, and I look forward to continuing to experiment with the "ecological" method in social planning.

In 2003, after I graduated with an MA from the School of Child and Youth Care at the University of Victoria, I started my PhD in the School of Community and Regional Planning (commonly known as urban planning) at the University of British Columbia. Coincidentally, my first project as a research assistant was embedded within the CHILD Project, under the supervision of my advisor, Dr. Gurstein. Also, one of my Master's supervisors was one of the principal investigators of the CHILD Project, providing a coincidental link to my former work.

I was on an inter- or multidisciplinary journey in my education, and this was mirrored and enhanced by the interdisciplinarity of the CHILD Project. My background (undergraduate) was in psychology, but I had been working on early childhood education and community support issues while doing my Masters. Previously, I had done community advocacy and worked in government on children's issues. Thus, I was well-positioned to understand or liaise between community and academia. My progression from my original interest in psychology to community context as a determinant of health and well-being was reflected in a thematic span that was central to the CHILD Project. Community and regional planning represented the culmination of a natural evolution for me, but at the same time, I found myself in a discipline that was not accustomed to drawing on psychology or early childhood education. The tension I experienced in trying to integrate my original interests into social planning were mirrored in the CHILD Project, providing a laboratory to understand the tensions in community planning.

The study I joined—the *Income Assistance Study* (see Chapter 4)—was also, in itself, interdisciplinary. We were interested in the impacts of the 2001 income assistance (welfare) cuts on lone-female parents with young children, and I have subsequently used this material to examine women's agency in the context of welfare reform. Our team's unit of analysis was the women's experiences, and our focus was the context of early childhood in the form of a particular type of family, the lone-parent low-income household. Our team consisted of two sociologists, a political scientist, an anthropologist, and a Women's Studies professor, and our community partners were research and advocacy bodies. Within this team, I was the only one with a psychology/development perspective, even though within CHILD there were many with developmental perspectives and training.

My dissertation changed focus during my involvement with the CHILD Project, so my reflections here focus on my learning about process more than the actual substance of my dissertation.

One of my first major learning experiences in the CHILD Project was triggered during the experience of the CHILD Project's midterm review, when I realized that the students had multiple roles that gave them unique perspectives on the CHILD Project experience. The funding agency's review team met with the entire CHILD Project team including about 25 MA and PhD students involved across all the CHILD Project studies at that time.

The reviewers were interested in the learning that graduate students were receiving; skills they might be acquiring; whether the overall CHILD Project's objective of creating an interdisciplinary environment was working as a training ground; and whether this might or could contribute to productive career development. They asked how many of the students were using CHILD Project data for their theses or dissertations. At this point, I learned that about half of the attending students were not using CHILD Project material as data, including students who were centrally involved with the CHILD Project. Up to that point, I had felt a bit like an outsider, because I was not at that point using data on the CHILD Project for my dissertation. This had played into a feeling of separation as I felt like I could go only so far in my participation, as I had felt that my participation was always about someone else's study, rather than my *own* work, per se. Having seen others' commitments, I realized that many of us were juggling multiple projects, and that this did not lessen our impact on or learning from the CHILD Project, but perhaps, instead, enhanced our experiences and our studies.

The reviewers then asked how many people were publishing on CHILD Project–related topics, and who was getting authorship. This question seemed to aim at understanding whether students were benefitting from the funding and to uncover how the CHILD Project supported their career development. There were many opportunities for equal engagement of the graduate students in the CHILD Project, and I had, throughout, opportunities to author or coauthor presentations and publications, or to use data for my dissertation. The reviewers inquired how we thought we were benefiting career-wise, what we were learning about, and whether we were truly part of the teams or whether we were treated as "staff." Most students felt completely valued by their teams, and there was a very warm feeling about this in the room. Finally, the reviewers wanted to know how we were invited to participate. This was not only of particular interest to the midterm reviewers—illustrated by the fact, that some of the midterm review's recommendations focussed on this aspect—but also of particular interest to me, and to a large extent, this story comes out of the awareness created by the discussions in the midterm review meeting with the other CHILD Project students.

The midterm review, and many other experiences, highlighted the multiple natures of our (students') roles. More than others, we students often got to see multiple sides of the research process. We were out in the community recruiting study participants, and working closely with our community partners, so we had a grounded community perspective. Many of us, in fact, came from community work. At the CHILD Annual Retreats or CHILD Learning Forums (see Chapter 3), we watched or were involved when the results of our studies were presented. We were immersed in our independent academic work. Because the interdisciplinary meetings required regularly reporting on project progress, processes that might otherwise have invisibly moved toward publication or funding reports were, instead, regularly discussed as part of open forums. Each meeting was an opportunity to reflect on others' reactions to our work, and to see how research findings were organized for presentation in an interdisciplinary setting. These moments offered the opportunity to reflect on processes from the multiple perspectives: from community and academic roles; from a grounded perspective of being immersed in data collection and familiarity with study participants; through "learning by watching" as the research designs evolved; and through watching our own individual and collective efforts being reacted to in an interdisciplinary academic setting. This was somewhat like taking the back off an analog watch and watching the movements. It is difficult to say that this provided a specific skill or career enhancement, but it sharpened my ability to articulate the movements between the stages of research and introduced me to many practical as well as theoretical dilemmas of scholarly work.

A critical learning experience, much discussed within the CHILD Project, was about how to communicate over and across disciplinary boundaries. This communication occurred within and between the graduate students as well as between students and faculty team leads, within teams, and between teams and the CHILD Project's overall leads. We graduate students had a "front row seat" for this interdisciplinary experiment. As I mentioned, inter- or multidisciplinarity was not new to me. However, what was new was to *practice* it within the academic setting. Trying to explain concepts and whole frameworks to people who had typically worked only within their fields (education, psychology, epidemiology, sociology, etc.) was a completely new challenge. I watched our group struggle to effectively communicate both the premise (the theoretical frame) and the results of our study, and I experienced the surprises and frustrations when members of some CHILD Project studies struggled to apply or integrate the work of other studies. This highlighted the difficulties of interdisciplinary communication, even within a sophisticated and adept group.

In addition to the communication struggles, I realized to what extent the orientation to research might be different in different disciplines. For example, conducting clinical intervention trials was seen, in some disciplines, as an unquestioned standard. Therefore, when confronted with critical questions from other disciplines pertaining to the limitations of clinical trials, researchers from those disciplines did, at first, not comprehend that this could be a question. Then they struggled to communicate their arguments—in this case, the need for clinical trials—convincingly beyond their disciplinary boundaries. At first, this seemed to be destabilizing. If fundamental aspects of one's disciplinary standards were questioned, did it not also question, in some way, people's entire career work in that field? As a consequence of this dynamic, the interdisciplinarity challenge moved rapidly from a project- or content-related communication issue to reflection on knowledge production, and then to a reflection on the value of one's personal career accomplishments and one's own career emphasis within one's own field of study.

My experience "with CHILD" shaped me and my future work through numerous concrete learning experiences. Some specific skills that I learned will be useful assets in my future career, such as learning about longitudinal research, or being involved in the publication process with a larger team. At another level, however, certain insights evolved in a more subtle manner. I continue to reflect on how to crystallize what makes my research unique and of interest to others, and how to effectively communicate my research questions and their significance to others with different perspectives. As a result, I deliberately seek to look at my research from multiple perspectives, and I intently watch and listen to how researchers, community practitioners, and policymakers conceptually frame and methodologically approach research questions in different ways. Finally, I have become aware of the different barriers, realities, and incentive structures with regard to research when it comes to community practitioners and professionals versus academic researchers. Learning from both my community partners and research supervisors, I have learned how to better communicate the relevance of each other's questions and contributions.

How, then, is the CHILD experience reflected in my current work, and can it be relayed back into my profession and discipline? How might I be a conduit for the interdisciplinary insights? My current academic home is the urban planning school in the College for Interdisciplinary Studies at UBC, which has a tradition of focussing on sustainability in ecological and human habitats. In spite of this, the greater field of urban planning does not have a focus (yet) on early childhood. However, in 2006, I attended the first ever round table on child care and planning in North America. This suggests a trend that may be reflected in increasing amount of research conducted on creating liveable cities, enhancing cross-cultural environments, providing housing and mitigating transportation barriers for families. The CHILD Project helped give me interdisciplinary expertise that may help me inform further work in this emerging area of interest, which draws on multiple disciplinary bases. The CHILD experience, although interdisciplinary itself, helped give me an intellectual theoretical home that may enhance my disciplinary home of urban planning. Thus, the encouragement I received through the CHILD

Project inspires me to continue my efforts to make urban planning more aware of its potential to positively affect the lives of children.

AFTERTHOUGHTS

What would happen if you took the [research] models of one [discipline] and applied them to [another]?
Bronfenbrenner, Kessel, Kessen, and White, 1988, p. 62

I have spent successively more time thinking about the question and less about the answer. Namely, is this a good question to ask in the first place? Why should I or anyone else care what the answer is?
Morgeson, Seligman, Sternberg, Taylor, and Manning, 1999, p. 113

[N]ew paradigms in our field tend to come primarily from disciplines other than our own [...]
Bronfenbrenner, Kessel, Kessen, and White, 1988, p. 62

These quotes recapitulate insights contained in the four stories of this chapter. The graduate students in the CHILD Project were repeatedly exposed to research meetings and discussions, in which research and practitioners from different disciplines exchanged their knowledge of research models and on their research questions. Growing out of this experience, the graduate students' dissertations projects (1) addressed questions from their respective disciplines using a method from another discipline (e.g., applying a bioecological approach to a sociological conceptualization of school readiness); (2) searched for ecologically valid answers (to "good questions") using applied research methods (e.g., deducing recommendations for screening and service practice from family case studies); and (3) pursued the vision to contribute to paradigm shifts in their own disciplines (e.g., by raising awareness for the primacy of child development concerns in urban planning).

In retrospect, some of the questions we are asking today may seem obvious, even if they were surprising a few years ago. Similarly, the application of new research methods to existing questions may seem natural now, even though we were not aware of the methods until recently. Finally, new ideas and paradigms sometimes have such a powerful and pervasive effect on a field that it is hard to imagine the field without it—even if one remembers the field without that paradigm.

The stories in this chapter illustrated in what ways the CHILD Project fostered openness to new ideas and methods, and in what ways it made us critically reevaluate our current paradigms. We believe that such openness and criticalness is a valuable principle for research in general, and a fundamental component of the interdisciplinary, collaborative research process—a process that needs to be continuously and deliberately renewed in our quest for "new, more differentiated, more precise," and "more valid scientific knowledge" on human development (Bronfenbrenner, 2001, p. 4).

CHAPTER 11

Conclusions and New Beginnings: What We Have Learned about the Rules, Rituals, and Realities of Interdisciplinary Research

Hillel Goelman, Jayne Pivik, and Martin Guhn

Yet, in order to live, to breathe and to generate novelty, human beings have had to create—by structural means—spaces and times in the calendar or, in the cultural cycles of their most cherished groups which cannot be captured in the classificatory nets of their quotidian, routinized spheres of action. These liminal areas of time and space—rituals, carnivals, dramas and, latterly, films—are open to the play of thought, feeling and will; in them are generated new models, often fantastic...

Turner, 1969, p. vii

Throughout this book we have attempted to describe the theory, the process, and the relevance of Bronfenbrenner's bioecological framework to the growing body of research on interdisciplinary research[1] on young children from the medical, health, and social sciences. While not conducted from a reconceptualist perspective, which is the major theoretical orientation of the *Critical Cultural Studies in Early Childhood* series in which this book appears, we see many areas of consistency between the reconceptualist perspective and the interdisciplinary perspective that guided the CHILD Project. This book contributes to the stated intention of this series to "open up new spaces for dialogue and reconceptualization" (Palgrave Press Brochure, 2010). In this chapter we discuss why this book will open an intellectual space where the reconceptualist and the interdisciplinary perspectives can inform and complement one another.

A basic assumption in this chapter is that neither the reconceptualist nor the bioecological approaches are neat, homogeneous, or monolithic schools of thought. Both approaches include diverse viewpoints on theory and practice. What we aim to accomplish in this concluding chapter is to summarize how the *rules* of interdisciplinary research and the use of meaningful and effective *rituals* among interdisciplinary researchers can help to successfully address many of the *realities* that impact on early child development. Woven throughout these rules, rituals, and realities was the two-part question that confronted all of the studies in the CHILD Project: *What can our study learn from the other studies* and *what can our study contribute to the other studies?*

The Realities Confronting Reconceptualist and Interdisciplinary Approaches to Research

Both reconceptualist and interdisciplinary research in early child development emphasize the importance of the social, demographic, economic, cultural, and policy contexts that frame and influence the lives of children and their families. Mac Naughton (2005) has encouraged researchers to consciously and conscientiously explore research questions and phenomena that pertain to minority populations and those that have traditionally been marginalized in studies of child development. She speaks of the importance of conducting research that would highlight the significance of enhancing equity and justice in society. Each of the studies in the CHILD Project had a strong social justice component, and to a large extent this was built into the CHILD Project by including community-based researchers as partners in the respective programs of research. The inclusion of community partners was intended to ensure that the data and the findings would be relevant to the children in their respective communities.

Yet, in the CHILD Project we found that unforeseen, subtle, and changing realities can have major impacts on the content and process of the research project. As noted in Chapter 2, the CHILD Project was funded by the Canadian federal government at a time when early childhood was high on the policy priority list of that government. Simultaneously, however, the newly elected provincial (state) government in British Columbia was developing its own neoliberal policy agenda that reflected itself in major cutbacks in government funds to many community-based health, social service, and education programs for young children and their families. When the university and community partners first met, the researchers were enthusiastic about the prospect of a five-year longitudinal research project while the community partners were dealing with budget cutbacks, staff layoffs, and program reductions. This tension was compounded when two of the community partners in the CHILD Project were actually competing for the same service delivery contract that was being tendered by the provincial government. These political realities had to be recognized and confronted by all partners in the CHILD Project, requiring the academic partners to demonstrate heightened sensitivity to community issues and community partners and to be frank about the increased challenges they faced in delivering child, youth, and family services to their clientele. We should note that by the time the CHILD Project concluded its work and began to produce policy recommendations, both the federal and provincial governments had seriously downgraded the policy importance of early childhood research and programs. Thus, political and policy realities were far different at the end of the project than they had been at the beginning.

Besides these external realities that contextualized the CHILD Project, we were continually becoming aware of new internal realities within the consortium that demanded attention and resolution. One of these powerful realities has been described by Reich and Reich (2006) as the problem of "cultural competence," which is derived from their analysis of academic disciplines as "cultures" with their own specific values, attitudes, metaphors, and, perhaps most importantly, their own distinct jargon and language. This reality exerted a powerful effect upon the interaction of researchers from various disciplines but also in the discourse between the academic and community partners in the CHILD Project (Chapter 9). In our own case we were struck by the fact that there were diverse views on what was meant by "interdisciplinarity." Reich and Reich argue that successful interdisciplinary collaborations can occur only when the participants take an active role in translating their culture to others and in attempting to learn about the cultures of their colleagues. They recommend a process of self-reflection that can be broken down into a number of components: self-reflection on their own personal and professional motivations for wanting to engage in interdisciplinary research; developing sensitivity to the needs and cultural orientations of colleagues from other disciplines; paying attention to their own language and the language of their colleagues; breaking down barriers based on idiosyncratic or discipline-specific language; paying attention to diverse models of research; attending to the distribution of power within the consortium and taking steps to ensure that power within the group is fairly allocated. Regarding this final point, they argue against the notion that they call "disciplinary policing," where one discipline attempts to define and evaluate other disciplines based on their own.

We have discussed the ways in which our different disciplinary cultures dealt with the cognitive and emotional realities in reference to the use of the term "developmental surveillance." We would argue that a concern with the "words of power and the power of words" can be found in numerous places in the reconceptualist literature such as when Swadener (2006) points to the language of exclusion and marginalization, in discussing issues of both gender and disability. "Single motherhood," for example, is often seen as a diagnosis or description of a set of economic and social pathologies. This language itself can lead to a "blame-the-victim" orientation, which fails to recognize the broader systemic, administrative, and political frameworks that limit the social and economic opportunities for these families. As Swadener puts it, many families with young children face the "persistent trilemma of health care, child care and employable skills/livable wages" (p. 123). Similarly, the CHILD Project conducted discussions in which we attempted to look beyond simplistic (and misleading) definitions in order to better understand the lives of our studies' participants in terms of the gendered and "othered" restrictions imposed upon them from the outside. Discussions with the participant mothers through member checks were also conducted in order to ensure that their language was being cited and quoted with accuracy and sensitivity. It was increasingly clear in our work that language was both a means of communicating our results and a critical instrument in shaping and interpreting our results.

Another powerful reality acknowledged by both reconceptualist and interdisciplinary perspectives was the strong emphasis each placed on cultural and ethnic diversity, or what Ball and Pence (2000) refer to as "bringing culture into focus" (p. 21) and the "bicultural co-construction of childhood" (p. 23). The lives of children and families are powerfully influenced by social class, histories of oppression, immigration, and refugee status. Both perspectives have cited the importance of early childhood services for Indigenous peoples in Canada and the United States. For example, Rhinehart (2005) has summarized the goal of early childhood programs for Native American children as follows: "To grow to their fullest potential, Native American children need strong and loving families and communities who care for their needs. Equally important, tribal children need a careful balance of teachings about their traditions, tribal values and languages" (p. 135). Among the features of Native early childhood programs, Rhinehart cites the importance of appropriate learning environments; the politics of language and culture; staffing for Native American early childhood programs and family and community partnerships. These same features were developed and implemented in the CHILD Project's *Indigenous Child* and *Aboriginal HIPPY Documentation Projects* (Chapter 5) and in the other studies that included Indigenous children. Interestingly, Rhinehart goes on to discuss the importance and sensitivity of adapting concepts and assessment techniques from mainstream early childhood programs, which are criticized in other reconceptualist writings (e.g., Kessler & Swadener, 1992). For example, she acknowledges the program standards developed by the National Association for the Education of Young Children (NAEYC) whose work is criticized by many for allegedly being to "universalistic" and for ignoring issues of cultural sensitivity. Further, Rhinehart does not uniformly condemn all forms of child tests and assessments. She argues carefully and strongly for the need of using standardized tests and assessments in appropriate and sensitive ways. Finally, we note Rhinehart's assertion that to date, "there have been few studies that focus specifically on Native American children" (p. 141). The two studies on Indigenous child development in the CHILD Project will, we believe, make a major contribution to realities and research in this area.

Our awareness of, and attention to, language provided one of the major breakthroughs in our research process. When we began the CHILD Project we articulated our major research question as "*What differences make a difference in early child development?*" This question was seen as appropriate by the researchers around the table. Yet one of our community partners, a woman who was the director of a province-wide early intervention program, proposed a subtle but important modification of the question: "What differences *can we make* that will make a difference in early child development?" The revised question was crucial for a number of reasons. First, it directly addressed the reality that programs and interventions were in the process of being cut and it reminded us that our research had to contribute to ongoing support for staff and programs that make differences in the lives of children and families. It also represented an important step in our own reality within the CHILD Project that reinforced how community partners can actively contribute to and, indeed, shape the nature of the research in which we were all engaged.

This change in the framing and focus of the questions raises an even more general issue. From a pragmatic perspective, it is important in early child development research to differentiate between variables that are modifiable (e.g., the availability of child care) and those that are not modifiable (e.g., gender). And if our vision is to promote children's well-being/development, we need to focus on the changeable influences/factors/variables. Our argument is that it is through collaborative, interdisciplinary research that researchers and professionals can identify, describe, and explain the wide range of factors that are changeable, and develop recommendations and suggestions that are of practical relevance.

In these examples we have seen some of the ways in which macro and micro levels of reality impacted on interdisciplinary and reconceptualist research. We now proceed to consider some of the rules that were developed and implemented to help us conduct the research while staying attuned and sensitive to external pressures and the demands of collaborative interdisciplinary research.

Cultural Competence and the Rules of Conducting Interdisciplinary and Reconceptual Research

Klein and Newell (1996) have written that interdisciplinary research "is a process of answering a question, solving a problem, or addressing a topic that is too broad or complex to be dealt with adequately by a single discipline or profession...and draws on disciplinary perspectives and integrates their insights through construction of a more comprehensive perspective" (p. 393–394). This statement captures many of the core elements of the interdisciplinarity used in the CHILD Project. First, it emphasizes that each of the participating disciplines in the collaboration was expected to conduct their research according to the highest levels of disciplinary rigor—the rules that governed disciplined inquiry within their field of knowledge. For example, neonatologists were not expected to immediately abandon biomedical research perspectives for qualitative methods and qualitative researchers were not expected to delve into statistical analyses. We did not interpret interdisciplinarity as an abandonment of the disciplines from which we all came, but as a means of integrating the knowledge generated by the respective disciplines.

One of the significant similarities between the reconceptualist and the bioecological approaches is the emphasis both place on multiple perspectives on early childhood. The two approaches share the view that developmental psychology, as the discipline within which most "developmental research" has been conducted, has heavily relied upon paradigms that emphasize individual differences, experimental methods, and positivist epistemologies. Further, in large part, psychology has ignored contributions from other disciplinary perspectives. Both approaches argue for an integration of mutually informative theoretical orientations, which in turn generate a wide range of methodological techniques for the collection and analysis of data. One of the guiding rules of the CHILD Project was the deliberate effort to bring diversity of theory and practice into its work.

Within the CHILD Project we included many different kinds of data and this reveals a specific approach to the rules of research that we adopted. While we acknowledge that the *exclusive* reliance on quantitative data, for example, might provide a narrow, skewed perspective on the phenomena we studied, we also believe that these data can be integrated into a meaningful synthesis with data generated through the qualitative tools of, for example, women's studies and Indigenous studies. Our aim was not to privilege one approach over another but, rather, to attempt to understand how a weaving together of different approaches could complement and extend the findings of any one approach. By adopting a multifaceted, multilevel interactive design, the CHILD Project attempted to integrate findings from a wide range of disciplines and methods and not to rely on any one specific discipline or set of methods. We note support for this notion within the reconceptualist community, where Dahlberg, Moss, and Pence (1999) have argued that postmodern approaches to early childhood research do not necessarily "imply rejection of quantification" or the development of a "comprehensive and reliable system of information" (p. 119). This integrative approach is gaining much currency in interdisciplinary studies as suggested by the increased visibility and importance of the *Journal of Mixed Methods Research* (e.g., Morgan, 2007; Teddlie & Yu, 2007; Cresswell & Tashakkori, 2007).

And what are the rules of interdisciplinary research? While there is no definitive taxonomy of such rules, the CHILD Project developed a number of suggested guidelines. As discussed in Chapter 8, the precise nature of integrating knowledge across disciplinary boundaries is the subject of much debate among interdisciplinary researchers and theorists. While definitions and taxonomies of interdisciplinarity abound (e.g., Reich & Reich, 2006), Repko (2008) has proposed a useful set of metaphors that convey the ways in which knowledge integration can be accomplished. For example, there would be rules that allow researchers to engage in "boundary crossing" by presenting methods and findings that complement or juxtapose data from other studies/disciplines. To begin to cross boundaries in safe and constructive ways, Repko cites the metaphor of "bridge building," where two bodies of knowledge, anchored firmly in their disciplinary foundations, are strong enough to support shared data, findings, and possible explanations. Even so, boundary crossing and bridge building can be seen as serving more of a descriptive function rather than an integrative or explanatory function. A more collaborative image of interdisciplinary research would be "map making," whereby researchers from different disciplines acknowledge the varied and complex topographies generated by their respective theories and methods. This collaboration allows both disciplines to construct and enlarge a new reality map that draws on these differing perspectives. Finally, there is the metaphor of "bilingualism" that recognizes how language itself can serve as a barrier to integrative research. By becoming functional (if not fluent) in the language of other disciplines, researchers can more easily negotiate meanings, ask and answer questions, and articulate areas of agreement and disagreement.

In the CHILD Project we observed how disciplinary expertise could meaningfully contribute to a broader interdisciplinary understanding of different aspects of early child development. While the *Child Care Policy Study,* for example, drew upon large-scale population health and administrative databases to explore child care use, quality, affordability, and accessibility, the qualitative studies on *Income Assistance, Parent Counselling, Outdoor Criteria,* and *The Playground Study* added important new dimensions to our understanding of the meaning of child care in the lives of children and families. Parents told personal stories that reflected their unique experiences in their attempts to find child care and the consequences of not finding quality and affordable child care. The administrative databases could not produce data that reflected the sense of isolation, deprivation, and vulnerability, which were reported by lone parent mothers with young children who were living on income assistance. We learned about the human face of funding cuts to child care services. We learned from the interviews and focus groups in these studies that as economic conditions change, as policies change, the impacts on children and families also change. The *Indigenous Child Project* and the *Aboriginal HIPPY Documentation Project* helped us to understand the kinds of child care programs that were needed in Indigenous communities, the challenges of meeting governmental regulations on training and licensing, and the difficulty in creating or accessing early childhood curricula that spoke to the cultural, linguistic, and historical needs of their community. The *Safe Spaces* and *Outdoor Criteria* provided a window on an understudied aspect of children's experiences in child care programs: how physical environments and educational programs can impact on children's peer relations in child care settings. *The Child and Youth Well-Being Study* gave voice to the child experience, enhanced our understanding of environmental influences on child health and provided yet another perspective. The pediatricians in the Developmental *Pathways Study* modified their recommendations for parents to enroll their children in child care and, in a parallel development, the Canadian Paediatric Society adopted an advocacy stance for more child care and more affordable child care. Taken together, each of these separate "pixels" contributes meaningful and important pieces of information that generate a fuller and more realistic picture of child care in the province over the five years of the CHILD Project.

This integrative understanding was greatly facilitated by consistent attention to our key stimulus questions: *What can our study learn from the other 10 studies* and *what can our study contribute to the other studies?* In wrestling with these questions we saw numerous examples of boundary crossing, bridge building, map making, and interdisciplinary bilingualism. In the following section we discuss how we engaged in these activities through the rituals that were the life-blood of the CHILD Project.

Realities, Rules, and Rituals

> The ritual, in fact, has the long term effect of emphasizing all the more trenchantly, the social definitions of the group.
>
> Turner, 1969, p. 172

Interdisciplinary approaches to research emphasize the importance of communication and collaboration among researchers, participants, and stakeholders in the design, analysis, and interpretation of research results. A high priority from the very inception of the CHILD Project was to design specific kinds of gatherings that would regularize and structure opportunities for ongoing discourse among all of these research partners. We have summarized these specific rituals throughout this book (primarily in Chapters 3, 6, 8, and 9), and in this chapter we consider the theoretical underpinnings of these rituals in the hope of contributing to the further development of such rituals in other interdisciplinary programs of research.

Our view is that these rituals have to be meaningful and important encounters that occur at expected and regular intervals. They take place in large groups and small groups and are designed to provide opportunities for critically examining methods, results, and applications from different perspectives. They provide opportunities for developing the kinds of "cultural competence" described by Reich and Reich (2006) earlier. This approach fits in very well with Klein's (1990) view that the interdisciplinary approach is more about process than product:

> Interdisciplinarity is neither a subject matter nor a body of content. It is a process for achieving an integrative synthesis, a process that usually begins with a problem, question, topic or issue. Individuals must work to overcome problems created by differences in disciplinary language and world view. (p. 188)

Precisely how do individuals do this work and overcome these problems? Our experience in the CHILD Project has convinced us of the value of ritual as a means of facilitating this process. A variety of disciplines and approaches including anthropology, social psychology, religious studies, and symbolic interactionism have contributed to our understanding of the process of ritual. Getz (2007), drawing on Turner (1969) and van Gennep (1909/1960), has proposed three distinct phases of scheduled "events" (e.g., meetings, retreats, rituals, CHILD Learning Forums) that serve to draw a community together: "preliminal", "liminal" and "postliminal." The preliminal phase is one in which the individuals in the group begin to separate themselves from their normal, daily routines and move into the special "time out of time" and the special place where the gathering will occur. The purpose of the preliminal period is to gain perspective and to focus upon the issues that are arising through the collaboration. For example, in our own experience, Chief Willie Charlie's opening blessing and storytelling enabled us to distance ourselves from the pressures of other tasks and responsibilities and to regain the "big picture" focus on the importance of appreciating the multiple realities of children's lives.

It is in the liminal phase that the substantive and symbolic interactions occur. A sense of group or "communitas" is invoked—shared commitment to the collective endeavor—among participants of equal status to minimize struggles over person or disciplinary power. Characteristic of the interactions during this phase are descriptions and interpretations of past events and hypotheses and predictions of future events, with emphases on self-discovery and reflective discourse. The sense of open and safe exploration is enhanced by a group commitment to restrain any episodes of "disciplinary policing." Our sharing of language, metaphors, methods, and findings was the main focus of this phase.

In taking leave of the gathering, participants may experience a combination of accomplishment, loss, renewal, and transformation. In our own experience, efforts were made to find ways of holding on to the cognitive and emotional benefits yielded by the gathering, creating expectations, and anticipation toward future gatherings.

The importance of process, reflection, and interaction are emphasized by numerous scholars. Romm (1998) has pointed out the critical role of reflexivity in interdisciplinarity practice. That is, beyond attention to disciplinary rules and rigor, it is crucial for interdisciplinary researchers to examine their own—and their colleagues'—research from different perspectives and to attempt to do the important and difficult work of synthesizing diverse perspectives into meaningful reflections of complex interactions of, in our case, biomedical, social, cultural, and policy perspectives. Petersen (1996) has pointed out the personal and academic risks that scholars take when engaging in interdisciplinary work, particularly in acknowledging the area of health promotion and what he refers to as the "politics of uncertainty." Marzano, Carss, and Bell (2006) echo Petersen's endorsements of interdisciplinary research and articulate many of the same recommendations regarding the importance of clear and consistent communication as essential to interdisciplinary and collaborative research.

These descriptions of ritual and of interdisciplinary discourse fit with the processes that we drew upon in understanding our data and creating new interpretations in the CHILD Project. Klein's (1990) discussion on the importance of meaningful interdisciplinary discourse reads in many ways like a description of one of our CHILD Learning Forums:

> "Of these different techniques, iteration and role clarification have proved especially useful. Iteration allows authors to become readers and critics by going over each other's work in order to achieve a coherent, common assessment. To facilitate interaction, a project director or team leader can act as a synthesizer. Role negotiation and role clarification allow team members to assess what they need and expect from each other while clarifying differences in methodology and ideology. Members of interdisciplinary teams are, in effect, translating specialized knowledge into a "synthetic product," acting as filters for each

other, consulting experts and the ultimate recipients of their work, whether they are students, patients, clients or other scholars. Making it through the long haul depends in no small part on identifying several factors: where difficulties lie, where and by whom goals are clarified and roles defined, what the levels of communication are inside and outside the group, how the group builds and maintains its identify and sense of purpose, what its capacity for change is, and how and by whom points are accessed and achievements measured." (p. 190)

Returning to our example of child care issues cited earlier, we found that the ritualized interactions both within and across each of the teams allowed for a creative collaboration and a better interdisciplinary understanding of the complexity of child care. The major community partner for the *Child Care Policy Study* was a community-based child care resource and referral center. While the center was not interested in the details of the data analyses, it was an invaluable source of information on the context and the meaning of the data that the academics were generating. In a regularly scheduled series called "Dinner and Data," the academics would present the most recent data analyses and the community partners used their knowledge of what was happening on the street, in the neighborhoods, in contract negotiations, in city council by-law discussions, and in the various ethnic communities to provide helpful interpretations of those data. The community partners were able to place the data in the context of previous policies and current concerns; they drew attention to what looked like insignificant "blips" in the data and explained why those data points were important to attend to. Through this Dinner and Data ritual, CHILD engaged in collaborative hypothesis generation, and allowed the community and university partners to hear about and explore alternative interpretations of data. Taken together, the many different studies in which child care data emerged and the ability to co-construct meaning with community partners brought together different disciplines, different methodologies, different sets of findings—and a more powerful realization of the interactive complexity that characterized child care in the province of British Columbia. Thus, in a more compressed time frame Dinner and Data was a ritual of sharing and exploration that allowed for deeper and more nuanced insights to be developed by all participants.

This degree of integration is consistent with a transdisciplinary approach to knowledge construction. While the research on interdisciplinarity is replete with discussions and definitions of inter-, multi-, and transdisciplinarity, it is the latter that some argue that emphasizes the ways in which the findings and results of one discipline can directly inform the findings and results of another discipline. We believe that through this kind of integrative analysis our findings will make a difference to children and will make a difference to those individuals in a wide range of professions and disciplines who themselves make a difference in the developmental pathways of young children and their families.

Through our various rituals, publications, and gatherings we were able to stay focused on the questions what each studied learned from and contributed to the other studies in the CHILD Project. In the following sections we turn our attention to what we have learned about collaborative interdisciplinary research as a whole and how what we learned might contribute to others who are interested in undertaking similar kinds of research initiatives.

New Beginnings and Recommendations

Starting and conducting collaborative, interdisciplinary inquiry does not involve following a recipe or painting by numbers. The activities listed below are those that worked for our specific collaboration and we discuss them here to give examples of some of the underlying principles that we believe should guide this kind of work.

A question that arises frequently is "How do you get started?" In our experience it was a combination of organic growth and development, along with periods of intensive, focused activity, and maintaining a self-reflexive stance throughout that allowed us to monitor our current progress at any given stage in light of where we had come from and where we hoped to go.

In the years leading up to the CHILD Project, many of the participants got to know each other through a series of seminars, workshops, and retreats, some of which were supported by a federal research infrastructure grant that was explicitly intended to build research teams. As the "UBC Child and Family Research Project," we began with informal lunch hour presentations by academics, community professionals, and graduate students where the only agenda was to learn about each other's work. We made a conscious effort to recruit people from different disciplines and professions and much of the contact was made through a "snowball" technique involving word of mouth. An interdisciplinary doctoral seminar was mounted that drew students from the medical, health, and social sciences. This core group applied to the university for funds to mount an interdisciplinary lecture series on early child development and the process of applying for funds, administering, and organizing the lecture series, and, finally, publishing the lectures (Goelman, Marshall, & Ross, 2004) helped to create a sense of cohesion and purpose. Our first recommendation, then, is to begin by building a process by which researchers and professionals from different fields can begin to learn about each other's interests and programs of research and, on an interpersonal level, created a positive comfort zone for all participants.

In the course of this preliminary activity the group began to explore the possibilities of collaboration but we realized early on that a more foundational issue was for the various researchers and professionals to begin to articulate the research problems within their own specific disciplines. The different groups were, however, strongly encouraged, to include both university academics and community partners. Thus, simultaneous with the early disciplinary activity, disciplinary groups were considering their own programs of research with the possibility that this program might fit into a collaboration of some sort a few steps down the road. The discussions within the disciplines tended to first focus on describing the research problem with which they wanted to engage by identifying the current *limits* of our knowledge in a given area; the possible *gaps* in our knowledge or gaps between the research and practice; or perhaps the *contradictions* that we faced between different theoretical, empirical, or practical approaches to child and family research. This discussion among potential academic and community research partners on the limitations, gaps, and contradictions within the research and professional literatures is a crucial phase of development in building multiteam, interdisciplinary research.

Based on the bioecological model of research, we strongly encourage research teams to explicitly articulate the multiple contexts that will either directly or indirectly impact on our results. As noted throughout this book, we emphasize the importance of consciously and conscientiously tracking the political, social, economic, demographic, cultural, policy, environmental, and social justice contexts that frame the research question and the methods, data analyses, and interpretations of the findings. The attention to context must also take into consideration the institutional, temporal, and financial contexts of both the universities involved in the research and the community agencies. It is important to determine to what extent the universities and agencies will support the research and the specific demands of collaborative interdisciplinary inquiry. Will the university provide any needed financial and infrastructure support? Will the community agencies see the research effort as relevant to their mandate?

Taken together, these preliminary steps must culminate in a consensus regarding the ways in which the partners see their research as making a difference in the lives of young children. In our experience, this phase of discussion and planning was perhaps the most crucial. Community partners were frank in telling their university partners that the academic research questions were either not compelling or relevant to their community mission. Research questions and methods had to be sharpened, added, deleted, or modified so that the research questions and methods made sense from both a research and a community perspective.

Once this level of intradisciplinary work was completed it was important for the different study teams to reconvene to both report on their proposed plan of research and to begin to discuss what the collaboration might offer. One very basic question that remained on the table during these discussions was, "Why collaborate in the first place?" That is, the potential collaborators had to articulate why they felt that the benefits of interdisciplinary collaboration were worth the high costs in terms of time, money, and energy to collaborate. In what ways would the collaboration overcome the limits, gaps, and contradictions that existed between the various disciplines? We explored the possibility of developing or using an overarching theoretical framework within which all disciplines and professions would feel equally comfortable. What were the areas that offered rich potential for theoretical or methodological collaboration and what were the areas where there was limited or no potential? The discussions moved quickly from general to specific questions:

- What are the proposed methods of research within and across the studies?
- What techniques or approaches will be used for data collection?
- What techniques or approaches will be used for data analysis?
- How will findings be explained, discussed, debated across the studies?

These were our earliest discussions on what each study could learn from and contribute to the other studies and allowed for the participants to begin to develop the clarity and direction needed to work together on a grant proposal to fund the work of the consortium.

Taken together, the early exploratory work and the later planning work brought us to a place where we could state the research questions for each study and the research questions for the collaborative. These gatherings also represented our early attempts at creating meaningful rituals of collaboration. A subcommittee of academics and professionals worked together to craft the grant proposal that was to fund the CHILD Project.

The grant proposal itself outlined a number of consultative processes including committees, communication vehicles, and community-building activities to provide the group with direction and a framework for the collaboration. However, it was only with the actual implementation of the study that we faced the task of creating the roles, rules, and rituals that would allow us to face the realities and the challenges of collaborative interdisciplinary research.

Early in the collaboration a number of key decisions must be made by the members of the consortium. For example, decisions must be made about the relationship between the central administration of the project. There must be clarity around the responsibilities of the coordination team of the entire project to the individual studies (e.g., allocations of budgets, communications, planning, and implementation of retreats) and the obligations of the individual studies (e.g., regular research and financial updates) to the central administration. The central administration team will convene regular executive committee meetings in order to consult with academic and community representatives of the studies to discuss both administrative and research-related issues. The central administration will bring proposals to the executive regarding the communication needs of the group and the various communication vehicles that will be developed in order to maintain ongoing contact with all consortium members. These communication vehicles should include oral, written, and online means at appropriate times and desired frequency.

Throughout this book we have discussed the importance of planning the rituals with the sensitivity and consciousness that recognizes that interdisciplinarity is an ongoing process rather than a specific outcome of product. In preparing for these gatherings it is important that all participants be aware of the preliminal, liminal, and postliminal phases of each ritual. It is critical that the gatherings value the diversity of disciplinary and professional voices around the table and that disagreement be dealt with in a respectful and constructive manner.

Built into the ongoing fabric of the consortium's work there must be a strong commitment to the kinds of reflexive activity and thinking that facilitates both individual and disciplinary decentering. This reflexive mode will facilitate individual studies attending to the work of other studies in the consortium and to consider the ways in which their own research contributes to and learns from the other studies in the consortium. It reminds each study of the importance of paying attention, on an ongoing basis, to the substance of the research progress being made by individual studies and by the consortium as a whole.

The recurrence of these self-reflexive activities in different stages in the life of the consortium acknowledges the reality that research, knowledge, and relationships change over time; that ideas themselves take time to deepen, to germinate and to inform; and to fully appreciate that the comfort zone and "accuracy" of one's own disciplinary lens can only be enhanced and sharpened with the addition of other lenses, other perspectives, and other ways of thinking. Collaborative, interdisciplinary research takes time, it takes knowledge, and it takes the ability to recognize both the opportunities and the limitations of one's own limitations.

Conclusions

In the Introduction to this book we wrote:

> *This introduction attempts to lay the groundwork for two levels of critical analysis in the book. At one level of analysis, the book discusses the design, implementation and findings of the 10 studies and what they contribute to our understanding of early child development. At another level, the book also attempts to describe what we learned about interdisciplinarity, about collaboration and, ultimately, what we learned about ourselves as researchers by conducting the CHILD Project.*

The final aspect of the learning—"about ourselves"—will be ongoing for a long time to come. While the formal network known as the CHILD Project does not continue to meet, to retreat, to share, to listen, and to learn together, we can say with certainty that the process of engaging in the rules and rituals of interdisciplinary research has made a profound impact on the faculty members, community professionals, and the graduate students who spent the better part of five years posing important self-reflective questions about what it was we were learning and what it was we were contributing. In our own ways, the individual members of the collaborative will continue to question, to problem-solve, and to think about the ways in which our work may even have an impact on the seven generations of children into the future whom Willie Charlie admonished us to hold close to our hearts and our minds.

Note

1. In this chapter we use the terms "interdisciplinary" and "bioecological" interchangeably.

References

Abdulrazzaq, Y. M., Kendi, A. A., & Nagelkerke, N. (2009). Soothing methods used to calm a baby in an Arab country. *Acta Paediatrica, 98,* 392–396. doi: 10.1111/j.1651-2227.2008.01029

Aboriginal Healing Foundation. (2008). *From truth to reconciliation: Transforming the legacy of residential schools.* Ottawa, ON: Aboriginal Healing Foundation.

Altman, I. (1987). Community psychology twenty years later: Still another crisis in psychology? *American Journal of Community Psychology, 15,* 613–627. doi:10.1007/BF00929914

Altman, I., & Rogoff, B. (1987). World views in psychology: Trait, interactional, organismic and transactional perspectives. In D. Stokols & I. Altman (Eds.), *Handbook of environmental psychology* (pp. 1–40). New York: John Wiley.

Alvarez, M. (2004). Caregiving and early infant crying in a Danish community. *Journal of Developmental and Behavioral Pediatrics, 25,* 91–98. doi: 0196–206X/00/2502-0091

American Academy of Pediatrics. (2001). Developmental surveillance and screening of infants and young children. *Pediatrics, 108,* 192–195.

American Academy of Pediatrics. (2006). Identifying infants and young children with developmental disorders in the medical home: An algorithm for developmental surveillance and screening. *Pediatrics, 118,* 405–420.

Anstett, S., & MCFI Screening Task Group. (2002, March). *Phase 1: Framework for MCFI Integrated Early Identification Screening program.* Discussion Paper prepared for the Eastern Fraser Valley "Make Children First Initiative" Implementation Committee.

Anstett, S., & MCFI Screening Task Group (2003, February). *Child development guide.* Vancouver, BC: MCFI Screening Task Group.

Arnett, J. (1989). Caregivers in day care centers: Does training matter? *Journal of Applied Developmental Psychology, 10,* 541–552.

Assembly of First Nations. (1988). *Tradition and Education: Towards a vision of our future.* Ottawa, ON: Assembly of First Nations/National Indian Brotherhood.

Aurora Research Institute. (2002). *Doing research in the Northwest Territories: A guide for researchers.* Inuvik, NT: Author.

Baker, M., & Tippin, D. (1999). *Poverty, social assistance and the employability of mothers: Restructuring the welfare state.* Toronto, ON: University of Toronto Press.

Baker, E., Homan, S., Schonhoff, R., & Kreuter, M. (1999). Principles of practice for academic/practice/community research partnerships. *American Journal of Preventive Medicine, 3,* 86–93. doi:10.1016/S0749-3797(98)00149-4

Ball, J. (2004). As if indigenous knowledge mattered: Transformative education in First Nations communities in Canada. *American Indian Quarterly, 28,* 454–479.

Ball, J. (2004, February). *Principles and protocols for research about First Nations children and communities in Canada.* Paper presented at the 33rd Annual Meeting of the Society for Cross-Cultural Research, San Jose, CA.

Ball, J. (2005a). Early childhood education and development programs as hook and hub for inter-sectoral service delivery in First Nations communities. *Journal of Aboriginal Health, 2,* 36–50.

Ball, J. (2005b). Nothing about us without us: Restorative research partnerships involving Indigenous children and communities in Canada. In A. Farrell (Ed.), *Exploring ethical research with children* (pp. 81–96). Berkshire, UK: Open University Press/McGraw Hill.

Ball, J., & Pence, A. (2000). A postmodernist approach to culturally grounded training in early childhood care and development. *Australian Journal of Early Childhood, 25,* 21–25.

Ball, J., & Janyst, P. (2007). Enacting research ethics in partnership with Indigenous communities in Canada: "Do it in a good way." *Journal of Empirical Research on Human Research Ethics,* 33–51. doi:10.1525/jer.2008.3.2.33

Bandura, A. (1986). *Social foundations of thought and action: A social cognitive theory.* Englewood Cliffs, NJ: Prentice Hall.

Barker, R. G. (1968). *Ecological psychology: Concepts and methods for studying the environment of human behavior.* Stanford, CA: Stanford University Press.

Bayley, N. (1993). *Bayley scales of infant development—Second edition.* San Antonio, TX: The Psychological Corporation.

Bayley, N. (2006). *Bayley scales of infant and toddler development.* San Antonio, TX: Harcourt Assessment.

Beatch, M. & Le Mare, L. (2007). Taking ownership: The implementation of a non-Aboriginal early education programme for on-reserve children. *The Australian Journal of Indigenous Education, 36,* 77–87.

Beauvais, C., & Jenson, J. (2003). *The well-being of children: Are there neighbourhood effects?* (Discussion paper No. 31). Ottawa, ON: Canadian Policy Research Network.

Becher, T. (1989). *Academic tribes and territories.* Milton Keynes, UK: Open University Press.

Bell, C. M. (1997). *Ritual: perspectives and dimensions.* Oxford: Oxford University Press.

Bennett, M., & Blackstock, C. (2002). *A literature review and annotated bibliography focusing on aspects of Aboriginal child welfare in Canada.* Ottawa: First Nations Child and Family Caring Society of Canada.

Benzaquen, A. S. (2004). Childhood, history, and the sciences of childhood. In H. Goelman, S. Ross, & S. Marshall (Eds.), *Multiple lenses, multiple images: Perspectives on the child across time, space, and disciplines* (pp. 14–37).Toronto, ON: University of Toronto Press.

Berkowitz, B., & Wadud, E. (2003). *Identifying community assets and resources* (Community Tool Box, Chap. 3, Sec. 8). Retrieved from Work Group on Health Promotion and Community Development at the University of Kansas website: http://ctb.ku.edu/en/tablecontents/section_1043.aspx

Binet, A. & Simon, T. (1914). *Mentally defective children.* London: Edward Arnold.

Bixler, R. D., Floyd, M. F., & Hammitt, W. E. (2002). Environmental socialization: Quantitative tests of the childhood play hypothesis. *Environment and Behavior, 34,* 795–818. doi:10.1177/001391602237248

Björklid, P., & Nordström, M. (2007). Environmental child-friendliness: Collaboration and future research. *Children, Youth and Environments, 17,* 388–401.

Blatchford, P. (1989). *Playtime in the primary school: problems and improvements.* Windsor: NFER-Nelson.

Bloch, M. N. (1992). Critical perspectives on the historical relationship between child development and early childhood education research. In S. A. Kessler & B. B. Swadener (Eds.), *Reconceptualizing the early childhood curriculum* (pp. 3–20). New York: Teachers College Press.

Bloch, M. N. (2000). Governing teachers, parents, and children through child development knowledge. *Human Development, 43,* 257–265. doi: 10.1159/000022685

Bloch, M. N., & Popkewitz, T. S. (2000). Constructing the parent, teacher, and child: Discourses of development. In L. Diaz Soto (Ed.), *The politics of early childhood education* (pp. 7–33). New York: Peter Lang.

Bradley, R. H., & Corwyn, R. F. (2002). Socioeconomic status and child development. *Annual Review of Psychology, 53,* 371–399. doi:10.1146/annurev.psych.53.100901.135233

Bradshaw, J., & Harland, A. (2006). *Social policy, employment and family change in a comparative perspective.* Cheltenham, UK: Edward Elgar.

Braga, L. W. (2007). Developmental perspectives: Culture and neuropsychological development during childhood. In B. P. Uzzell, M. O. Ponton, & A. Ardila (Eds.), *International handbook of cross-cultural neuropsychology.* Mahwah, NJ: Lawrence Erlbaum Associates.

Bricker, D., Squires, J., & Mounts, L. (1999). *Ages & stages questionnaires: A parent-completed, child-monitoring system.* Baltimore: Paul H. Brookes.

British Columbia Aboriginal Network on Disability Society. (1996). *Identification of barriers to post-secondary training and employment.* Vancouver, BC: Author.

British Columbia Centre for Ability. (2010). *Services for infants, toddlers and pre-school children.* Retrieved from BC Centre for Ability website: http://www.centreforability.bc.ca/?page=12

British Columbia Legislative Committee. (2006). *Select standing committee on health strategy for combating childhood obesity and physical inactivity in British Columbia*. Retrieved from the British Columbia Legislative Committee website: http://www.leg.bc.ca/cmt/38thparl/session-2/health/reports/Rpt-Health-38-2-29Nov2006.pdf.

British Columbia Ministry of Education (2000a). *Individualized Educational Plan*. Retrieved August 15, 2007 from http://www.bced.gov.bc.ca/specialed/iepssn/.

British Columbia Ministry of Health, Living and Support (2010, June). *Health screening now available to more British Columbia children*. Retrieved from the Province of British Columbia website: http://www2.news.gov.bc.ca/news_releases_2009–2013/2010HLS0035-000768.htm

Bronfenbrenner, U. (1977a). Toward an experimental ecology of human development. *American Psychologist, 32*, 513–531.

Bronfenbrenner, U. (1977b). *Who needs parent education? Position paper for the working conference on parent education*. Flint, Michigan: Charles Stewart Mott Foundation.

Bronfenbrenner, U. (1979). *The ecology of human development: experiments by nature and design*. Cambridge, MA: Harvard University Press.

Bronfenbrenner, U. (2001). The theory of human development. In N. J. Smelser & P. B. Baltes (Eds.), *International encyclopedia of the social and behavioral sciences* (Vol. 10, pp. 6963–6970). New York: Elsevier.

Bronfenbrenner, U. (Ed.). (2005). *Making human beings human: Bioecological perspectives on human development*. Thousand Oaks, CA: Sage.

Bronfenbrenner, U., & Morris, P. A. (2006). The bioecological model of human development. In W. Damon & R. M. Lerner (Eds.), *Handbook of child psychology* (6th ed., Vol. 1, pp. 793–828). Hoboken, NJ: John Wiley.

Bronfenbrenner, U., Kessel, F., Kessen, W., & White, S. (1988). Toward a critical history of development: A propaedeutic discussion. *American Psychologist, 41*, 1218–1230.

Brooks-Gunn, J., & Duncan, J. (1997). The effects of poverty on children and youth. *The Future of Children, 7*, 55–71.

Brooks-Gunn, J., & Duncan, J. (1997). The effects of poverty on children and youth. *The Future of Children, 7*, 55–71.

Brooks-Gunn, J., Duncan, G. J., Klebanov, P. K., & Sealand, N. (1993). Do neighbourhoods influence child and adolescent behavior? *American Journal of Sociology, 99*, 353–395.

Brown, J. G., & Burger, C. (1984). Playground designs and preschool children's behaviors. *Environment and Behavior, 16*, 599–626. doi:10.1177/0013916584165004

Browning, D. M., & Solomon, M. Z. (2005). The initiative for pediatric palliative care: An interdisciplinary educational approach for healthcare professionals. *Journal of Pediatric Nursing, 20*, 326–334. doi: 10.1016/j.pedn.2005.03.004

Campaign 2000. (2006). *Decision time for Canada: Let's make poverty history*. [online publication], Retrieved from Campaign 2000 website: www.campaign2000.ca/re/re05/05NationalReportCard.pdf.

Campbell, S. D., & Frost, J. L. (1985). The effects of playground type on the cognitive and social play behaviors of grade two children. In J. L. Frost & S. Sunderlin (Eds.), *When children play* (pp. 81–88). Wheaton, MD: Association for Childhood Education International.

Canadian Centre for Justice. (2001). *Aboriginal peoples in Canada*. Statistics Profile Series. Ottawa, ON: Minister of Industry.

Canadian Institutes of Health Research. (2007). *CIHR guidelines for health research involving Aboriginal people*. Retrieved from the Canadian Institutes of Health Research website: http://www.cihr-irsc.gc.ca/e/documents/ethics_aboriginal_guidelines_e.pdf

Canadian Paediatric Society. (2010). *Canadian paediatric surveillance program*. Retrieved from Canadian Paediatric Society website: http://www.cps.ca/English/surveillance/CPSP/About/index.htm.

Canam, C., Dahinten, V. S., & Ford, L. (2007, June). *Evaluation of a universal developmental screening program: An ecological approach*. Paper presented at the 19th IUHPE World Conference. Vancouver, BC.

Canella, G. S. (1997). *Deconstructing early childhood education: Social justice and revolution*. New York: Peter Lang.

Caragata, L. (2009). Lone mothers: Policy responses to build social inclusion. In M. G. Cohen & J. Pulkingham (Eds.), *Public policy for women: The state, income security and labour market issues* (pp. 162–183). Toronto ON: University of Toronto Press.

Carlton, A., & Winsler, M. P. (1999). School readiness: The need for a paradigm shift. *School Psychology Review, 28*, 338–352.

Carr, M., Hatherly, A., Lee, W., & Ramsey, K. (2003). Te Whāriki and assessment: A case study of teacher change. In J. Nuttall (Ed.), *Weaving Te Whāriki. Aotearoa New Zealand's early childhood curriculum document in theory and practice* (pp. 187–212). Wellington, NZ: New Zealand Council for Educational Research.

Castellano, M. B. (2002). *Aboriginal family trends: Extended families, nuclear families, families of the heart*. Retrieved from the Vanier Institute of the Family website: http://www.vifamily.ca/library/cft/aboriginal.html

Castellano, M. B. (2004). Ethics of Aboriginal research. *Journal of Aboriginal Health, 1*, 98–114.

Ceppi G. & M. Zini, (1998). Design Tools. In G. Ceppi, & M. Zini (Eds.), *Children, spaces, relations: Metaproject for an environment for young children* (pp. 35–110). Modena, Italy: Grafiche Rebecchi Ceccarelli.

Chamberlayne, R., Green, B., Barer, M. L., Hertzman, C., Lawrence, W. J., & Sheps, S. B. (1998). Creating a population-based linked health database: A new resource for health services research, *Canadian Journal of Public Health, 89*, 270–273.

Chandler, M. J., & Lalonde, C. E. (1998). Cultural continuity as a hedge against suicide in Canada's First Nations. *Transcultural Psychiatry, 35*, 2, 191–219. doi:10.1177/136346159803500202

Charters-Vogt, O. (1999) Indian control of Indian education: The path of the Upper Nicola Band. *Canadian Journal of Native Education, 23*, 64–99.

Chase-Lansdale, L. P., & Gordon, R. A. (1996). Economic hardship and the development of five- and six-year-olds: Neighbourhood and regional perspectives. *Child Development, 67*, 3338–3367. doi:10.2307/113178

Chawla, L. (2002). *Growing up in an urbanizing world*. London, UK: UNESCO/Earthscan.

Chawla, L., & Heft, H. (2002). Children's competence and the ecology of communities: A functional approach to the evaluation of participation. *Journal of Environmental Psychology, 22*, 201–216. doi:10.1006/jevp.2002.0244

Chen, E., Fisher, E. B., Bacharier, L. B., & Strunk, R .C. (2003). Socioeconomic status, stress, and immune markers in adolescents with asthma. *Psychosomatic Medicine, 65*, 984–992.

The CHILD Project. (2003). *Introductory CHILDTalk Paper*. (Report No. 1). Vancouver, BC: CHILDTalk.

The CHILD Project. (2004a). *Developmental Pathways CHILDTalk Paper*. Vancouver, BC: CHILDTalk.

The CHILD Project. (2004b). *Indigenous CHILD CHILDTalk Paper* Vancouver, BC: CHILDTalk.

The CHILD Project. (2004c). *Infant Neuromotor CHILDTalk Paper*. Vancouver, BC: CHILDTalk.

Chun, D. E., & Gavigan, S. A. (2004). Welfare law, welfare fraud, and the moral regulation of the "never deserving" poor. *Social and Legal Studies, 13*, 219–243. doi:10.1177/0964663904042552

Chung, J. (2004). Preschool Literacy Program Piloted in Vancouver. *Raven's Eye, 9*.

Cohen, M. G., & Pulkingham, J. (2009). Introduction: Going too far? Feminist public policy in Canada. In M. G. Cohen & J. Pulkingham (Eds.), *Public policy for women: The state, income security and labour market issues* (pp. 3–48). Toronto, ON: University of Toronto Press.

Cole, P. (2002). Aboriginalizing methodology: Considering the canoe. *Qualitative Studies in Education, 15*, 447–459. doi:10.1080/09518390210145516

Coleman, M. R., Buysse, V., & Netzel, J. (2006). *Recognition and response: An early intervening system for young children at-risk for learning disabilities*. Chapel Hill, NC: FGP Child Development Center.

Committee on Community Health Services (2005). The pediatrician's role in community pediatrics. *Pediatrics, 115*, 1092–1094. doi: 10.1542/peds.2004-2680

Community-Campus Partnerships for Health Summit (2006, April). Achieving the Promise of Authentic Community-Higher Education Partnerships: A Community Partner Summit Executive Summary. Racine, WI.

Connor, S. (2001). Using community mapping to enhance child development. *Education Canada, 40*, 24–26.

Connor, S., & Brink. S. (1999). *Understanding the early years-community impacts on child development* (Working Paper No. W-099–6E). Ottawa,

ON: Applied Research Branch, Strategic Policy, Human Resources Development Canada.

Cordier, S., Chevrier, C., Robert-Gnansia, E., Lorente, C., Brula, P., & Hours, M. (2004). Risk of congenital anomalies in the vicinity of municipal solid waste incinerators. *Occupational and Environmental Medicine, 61*, 8–15.

Coulton, C. (1979). Developing an instrument to measure person-environment fit. *Journal of Social Service Research, 3*, 159–173. doi:10.1300/J079v03n02_02

Council on Children with Disabilities (2006), Identifying infants and young children with developmental disorders in the medical home. *Pediatrics, 18*, 405–420. doi: 10.1542/peds.2006-1231

Creswell, J. W. (2003). *Research design: Qualitative, quantitative, and mixed approaches.* Thousand Oaks, CA: Sage.

Currie, M., King, G., Rosenbaum, P., Law, M., Kertoy, M., & Specht, J. (2005). A model of impacts of research partnerships in health and social services. *Evaluation and Program Planning, 28*, 400–412. doi:10.1016/j.evalprogplan.2005.07.004

Cynader, M. S., & Frost, B. J. (1999). Mechanisms of brain development: Neuronal sculpting by the physical and social environment. In D. P. Keating & C. Hertzman (Eds.), *Developmental health and the wealth of nations: Social, biological and educational dynamics* (pp. 153–184). New York: Guilford Press.

D'Amour, D., Ferrada-Videla, M., Rodriguez, L., & Beaulieu, M. (2005). The conceptual basis for interprofessional collaboration: Core concepts and theoretical frameworks. *Journal of Interprofessional Care, 19*, 116–131. doi: 10.1080/13561820500082529

Dahinten, V. S. (2007a, April). *The process and impact of developmental screening with the Nipissing Developmental Screen.* Paper presented at the Healthy Child Developmental meeting of the Fraser Health Authority, New Westminster, BC.

Dahinten, V. S. (2007b, October). *Screening for at-risk children and developmental delays.* Paper presented at the New Brunswick Early Childhood Initiatives Review Committee meeting, Fredericton, NB.

Dahinten, V. S., Ford, L., & Lapointe, V. (2004, May). *Validation of the Nipissing district developmental screen for use with infants and toddlers.* Poster presented at the 12th Annual Meeting of the Society for Prevention Research, Quebec City, PQ.

Dahinten, V. S., Ford, L., Canam, C., Lapointe, V. R., & Merkel, C. (2007, March). The Chilliwack developmental screening study. In J. Houbé (Chair), *The ecology of early screening and follow-up programs.* Symposium paper presented at the 2007 Biennial Meeting of the Society for Research in Child Development, Boston, MA.

Dahinten, V. S., Ford, L., Canam, C., Lapointe, V. R., Merkel, C., Van Leeuwen, S. et al. (2004, July) *The Kids First Project: A partnership to promote early school readiness.* Poster presented at the 2004 APA Annual Convention, Honolulu, HI.

Dahlberg, G., Moss, P., & Pence, A. (1999). *Beyond quality in early childhood education and care: Postmodern perspectives.* Philadelphia, PA: RoutledgeFalmer.

D'Amour, D., Ferrada-Videla, M., Rodriguez, L., & Beaulieu, M. (2005). The conceptual basis for interprofessional collaboration: Core concepts and theoretical frameworks. *Journal of Interprofessional Care, 19,* 116–131. doi: 10.1080/13561820500082529

Darwin, C. (1871). *The descent of man.* London, UK: John Murray.

Dighe, J. (1993). Children and the earth. *Young Children, 48,* 58–63.

DiLauro, M. D. (2004). Psychosocial factors associated with types of child maltreatment. *Child Welfare, 83,* 69–99.

Disease Control Priorities Project. (2008). *Public health surveillance: The best weapon to avert epidemics.* Retrieved from the Disease Control Priorities Project website: http://www.dcp2.org/file/153/dcpp-surveillance.pdf.

Doherty G., Forer, B, Lero, D., Goelman, H., & LaGrange, A. (2006). Predictors of quality in family child care. *Early Childhood Research Quarterly, 21,* 296–312. doi: 10.1016/j.ecresq.2006.07.006

Down, J. L. H. (1867). Observations on an Ethnic Classification of Idiots. *Journal of Mental Scienc,13,* 121–123.

Drotar, D., Stancin, T., & Dworkin, P. (2008). *Pediatric developmental screening: Understanding and selecting screening instruments.* Retrieved from The Commonwealth Fund website: http://mobile.commonwealthfund.org/

Duncan, G. J., Brooks-Gunn, J. P., & Klebanov, P. K. (1994). Economic deprivation and early-childhood development. *Child Development, 65,* 296–318. doi:10.2307/1131385

Dworkin, P. H. (1993) Detection of behavioral, developmental, and psychosocial problems in pediatric primary care practice. *Current Opinion in Pediatrics, 15,* 531–536.

Dworkin, P. & Glascoe, F. P. (2005). *Developmental screening and developmental surveillance: An either/or proposition?* Retrieved from Developmental Pediatrics Online website: http://www.dbpeds.org/articles/detail.cfm?TextID=139

Edin, K., & Lein, L. (1997). *Making ends meet: How single mothers survive welfare and low-wage work.* New York: Russell Sage Foundation.

Edwards, C. P. (1993). *Hundred languages of children: the Reggio Emilia approach to early childhood education.* Norwood, NJ: Ablex.

Eisenberg, L. (1998). Nature, niche, and nurture: The role of social experience in transforming genotype into phenotype. *Academic Psychiatry, 22,* 213–222.

Ellen, I., & Turner, M. (1997). Does neighbourhood matter? Assessing recent evidence. *Housing Policy Debate, 8,* 833–866. doi:10.1080/10511482.1997.9521280

Ellis, C. (2004). *The ethnographic I.* New York: Altamira Press.

Ermine, W. (1995). Aboriginal epistemology. In M. Battiste & J. Barman (Eds.), *First Nations education in Canada: The circle unfolds* (pp. 101–112). Vancouver, BC: UBC Press.

Evans, G. W. (2004). The environment of childhood poverty. *American Psychologist, 59,* 77–92. doi:10.1037/0003-066X.59.2.77

Evans, G. W. (2006). Child development and the physical environment. *Annual Review of Psychology, 57,* 423–451. doi:10.1146/annurev.psych.57.102904.190057

Evans, G. W., Boxhill, L., & Pinkava, M. (2008). Poverty and maternal responsiveness: The role of maternal stress and social resources. *International Journal of Behavioral Development, 32,* 232–237. doi:10.1177/0165025408089272

Faber Taylor, A., Kuo, F., & Sullivan, W. (2001). Coping with ADD: The surprising connects to green play settings. *Environmental Behavior, 33,* 54–77.

Fawcett, S. B., Paine-Andrews, A., Fransciso, V. T., Schultz, J. A. et al. (1995). Using empowerment theory in collaborative partnerships for community health and development. *American Journal of Community Psychology, 23,* 677–697. doi:10.1007/BF02506987

Figueria-McDonough, J. (1998). Environment and interpretation: Voices of young people in poor inner-city neighbourhoods. *Youth and Society, 30,* 123–163. doi:10.1177/0044118X98030002001

Finlay, J. (1988). Sharing and caring. *Nature Study, 42,* 28.

First Call BC Campaign 2000. (2009). *2009 Child Poverty Report Card.* Retrieved from the First Call BC website: http://www.firstcallbc.org/. Vancouver, BC.

Fjortoft, I. (2001). The natural environment as a playground for children: The impact of outdoor play activities in pre-primary school children. *Early Childhood Education, 29,* 111–117. doi:10.1023/A:1012576913074

Ford, L., & Dahinten, V. S. (2005). The use of intelligence tests in the assessment of preschoolers. In D. Flanagan, & P. Harrison (Eds.), *Contemporary intellectual assessment* (2nd ed, pp. 487–503). New York: Guildford Press.

Ford, L., Negreiros, J., & Shim, V. (in press). A framework for conceptualizing cognitive assessment in early childhood. *Psychology in the Schools.*

Forer, B., Goelman, H., & Kershaw, P. (2007, March). The outcomes and process of studying the ecology of child care policies and programs. In K. Marfo (Chair), *Urie Bronfenbrenner, Interdisciplinarity and the CHILD Project.* Symposium paper presented at the 2007 Biennial Meeting of the Society for Research in Child Development, Boston, MA.

Fournier, S., & Crey, E. (1997). *Stolen from our embrace: The abduction of First Nations children and the restoration of Aboriginal communities.* Vancouver, BC: Douglas & McIntyre.

Frost, J. L., Wortham, S. C., & Reifel, S. (2001). *Play and child development.* Upper Saddle River, NJ: Merrill-Prentice Hall.

Fuller, S., Kershaw, P., & Pulkingham, J. (2008). Constructing "active citizenship": Single mothers, welfare and the logic of voluntarism. *Citizenship Studies, 12*, 157–176. doi:10.1080/13621020801900119

Gajda, R. (2004). Utilizing collaboration theory to evaluate strategic alliances. *American Journal of Evaluation, 25*, 65–77. doi:10.1177/109821400402500105

Gaver, W. W. (1996). Situating action II: Affordances for interaction: The social is material for design. *Ecological Psychology, 8*, 111–129. doi:10.1207/s15326969eco0802_2

Getz, D. (2007). *Event studies: Theory, research and policy for planned events*. Oxford, UK: Elsevier.

Gibson, J. J. (1977). The theory of affordances. In R. Shaw & J. Bransford (Eds.), *Perceiving, acting, and knowing: Toward an ecological psychology* (pp. 67–82). Hillsdale, NJ: Erlbaum.

Gibson, J. J. (1979). *The ecological approach to visual perception*. Boston, MA: Houghton Mifflin.

Gill, T. (2008). Space-oriented children's policy: Creating child-friendly communities to improve children's well-being. *Children & Society, 22*, 136–142. doi:10.1111/j.1099-0860.2007.00139.x

Glascoe F. P. (1999). Toward a model for an evidenced-based approach to developmental/ behavioral surveillance, promotion and patient education. *Ambulatory Child Health, 5*, 197–208.

Glascoe, F. P. (2001). Evidence-based approach to developmental and behavioural surveillance using parents' concerns. *Child: Care, Health, and Development, 26*, 137–149. doi: 10.1046/j.1365-2214.2000.00173.x

Glascoe, F. P. (2006). *Commonly used screening tools*. Retrieved from Developmental Pediatrics Online website: http://www.dbpeds.org/tools/temporarypdf/Commonly usedscreeningtools-20090401204133.pdf

Glascoe, F. P., Foster, E. M., & Wolrich, M. L. (1997). An economic analysis of developmental detection methods. *Pediatrics, 99*, 830–837. doi:10.1542/peds.99.6.830

Göb, R., McCollin, C., & Fernada Ramalhoto, M. (2007). Ordinal methodology in the analysis of Likert scales. *Quality & Quantity, 41*, 601–626. doi:10.1007/s11135-007-9089-z

Gockel, A., Russell, M., & Harris, B. (2008). Providing nurturing family relationships: Parent perspectives on effective family preservation services. *Child Welfare, 87*, 91–113.

Goddard, H. H. (1912). The height and weight of feeble-minded children in American institutions. *The Journal of Nervous and Mental Disease, 39*, 4, 217–235.

Goelman, H. (2000). Training, quality and the lived experience of child care. In G. Cleveland & M. Krashinsky (Eds.), *Our children's future: Child care policy in Canada* (pp. 142–168). Toronto, ON: University of Toronto Press.

Goelman, H. (2007, March). The CHILD Project. In K. Marfo (Chair), *Urie Bronfenbrenner, Interdisciplinarity and the CHILD Project*. Symposium paper presented at the 2007 Biennial Meeting of the Society for Research in Child Development, Boston, MA.

Goelman, H. (2008, June). *Early learning and child care programs as cornerstones of child health and development.* Address given at the Symposium on Promoting Healthy Child and Youth Development presented at the 19th World Conference of The International Union for Health Promotion and Education, Vancouver, BC.

Goelman, H., Marshall, S. K., & Ross, S. (Eds.). (2004). *Multiple lenses, multiple images: Perspectives on the child across time, space, and disciplines.* Toronto, ON: University of Toronto Press.

Goelman, H., Doherty, G., Lero, D., LaGrange, A., & Tougas, J. (2000). *You bet I care! Caring and learning environments: Quality in child care centers across Canada.* Guelph, ON: Centre for Families, Work and Well-Being at the University of Guelph.

Goelman, H., Andersen, C. Anderson, J., Gouzouasis, P., Kendrick, M., Kindler, A. M., & Porath, M. (2002). Early childhood education. In W. M. Reynolds, G. E. Miller, & I. Weiner (Eds.), *Comprehensive handbook of psychology, Volume Seven: Educational psychology* (pp. 285–332). New York: John Wiley.

Goelman, H., Forer, B., Kershaw, P., Doherty, G., Lero, D., & LaGrange, A. (2006). Towards a predictive model of quality in Canadian child care centres. *Early Childhood Research Quarterly, 21,* 280–295. doi: 10.1016/j.ecresq.2006.07.005

Goelman, H., Synnes, A., Houbé, J., Klassen, A., Pighini, M., & Brynelsen, D. (2007, June). *The design and implementation of a two-phase study of the developmental trajectories of at-risk children.* Paper presented at the 2nd ISEI Conference of The International Society on Early Intervention: Research in Education and Rehabilitation Sciences. Zagreb, Croatia.

Goelman, H., Andersen, C. Anderson, J., Gouzouasis, P., Kendrick, M., Kindler, A. M., Porath, M. (2002). Early childhood education. In W. M. Reynolds, G. E. Miller & I. Weiner (Eds.), *Comprehensive handbook of psychology, volume seven: Educational psychology* (pp. 285–332). New York: John Wiley.

Goelman, H. & The CHILD Project. (2008). Three complementary community-based approaches to the early identification of young children at risk for developmental delays/disorders. *Infants and Young Children, 21,* 306–323. doi: 10.1097/01.IYC.0000336543.45003.0e

Gornick, T. F., & Meyers, M. L. (2003). *Families that work: Policies for reconciling parenthood and employment.* New York: Russell Sage.

Goulet, L., Dressyman-Lavallee, M., & McCleod, Y. (2001). Early childhood education for Aboriginal children: Opening petals. In K. P. Binda & S. Calliou (Eds.), *Aboriginal education in Canada: A study in decolonization* (pp. 137–153). Mississauga, ON: Canadian Educators' Press.

Greaves, L. S., Pederson, A., Varcoe, C., Poole, N., Morrow, M., Johnson, J., & Irwin, L. (2002). Mothering under duress: Women caught in a web of discourse. *Journal of the Association for Research on Mothering, 6*, 1–27.

Greenwood, M. (2006). Children are a gift to us: Aboriginal-specific early childhood programs and services in Canada. *Canadian Journal of Native Education, 29*, 12–28.

Grenier, D., & Leduc, D. (2008). Let's put a national child care strategy back on the agenda. *Paediatrics and Child Health, 13*, 837.

Groark, C. J., & McCall, R. B. (1996). Building successful university-community human service agency collaborations. In C. B. Fisher, J. P. Murray, & I. E. Sigel (Eds.), *Applied developmental science: Graduate training for diverse disciplines and educational settings* (pp. 237–251). Norwood, NJ: Ablex.

Guhn, M., & Goelman, H. (in press). Bioecological theory, early child development, and the validation of the population-level Early Development Instrument. *Social Indicators Research*.

Gummerum, M., Herrington, S., Schonert-Reichl, K. A., & Lesmeister, C. (2007, March). The ecology of children's social play in outdoor play spaces. In K. Marfo (Chair), *Urie Bronfenbrenner, Interdisciplinarity and the CHILD Project*. Symposium paper presented at the 2007 Biennial Meeting of the Society for Research in Child Development, Boston, MA.

Guralnick, M. (Ed.). (2005). *The developmental systems approach to early intervention*. Baltimore, MD: Paul H. Brooks.

Gurstein, P., & Goldberg, M. (2008). *Precarious & vulnerable: Lone mothers on income assistance*. Retrieved from SPARC BC website: http://www.sparc.bc.ca/resources-and-publications/category/44-income-assistance.

Gurstein, P., & Vilches, S. (2009). Re-visioning the environment of support for lone mothers in extreme poverty. In M. G. Cohen & J. Pulkingham (Eds.), *Public policy for women: The state, income security and labour market issues* (pp. 226–247). Toronto, ON: University of Toronto Press.

Haig-Brown, C. (1988). *Resistance and renewal: Surviving Indian residential school*. Vancouver, BC: Tillacum Press.

Haikkola, L., Pacilli, M., Horelli, L., & Prezza, M. (2007). Interpretations of urban child-friendliness: A comparative study of two neighborhoods in Helsinki and Rome. *Children, Youth and Environment, 17*, 319–351.

Haney, W., Russell, M., Gulek, C., & Fierros, E. (1998). Drawing on education: Using student drawings to promote middle school improvement. *Schools in the Middle, 7*, 38–43.

Hanson, M. J. (2004). Disability in childhood: Views within the context of society. In H. Goelman, S. K. Marshall, & S. Ross (Eds.), *Multiple lenses, multiple images: Perspectives on the child across time, space, and disciplines* (pp. 109–121).Toronto, ON: University of Toronto Press.

Hardley, H., & Crowe, G. (1991). *Lone parenthood: Coping with constraints and making opportunities*. London, UK: Harrester Wheatsheaf.

Harms, T., & Clifford, R. M. (1990). *Infant/toddler environment rating scale*. New York: Teachers College Press.

Harms, T., Clifford, R. M., & Cryer, D. (1998). *Early childhood environment rating scale: Revised edition*. New York: Teachers College Press.

Harris, B., Russell, M., & Gockel, A. (2007). The impact of poverty on First Nations mothers attending a parenting program. *First Peoples Child & Family Review, 3*, 21–30.

Harris, S. R., Megens, A. M., Backman, C. L., & Hayes, V. (2003). Development and standardization of the Harris Infant Neuromotor Test. *Infants and Young Children, 16*, 143–151. doi:10.1097/00001163-200304000-00006

Hart, C. H., & Sheehan, R. (1986). Preschoolers' play behavior in outdoor environments: Effects of traditional and contemporary playgrounds. *American Educational Research, 23*, 668–678. doi:10.3102/00028312023004668

Harvey, M. R. (1989). Children's experiences with vegetation. *Children's Environments Quarterly, 6*, 36–43.

Heft, H. (1988). Affordances of children's environments: A functional approach to environmental description. *Children's Environments Quarterly, 5*, 29–37.

Herrington, S. (1997). The received view of play and the subculture of infants. *Landscape Journal, 16*, 149–160. doi:10.3368/lj.16.2.149

Herrington, S. (2004). Muscle memory: Reflections on the North American schoolyard. In H. Goelman, S. K. Marshall, & S. Ross (Eds.), *Multiple lenses, multiple images: Perspectives on the child across time, space, and disciplines* (pp. 91–108). Toronto, ON: University of Toronto Press.

Herrington, S. (2008). Perspectives from the ground: Early childhood educators' perceptions of outdoor play spaced at child care centres. *Children, Youth and Environments, 18*, 64–83.

Herrington, S., & Lesmeister, C. (2006). The design of landscapes at child-care centres: Seven Cs. *Landscape Research, 31*, 63–82. doi: 10.1080/01426390500448575

Herrington, S., & Nichols, J. (2007). Outdoor play spaces in Canada: The safety dance of standards as policy. *Critical Social Policy, 27*, 128–138. doi: 10.1177/0261018307072210

Herrington, S., & Studtmann, K. (1998). Landscape interventions: New direction for the design of children's outdoor play environments. *Landscape and Urban Planning, 42*, 191–205. doi:10.1016/S0169-2046(98)00087-5

Herrington, S., Lesmeister, C., Nicholls, J., & Stefiuk, K. (2007). *Seven C's*. Retrieved from Westcoast Child Care Resources website: http://westcoast.ca/playspaces/outsidecriteria/index.html.

Hertzman, C., McLean, S., Kohen, D., Dunn, J., & Evans, T. (2002). *Early development in Vancouver: Report of the Community Asset Mapping Project (CAMP)*. Retrieved from Human Early Learning Partnership, University of British Columbia website: http://ecdportal.help.ubc.ca/publications.htm

Heymann, J., Hertzman, C., Barer, M. L., & Evans, R. G. (Eds.). (2006). *Healthier societies: From analysis to action*. New York: Oxford University Press.

HIPPY International (n.d.). *About the HIPPY international network.* Retrieved from the HIPPY international website: http://www.hippy.org.il/html/about_international.html.

Hoch, J., Pellegrini, A. D., & Symons, F. (2004). *Observing children in their natural worlds: a methodological primer.* Mahwah, NJ: Lawrence Erlbaum Associates.

Horelli, L. (1998). Creating child-friendly environments: case studies on children's participation in three European countries. *Childhood, 5,* 225–239. doi:10.1177/0907568298005002008

Horelli, L. (2002). A methodology of participatory planning. In R. Bechtel & A. Churchman (Eds.), *Handbook of environmental psychology* (pp. 607–628). New York: John Wiley.

Horelli, L. (2007). Constructing a theoretical framework for environmental child-friendliness. *Children, Youth and Environments, 17,* 268–292.

Houbé, J., Lisonkova, S., Klassen, A., Synnes, A. R., & Lee, S. K. (2004, May). *Canadian neonatal network: Patterns of health care utilization among children four years after discharge from NICU.* Poster presentation at the Pediatric Academic Societies Meeting. San Francisco, CA.

Indian and Northern Affairs Canada. (2008). *Early childhood development: Programs and initiatives.* Retrieved from the Indian and Northern Affairs Canada website: http://www.ainc-inac.gc.ca/hb/sp/ecd/index-eng.asp.

Interagency Advisory Panel on Research Ethics. (2003). Section 6: Research involving Aboriginal peoples. In *Tri-council policy statement: Ethical conduct for research involving humans.* Ottawa, ON: Author.

International classification of diseases, 9th revision, clinical modification, fourth revision, color coded. (1995). Los Angeles, CA: Practice Management Information Corporation.

Israel, B. A., Krieger, J., Vlahov, D., Ciske, S., Foley, M., Fortin, P., Guzman, J. R., Lichtenstein, R., McGranaghan, R., Palermo, A., & Tang, G. (2006). Challenge and facilitating factors in sustaining community-based participatory research partnerships: Lessons learned from Detroit, New York City, and Seattle Urban Research Centres. *Journal of Urban Health, 83,* 1022–1040. doi:10.1007/s11524-006-9110-1

Janus, M., & Offord, D. (2007). Development and psychometric properties of the Early Development Instrument (EDI): A measure of children's school readiness. *Canadian Journal of Behavioural Science, 39,* 1–22. doi:10.1037/cjbs2007001

Janz, K. F., Burns, T. L., Torner, J .C., Levy, S. M., Paulos, R., Willing, M. C., & Warren, J. J. (2001). Physical activity and bone measures in young children: The Iowa bone development study. *Pediatrics, 107,* 1387–1393. doi:10.1542/peds.107.6.1387

Jaramillo, A., Schonert-Reichl, K. A., & Gummerum, M. (2007, October). *Fostering social, emotional, and moral understanding during the preschool years.* Paper presented at the annual meeting of the Association for Moral Education, New York.

Jencks, C., & Mayer, S. (1990). The social consequences of growing up in a poor neighbourhood. In L. E. Lynn & M. G. McGeary (Eds.), *Inner city poverty in the United States*. Washington, DC: National Academy Press.

Johnson, J. E., Christie, J. F. & Yawkey, T. D. (1999). *Play and early childhood development*. Boston, MA: Allyn and Bacon.

Johnson, R. B., & Onwuegbuzie, A. J. (2004). Mixed methods research: A research paradigm whose time has come. *Educational Researcher, 33*, 14–26. doi:10.3102/0013189X033007014

Joint Special Report by the Representative for Children and Youth and the Office of the Provincial Health Officer. (2007). *Health and well-being of children in care in British Columbia: Educational experience and outcomes*. Retrieved from the BC Ministry of Healthy Living and Sport website: http://www.hls.gov.bc.ca/pho/pdf/joint_special_report.pdf

Kamerman, S. B. (2000). Early childhood intervention policies: An international perspective. In J. P. Shonkoff & S. J. Meisels (Eds.), *Handbook of early childhood intervention* (2nd ed.) (pp. 613–629). Cambridge: Cambridge University Press.

Kamerman, S. B., & Kahn, A. J. (1988). *Mothers alone: Strategies for a time of change*. Dover, MA: Auburn House.

Kamerman, S. B., & Kahn, A. J. (1989). Family policy: Has the United States learned from Europe? *Policy Studies Review, 18*, 58–98. doi:10.1111/j.1541-1338.1989.tb00981.x

Kaplan, R. (1991). Environmental description and prediction: a conceptual analysis. In T. Garling & G. Evans (Eds.), *Environment, Cognition and Action* (pp. 19–34). New York: Oxford University Press.

Kaplan, R., & Kaplan, S. (1989). *The experience of nature*. New York: Cambridge University Press.

Kaplan, S. (1983). A model of person-environment compatibility. *Environment and Behavior, 15*, 311–344. doi:10.1177/0013916583153003

Keating, D. P., & Hertzman, C. (Eds.). (1999). *Developmental health and wealth of nations: Social, biological, and educational dynamics*. New York: Guilford Press.

Keller, H., Abels, M., Lamm, B., Yovsi, R. D., Voelker, S., & Lakhani, A. (2005). Ecocultural effects on early infant care: A study in Cameroon, India, and Germany. *Ethos, 33*, 512–514. doi: 10.1525/eth.2005.33.4.512

Kershaw, P., Forer, B., & Goelman, H. (2005). Hidden fragility: Closure among licensed child care services in BC. *Early Childhood Research Quarterly, 20*, 417–432. doi:10.1016/j.ecresq.2005.10.003

Kershaw, P., Irwin, L., Trafford, K., & Hertzman, C. (2005). *The British Columbia atlas of child development*. Victoria, BC: Western Geographic Press.

Kershaw, P., Pulkingham, J., & Fuller, S. (2008). Expanding the subject: Violence, care, and (in)active male citizenship. *Social Politics: International Studies in Gender, State, & Society, 15*, 182–206. doi:10.1093/sp/jxn009

Kessel, F., & Rosenfield, P. L. (2008). Preface to the new edition. In F. Kessel, P. L. Rosenfield, & N. B. Anderson (Eds.), *Interdisciplinary research: Case studies from health and social science* (pp. ix–xx). New York: Oxford University Press.

Kessler, S., & Swadener, B. B. (1992). *Reconceptualizing the early childhood curriculum: Beginning the dialogue.* New York: Teachers College Press.

King, G., Currie, M., Smith, L., Servais, M., & McDougall, J. (2008). A framework of operating models for interdisciplinary research programs in clinical service organizations. *Evaluation and Program Planning, 31,* 160–173. doi:10.1016/j.evalprogplan.2008.01.003

King, T. (2005). *The Truth about stories: A native narrative.* Minneapolis, MN: University of Minnesota Press.

Kirby, M. (1989). Nature as refuge in children's environments. *Children's Environments Quarterly, 6,* 7–12.

Kirkness, V. (1998). Our peoples' education: Cut the shackles; Cut the crap; Cut the mustard. *Canadian Journal of Native Education, 22,* 10–15.

Klein, J. T. (1990). *Interdisciplinarity: History, theory, and practice.* Detroit, MI: Wayne State University Press.

Klein, J. T. (2006). Afterword: The emergent literature on interdisciplinary and transdisciplinary research evaluation. *Research Evaluation, 15,* 75–80. doi: 10.3152/147154406781776011.

Klein, J. T. & Newell, W. T. (1996). Advancing interdisciplinary studies. In J. G. Gaff and J. L. Ratcliff (Eds.), *Handbook of the undergraduate curriculum: A comprehensive guide to purposes, structures, practices, and change.* San Francisco, CA: Jossey-Bass.

Kockelmans, J. J. (1979). *Interdisciplinary and higher education.* University Park, PA: State University Press.

Kone, A., Sullivan, M., Senturia, K. D., Chrisman, N., Ciske, S. J., & Krieger, J. W. (2000). Improving collaboration between researchers and communities. *Public Health Reports,* March–June, 243–248. doi:10.1093/phr/115.2.243

Kretzmann, J. P., & McKnight, J. L. (1993). *Building communities from the inside out.* Evanston, Illinois: Asset-Based Community Development Institute, Northwestern University.

Kuh, D., & Ben-Shlomo, Y. (Eds.). (2004). *A life course approach to chronic disease epidemiology* (2nd ed.). Oxford, UK: Oxford University Press.

Kuo, F., & Faber-Taylor, A. (2004). A potential natural treatment for attention-deficit/hyperactivity disorder: Evidence from a national study. *American Journal of Public Health, 94,* 1580–1586. doi:10.2105/AJPH.94.9.1580

Kylin, M. (2003). Children's dens. *Children, Youth and Environments, 13,* 1–25.

Kyttä, M. (2002). The affordances of children's environments. *Journal of Environmental Psychology, 22,* 109–123. doi:10.1006/jevp.2001.0249

Kyttä, M. (2004). The extent of children's independent mobility and the number of actualized affordances as criteria for child-friendly environments,

Journal of Environmental Psychology, 24, 179–198. doi:10.1016/S0272-4944(03)00073-2

Kyttä, M., Kaaja, M., & Horelli L. (2004). An internet-based design game as a mediator of children's environmental visions. *Environment & Behavior, 36,* 127–131. doi:10.1177/0013916503254839

Ladd, G. W., Price, J. M., & Hart, C. H. (1988). Predicting preschoolers' peer status from their playground behaviors. *Child Development, 59,* 986–992. doi:10.2307/1130265

Land, A. (2001). Lone mothers, employment and child care. In J. Millar & K. Rowlingson (Eds.), *Lone parents, employment and social policy: Cross-national comparisons* (pp. 233–253). Bristol, UK: The Policy Press.

Lattuca, L. R. (2001). *Creating interdisciplinary research and teaching among college and university faculty.* Nashville, TN: Vanderbilt University Press.

Learning Assistance Teaching Association of British Columbia. (2002). *Learning Assistance Handbook, 7,* 1. Kelowna, BC: The Vital Link Publications.

Lee, L., & Harris, S. R. (2006). Psychometric properties and standardization samples of four screening tests for infants and young children: A review. *Pediatric Physical Therapy, 17,* 140–147. doi:10.1097/01.PEP.0000163078.03177.AB

Le Mare, L. (2005, March). *The importance of the early years: Lessons from the Romanian Adoption Project and HIPPY in Aboriginal communities.* Paper presented at the meeting of BC Deputy Ministers sponsored by the British Columbia University President's Council, Victoria, BC.

Leventhal, T., & Brooks-Gunn, J. (2000). The neighborhoods they live in: The effects of neighborhood residence on child and adolescent outcomes. *Psychological Bulletin, 126,* 309–337. doi: 10.1037/0033-2909.126.2.309

Lewin, K. (1948). *Resolving social conflicts.* New York: Harper.

Lewin, K. (1951). *Field theory in social science.* New York: Harper & Brothers.

Lewis, J. (2001). Orientation to work and the issue of care. In J. M. Miller & K. Rowlingson (Eds.), *Lone parents, employment and social policy: Cross-national comparisons,* (pp. 153–168). Bristol, UK: The Policy Press.

Lillard, A. S. (2001). Explaining the connection: Pretend play and theory of mind. In S. Reifel (Ed.), *Theory in context and out, vol. 3, play and culture studies,* (173–178). Westport, CT: Ablex.

Lindsey, E., & McGuinness, L. (1998). Significant elements of community involvement in participatory action research: Evidence from a community project. *Journal of Advanced Nursing, 28,* 1106–1114. doi:10.1046/j.1365-2648.1998.00816.x

Linney, J. A. (2000). Assessing ecological constructs and community context. In J. Rappaport & J. Seidman (Eds.), *Handbook of community psychology.* New York, NY: Kluwer Academic/Plenum.

Lombard, A. (1981). *Success begins at home: Educational foundations for preschoolers.* Lexington, MA: Lexington Books.

Mac Naughton, G. (2005). *Doing Foucault in early childhood studies: Applying poststructural ideas.* New York: Routledge.

Maton, K. I., Perkins, D. D., Altman, D. G., Gutierrez, L., Kelly, J. G., Rappaport, J., & Saegert, S. (2006). Community-based interdisciplinary research: Introduction to the special issue. *American Journal of Community Psychology, 38*, 1–7. doi: 10.1007/s10464-006-9063-2

Marzano, M., Carss, D. N., & Bell, S. (2006). Working to make interdisciplinarity work: Investing in communication and interpersonal relationships. *Journal of Agricultural Economics, 57*, 185–197. doi: 10.1111/j.1477-9552.2006.00046.x

Maufette, A. G., Frechette, L., & Robertson, D. (1999). *Revisiting children outdoor environments: A focus on design, play and safety.* Hull, QC: Gauvin Presses.

Mayson, T. A., Hayes, V. E., Harris, S. R., & Backman, C. L. (2009). Comparison of two methods of teaching early childhood professionals to score a developmental screening test. *Journal of Allied Health, 38*, 102–107.

McGillvray, A. (2004). Childhood in the shadow of parens patriae. In H. Goelman, S. K. Marshall, & S. Ross (Eds.), *Multiple lenses, multiple images: Perspectives on the child across time, space, and disciplines* (pp. 38–72).Toronto, ON: University of Toronto Press.

McKendrick, J. (1998). The "big picture": Quality in lives of lone parents. In R. Ford & J. Millar (Eds.), *Private lives and public responses: Lone parenthood and future policy in the UK* (pp. 79–103). London, UK: Policy Studies Institute.

McLanahan, S. G., & Sandefur, G. (1994). *Growing up with a single parent: What helps, what hurts.* Cambridge, MA: Harvard University Press.

McNulty, B. A., & Miller, L. J. (1996). A values-based model of infant and toddler assessment. In S. J. Meisels & E. Fenichel (Eds.), *New visions for the developmental assessment of infants and young children* (pp. 347–360). Washington, DC: National Center for Infants, Toddlers and Families.

Meisels, S. J., & Atkins-Burnett, S. (2000). The elements of early childhood assessment. In J. P. Shonkoff & S. J. Meisels (Eds.), *Handbook of early childhood intervention* (2nd ed., pp. 231–257). New York: Cambridge University Press.

Mi'kmaq Ethics Watch. (2007). *Principles and guidelines for researchers conducting research with and/or among Mi'kmaq people.* Retrieved from the St. Frances Xavier University website: http://www.stfx.ca/Research/rgo/Documents/Mi'kmaqEthicsProcedures1.doc

Miller, J. R. (1996). *Shingwauk's vision: A history of native residential schools.* Toronto, ON: University of Toronto Press.

Minkler, M. (2005). Community-based research partnerships: Challenges and opportunities. *Journal of Urban Health, 82*, ii3–12. doi:10.1093/jurban/jti034

Mistry, J., & Diaz, V. (2004). Multiple constructions of childhood. In H. Goelman, S. Ross, & S. Marshall (Eds.), *Multiple lenses, multiple images:*

Perspectives on the child across time, space, and disciplines (pp. 147–167). Toronto, ON: University of Toronto Press.

Moore, R. C. (1986). *Childhood's domain: Play and place in child development.* London, UK: Croom Helm.

Moore, R. C. (1993). *Plants for play: A plant selection guide for children's outdoor environments.* Berkeley, CA: MIG Communications.

Moore, R. C., & Young, F. (1978). Childhood outdoors. In I. Altman & J. F. Wohlwill (Eds.), *Children and Environment* (pp. 83–130). New York: Plenum Press.

Moore, R. C., & Wong H. (1997). *Natural learning: Rediscovering nature's way of teaching.* Berkeley, CA: MIG Communications.

Moore, R. C., Goltsman, S. M., & Iacofano, D. S. (1992). *Play for all guidelines: planning, designing and management of outdoor play settings for all children* (2nd ed.). Berkeley, CA: MIG Communications.

Morgan, D. (2007). Paradigms lost and pragmatism regained: Methodological implications of combining qualitative and quantitative methods. *Journal of Mixed Methods Research, 1,* 48–76. doi:10.1177/2345678906292462.

Morgeson, F., Seligman, M. E. P., Sternberg, R. J., Taylor, S. E., Manning, C. M. (1999). Lessons learned from a life in psychological science: Implications for young scientists. *American Psychologist, 54,* 106–116.

Morin, H. (2004). *Student performance data and research tools to ensure Aboriginal student success.* Retrieved from BC Ministry of Education website: http://www.bced.gov.bc.ca/abed/research/ab_student_success.pdf

Morrison, N. C. (1995). Successful single-parent families. *Journal of Divorce & Remarriage, 22,* 205–219. doi:10.1300/J087v22n03_13

Mustard, F., McCain, M. N., & Bertrand, J. (2000). Changing beliefs to change policy: The early years study. *ISUMA:Canadian Journal of Policy Research, 1,* 76–79.

Myrick, R., Lemelle, A., Aoki, B., Truax, S., & Lemp, G. (2005). Best practices for community CBPR. *Aids Education and Prevention, 17,* 400–404. doi: 10.1177/1524839908329120

National Aboriginal Health Organization. (2002). *Governance of research involving human subjects: Research brief.* Retrieved from National Aboriginal Health Organization website: http://16016.vws.magma.ca/english/pdf/re_briefs3.pdf Nichols, J. (2010). Personal communication. July 8, 2010.

Olds, A. R. (2000). *Child care design guide.* New York: McGraw-Hill.

Panagiotopoulos, C., Rozmus, J., Gagnon, R. E., & Macnab, A. J. (2007). Diabetes screening of children in a remote First Nations community on the west coast of Canada: Challenges and solutions. *Rural and Remote Health, 7,* 771.

Panksepp, J. (1998). *Affective Neuroscience: The Foundations of Human and Animal Emotions.* New York: Oxford University Press.

Papps, E., & Ramsden, I. (1996). Cultural safety in nursing: The New Zealand experience. *International Journal for Quality in Health Care, 8,* 491–497. doi:10.1016/S1353-4505(96)00080-4

Parker, E. A., Isreal, B. A., Williams, M., Brakefield-Caldwell, W., Lewis, T. C., Robins, T., Ramirez, E., Rowe, Z., & Keeler, G. (2003). Community action against asthma. Examining the partnership process of a community based participatory research project. *Journal of General Internal Medicine, 18,* 558–567. doi:10.1046/j.1525-1497.2003.20322.x

Parten, M. B. (1932). Social participation among preschool children. *Journal of Abnormal Psychology, 27,* 243–269.

Pellegrini, A. D. (1995). *School recess and playground behavior: Educational and developmental roles.* New York: University of New York Press.

Pellegrini, A. D., Horvat, M., & Huberty, P. (1998). The relative cost of children's physical play. *Animal Behaviour, 55,* 1053–1061. doi:10.1006/anbe.1997.0658

Pelton, L. H. (1989). *For reasons of poverty.* New York: Praeger.

Petersen, A. R. (1996). Risk and regulated self: The discourse of health promotion as politics of uncertainty. *Journal of Sociology, 32,* 44–57. doi: 0.1177/144078339603200105

Phoenix, A. (1996). Social construction of lone motherhood: A case of competing discourses. In E. B. Silva (Ed.) *Good enough mothering? Feminist perspectives on lone motherhood* (pp. 175–190). London, UK: Routledge.

Piaget, J. (1962). *Play, dreams, and imitation in childhood.* New York: W. W. Norton.

Piaget, J., & Inhelder, B. (2000). *The psychology of the child.* New York: Basic Books.

Pianta, R. C. & McCoy, S .J. (1997). The first day of school: The predictive validity of early school screening. *Journal of Applied Developmental Psychology, 18,* 1–22. doi:10.1016/S0193-3973(97)90011-3

Pighini, M. (2008). *A multiple case study of the children and families in the Infant Development Program of British Columbia.* (Doctoral dissertation, The University of British Columbia). Retrieved from http://circle.ubc.ca/handle/2429/5308

Pinto-Martin, J. A., Dunkle, M., Earls, M., Fliedner, M., & Landes, C. (2005). Developmental stages of developmental screening: Steps to implementation of a successful program. *American Journal of Public Health, 95,* 1928–1932. doi: 10.2105/AJPH.2004.052167

Piper, M. C., Pinnell, L. E., Darrah, J., Maguire, T., & Byrne, P. J. (1992). Construction and validation of the Alberta Infant Motor Scale (AIMS). *Canadian Journal of Public Health, 83* (Suppl. 2), S46–S50.

Piquemal, N. (2000). Four principles to guide research with Aboriginals. *Policy Options, 21,* 49–51.

Pivik, J. (1997). *Facilitating collaborative research: Strategies from the health researcher's perspective.* Toronto, ON: Educating Future Physicians of Ontario.

Pivik, J. (2004a). *Empirically based examination of the mechanisms, models and impact of involving consumers in health decision-making* (Comprehensive Examination). University of Ottawa, Canada.

Pivik, J. (2004b). Practical strategies for facilitating meaningful citizen involvement in health planning. In P. Forest, T. McIntosh, & G. P. Marchildon (Eds.), *Changing health care in Canada* (pp. 312–348). Toronto, ON: University of Toronto Press.

Pivik, J. (2006). *Program evaluation of the Supporting Interdisciplinary Practice: The family physician/nurse practitioner educational and mentoring program.* Ontario: The Ministry of Health and Long Term Care.

Pivik, J., & Goelman, H. (in press). Evaluation of a community-based participatory research consortium focused on child health and well-being. *Health Education & Behavior.*

Pivik, J., & Weaver, L. (1997). *Facilitating community participation in health care planning: Recommendations from consumers and health professionals.* Kingston, ON: Health Information Partnership.

Pivik, J., Rode, E., & Ward, C. (2004). A consumer involvement model for health technology assessment, *Health Policy, 69,* 253–268. doi:10.1016/j.healthpol.2003.12.012

Plowfield, L., Wheeler, E., & Raymond, J. (2005). Time, tact, talent, and trust: Essential ingredients of effective academic-community partnerships. *Nursing Education Perspectives, 26,* 217–220. doi: 10.1043/1094-2831(2005)026

Poole, R. (1972). *Towards deep subjectivity.* London, UK: Harper & Row.

Polivka, B. J., Lovell, M., & Smith, B. A. (1998). A qualitative assessment of inner city elementary school children's perceptions of their neighborhood. *Public Health Nursing, 15,* 171–179. doi:10.1111/j.1525-1446.1998.tb00336.x

Prout, A. (2005). *The future of childhood: towards the interdisciplinary study of children.* London: RoutledgeFalmer, 2005.

Provincial Health Services Authority. (2010). *BC early hearing program.* Retrieved from the Provincial Health Services Authority website: http://www.phsa.ca/AgenciesAndServices/Services/BCEarlyHearing/default.htm

Raina, P., O'Donnell, M., Rosenbaum, P., Brehaut, J., Walter, S. D., Russell, D., Swinton, M., Zhu, B., & Wood, E. (2005). The health and well-being of caregivers of children with cerebral palsy. *Pediatrics, 115,* 626–636. doi: 10.1542/peds.2004-1689

Ramey, S. L., & Ramey, C. T. (1997). The role of universities in child development. In H. J. Walberg, O. Reyes & R. P. Weissberg (Eds.), *Children and youth: Interdisciplinary perspectives* (pp. 13–43). Chicago, IL: Sage.

Reed, B. J., Schumaker, A., & Woods, S. (2000). Collaborative models for metropolitan university outreach: The Omaha experience. *Cityscape: A Journal of Policy Development and Research, 5,* 197–207.

Reich, S. M. & Reich, J. A. (2006). Cultural competence in interdisciplinary collaborations: A method for respecting diversity in research partnerships. *American Journal of Community Psychology, 1–2,* 38–62.

Reimea, T. B., Tub, A. W., Lee, S. K., & the Canadian Neonatal Network. (2007). Treatment differences between Aboriginal and white infants admitted to Canadian neonatal intensive care units. *Paediatric and Perinatal Epidemiology, 21,* 532–540. doi:10.1111/j.1365-3016.2007.00874.x

Reimer Kirkham, S., Smye, V., Tang, S., Anderson, J. M., Browne, A., and Coles, R. (2002). Rethinking cultural safety. *Research in Nursing and Health, 25,* 222–232.

Repko, A. F. (2008). *Interdisciplinary research: Process and theory.* Thousand Oaks, CA: Sage.

Rhinehart, N. M. (2005). Native American perspectives: Connected to one another and to the greater universe. In L. D. Soto (Ed.), *The politics of early childhood education* (pp. 135–142). New York: Peter Lang.

Richardson, R. (1997). *Fields of play: Constructing an academic life.* New Brunswick, NJ: Rutgers University Press.

Rissotto, A., & Tonucci, F. (2002). Freedom of movement and environmental knowledge in elementary school children. *Journal of Environmental Psychology, 22,* 65–78. doi:10.1006/jevp.2002.0243

Rivkin, M. S. (1995). *The great outdoors: Restoring children's right to play outside.* Washington, DC: National Association for the Education of Young Children.

Romm, N. (1998). Interdisciplinarity practice as reflexivity. *Systemic Practice and Action Research, 11,* 63–77.

Rowlingson, K., & McKay, S. (2002). *Lone parent families: Gender, class and state.* Essex, UK: Pearson Educational.

Rowlingson, K., & Miller, J. (1998). Supporting employment: Emerging policy and practices. In J. Millar & K. Rowlingson (Eds.), *Lone parents, employment and social policy: Cross-national comparisons* (pp. 255–236). Bristol, UK: The Policy Press.

Roseneil, S., & Mann, K. (1996). Unpalatable choices and inadequate families: Lone mothers and the underclass debate. In E. B. Silva (Ed.), *Good enough mothering? Feminist perspectives on lone motherhood,* (pp. 191–210). New York: Routledge.

Royal Commission on Aboriginal Peoples. (1996). *Gathering strength: Report on the Royal Commission on Aboriginal Peoples.* Ottawa, ON: Canada Communication Group.

Rubin, K. H., Maioni, T. L., & Hornung, M. (1976). Free play behavior in middle and lower class preschoolers. Parten and Piaget revisited. *Child Development, 27,* 414–419. doi:10.2307/1128796

Rubin, K. H., Watson, K. S., & Jambor, T. W. (1978). Free-play behaviours in preschool and kindergarten children. *Child Development, 49,* 534–536. doi:10.2307/1128725

Russell, H. (1973). *A teacher's guide: Ten-minute field trips using school grounds for environmental studies.* Chicago, IL: J. G. Ferguson.

Russell, M., Gockel, A., & Harris, B. (2007). Parent perspectives on intensive intervention for child maltreatment. *Child and Adolescent Social Work, 24,* 101–120. doi: 10.1007/s10560-006-0068-3

Russell, M., Harris, B., & Gockel, A. (2008a). Canadian lone mothers describe parenting needs: European solutions explored. *Canadian Social Work Review, 25,* 169–185.

Russell, M., Harris, B., & Gockel, A. (2008b). Parenting in poverty: Perceptions of high risk parents. *Journal of Children and Poverty, 14,* 83–98. doi:10.1080/10796120701871322

Salter, L., & Hearn, A. (1996). *Outside the lines: Issues in interdisciplinary research.* Montreal, QC: McGill-Queen's Press.

Sand, S., Silverstein, M., Glascoe, F .P., Gupta, V. B., Tonniges, T. P., & O'Connor K. G. (2005). Pediatricians' reported practices regarding developmental screening: Do guidelines work? Do they help? *Pediatrics, 116,* 174–179. doi: 10.1542/peds.2004-1809

Scher, A., Tse, L., Harris, S., Hayes, V., & Tardif, M. (2007, March). Sleep habits and early neuromotor attainments. In J. Houbé (Chair), *The ecology of early screening and follow-up programs.* Symposium paper presented at the 2007 Biennial Meeting of the Society for Research in Child Development, Boston, MA.

Schiariti, V., Matsuba, C., Houbé, J. S., & Synnes, A. R. (2008a). Severe retinopathy of prematurity and visual outcomes in British Columbia: A 10-year analysis. *Journal of Perinatology, 28,* 566–572. doi: 10.1038/jp.2008.34

Schiariti, V., Klassen, A. F., Houbé, J. S., Synnes, A., Lisonkova, S., & Lee, S. K. (2008b). Perinatal characteristics and parents' perspective of health status of NICU graduates born at term. *Journal of Perinatology, 28,* 368–376. doi: 10.1038/jp.2008.9

Schnarch, B. (2004). Ownership, control, access, and possession (OCAP) or self-determination applied to research: A critical analysis of contemporary First Nations research and some options for First Nations communities. *Journal of Aboriginal Health, 1,* 80–95.

Schore, A. N. (1994). *Affect regulation and the origin of the self: The neurobiology of emotional development.* Hillsdale, NJ: Lawrence Erlbaum.

Scott, D. (2004). Spirituality and children: Paying attention to experience. In H. Goelman, S. K. Marshall, & S. Ross (Eds.), *Multiple lenses, multiple images: Perspectives on the child across time, space, and disciplines* (pp. 168–198).Toronto, ON: University of Toronto Press.

Seligman, M. E. P. (1972). Learned Helplessness. *Annual Review of Medicine, 23,* 407–412. doi:10.1146/annurev.me.23.020172.002203

Sen, A. (2000). *Social exclusion: Concept, application, and scrutiny.* Social development papers, No. 1. Manila: Asian Development Bank.

Sherlock, R. L., Synnes, A. R., Grunau, R. E., Holsti, L., Hubber-Richard, P., Johannesen, D., & Whitfield, M. F. (2008). Long-term outcome after neonatal intraparenchymal echodensities with porencephaly. *Archives of Disease in Childhood—Fetal and Neonatal Edition, 93,* F127–F131. doi:10.1136/adc.2006.110726

Shonkoff, J. P. (2000). Science, policy and practice: Three cultures in search of a shared mission. *Child Development 7,* 181–187. doi: 10.1111/1467-8624.00132

Shonkoff, J. P. (2007, March). Teaching, not preaching, as a strategy for social change. In J. W. Hagen (Chair), *Making a difference lecture in honor of Esther Thelen.* Presentation at the 2007 Biennial Meeting of the Society for Research in Child Development, Boston, MA.

Shonkoff, J. P. & Phillips, D. A. (Eds.). (2000). *From neurons to neighborhoods: The science of early child development*. Washington, DC: National Academy Press.

Shoultz, J., Oheha, M. F., Magnussen, L., Hla, M., Bress-Suanders, Z., Dela Cruz, M., & Douglas, M. (2006). Finding solutions to challenges faced in community-based participatory research between academic and community organizations. *Journal of Interprofessional Care, 20*, 133–144. doi:10.1080/13561820600577576

Shulman, L. S. (1988). Disciplines of inquiry in education. In R. M. Jaeger (Ed.), *Complementary methods for research in education* (pp. 3–17). Washington, DC: American Educational Research Association.

Sigel, I. E. (1996). Applied developmental science training should be grounded in a social-cultural framework. In C. B. Fisher, J. P. Murray, & I. E. Sigel (Eds.), *Applied developmental science: Graduate training for diverse disciplines and educational settings* (pp. 189–221). Norwood, NJ: Ablex.

Skinner, B. F. (1971). *Beyond freedom and dignity*. Harmondsworth, UK: Penguin.

Smilansky, S., & Shefatya, L. (1990). *Facilitating play: A medium for promoting cognitive, socio-emotional and academic development in young children*. Gaithersburg, MD: Psychosocial and Educational Publications.

Smith, L. T. (2002). *Decolonizing methodologies: Research and Indigenous Peoples* (5th ed.). London, UK: Zed Books.

Smith, V., Schonert-Reichl, K. A., Lawlor, M. S., & Jaramillo, A. (2008, November). Evaluating the effectiveness of universal social and emotional competence promotion programs: Theoretical, contextual, and practical considerations in conducting evaluation research in educational settings. In B. Sokol (Chair), *Goodness of fit: design considerations for evaluating socio-emotional learning (SEL) programs*. Symposium conducted at the annual meeting of the Association for Moral Education, South Bend, IN.

Smolewski, M., & Wesley-Esquimaux, C. C. (2003). *Historic trauma and Aboriginal healing*. Ottawa, ON: Aboriginal Healing Foundation Research Series.

Sokoloff, N. (2004). The voices of children in literature. In H. Goelman, S. K. Marshall, & S. Ross (Eds.), *Multiple lenses, multiple images: Perspectives on the child across time, space, and disciplines* (pp. 73–90).Toronto, ON: University of Toronto Press.

Soto, L. D. (Ed.) (2005). *The politics of early childhood education: Re-thinking childhood*. New York: Peter Lang.

Spenser, N., & Baldwin, N. (2005). Economic, cultural and social contexts of neglect. In J. Taylor & B. Daniels (Eds.), *Child neglect: Practice issues for health and social care*. (pp. 26–42). London, UK: Jessica Kingsley.

St. James-Roberts, I. (1989). Persistent crying in infancy. *Journal of Child Psychology and Psychiatry, 30*, 189–195. doi: 10.1111/j.1469-7610.1989.tb00233.x

St. James-Roberts, I., Alvarez, M., Csipke, E., Abramsky, T., Goodwin, J., & Sorgenfrei, E. (2006). Infant crying and sleeping in London, Copenhagen, and when parents adopt a "proximal" form of care. *Pediatrics, 117,* 1146–1155. doi:10.1542/peds.2005-2387

Stairs, A. H., & Bernhard, J. K. (2002). Considerations for evaluating "good care" in Canadian Aboriginal early childhood settings. *McGill Journal of Education, 37,* 309–331.

Stamp, G., Champion, S., Anderson, G., Warren, B., Stuart-Butler, D., Doolan, J., Boles, C., Callaghan, L., Foale, A., & Muyambi, C. (2008). Aboriginal maternal and infant care workers: Partners in caring for Aboriginal mothers and babies. *Rural and Remote Health, 8,* 1–12.

Statistics Canada. (2007). *Family portrait: Continuity and change in Canadian families and households in 2006.* National Portrait: Census Families. Retrieved from the Statistics Canada website: www.12.statcan/can/english/census06/analysis/famhouse/cenfam3cfm.

Stemler, S. (2001). An overview of content analysis. *Practical Assessment, Research & Evaluation, 7,* 17. Retrieved from PARE website: http://PAREonline.net/getvn.asp?v=7&n=17

Stokols, D. (1977). *Perspectives on environment and behavior.* New York: Plenum.

Stokols, D. (1979). A congruence analysis of human stress. In I. G. Sarason & C. D. Spielberger (Eds.), *Stress and Anxiety, Vol. 6.* (pp. 27–53). New York: John Wiley.

Stokols, D. (2006). Towards a science of transdisciplinary action research. *American Journal of Community Research, 38,* 63–77. doi: 10.1007/s10464-006-9060-5

Strelnick, A. H., Bateman, W. B., Jones, C., Shepherd, S. D., Massad, R. J., Townsend, J. M., Grossman, R., Korin, E., & Schorow, M. (1988). Graduate primary care training: A collaborative alternative for family practice, internal medicine, and pediatrics. *Annals of Internal Medicine, 109,* 324–334.

Stringer, E. T. (1996). *Action research: a handbook for practice.* Thousand Oaks, CA: Sage.

Stroick, S., & Jensen, J. (1999). *What is the best policy mix for Canada's young children?* (CPRN Study No. F-09). Ottawa, ON: Canadian Policy Research Networks.

Suarez-Balcazar, Y., Harper, G., & Lewis, R. (2005). An interactive and contextual model of community-university collaborations for research and action. *Health Education and Behavior, 32,* 84–101. doi:10.1177/1090198104269512

Sundrum, R., Logan, S., Wallace, A., & Spencer, N. (2005). Cerebral palsy and socioeconomic status: A retrospective cohort study. *Archives of Disease in Childhood, 90,* 15–18. doi: *10.1136/adc.2002.018937*

Super, C. M. & Harkness, S. (2002). Culture structures the environment for development. *Human Development, 45,* 270–274. doi: 10.1159/000064988

Swadener, B. B. (2006). "At risk" or "at promise"? From deficit constructions of the "Other Childhood" to possibilities for authentic alliances with children and families. In L. D. Soto (Ed.). *The politics of early childhood education* (pp. 117–134). New York: Peter Lang.

Swift, K. (1995). *Manufacturing "bad mothers": A critical perspective on child neglect.* Toronto, ON: University of Toronto Press.

Synnes, A., Houbé, J., & Klassen, A. (2007, March). Developmental Pathways of At-Risk Neonates Study. In J. Houbé (Chair), *The ecology of early screening and follow-up programs.* Symposium paper presented at the 2007 Biennial Meeting of the Society for Research in Child Development, Boston, MA.

Synnes A. R., Buchanan, L., Ruth, C., & Albersheim, S. (2008). Management of the newborn delivered at the threshold of viability. *British Columbia Medical Journal, 50,* 498–508.

Synnes, A. R., Lisonkova, S., Houbé, J. S., Klassen, A., & Lee, S. K. (2004, May). *Canadian Neonatal Network: Targeting follow-up needs of premature survivors.* Poster presentation at the Pediatric Academic Societies meeting, San Francisco, CA.

Synnes, A. R, MacNab, Y. C., Qiu, Z., Ohlsson, A., Gustafson, P., Dean, C., Lee, S. K., & the Canadian Neonatal Network (2006). Neonatal intensive care unit characteristics affect the incidence of severe intraventricular hemorrhage. *Medical Care, 44,* 754–759. doi: 10.1097/01.mlr.0000218780.16064.df

Synnes, A. R., Berry, M., Huw, J., Pendray, M., Stewart, S., Lee, S. K., & the Canadian Neonatal Network (2004). Infants with congenital anomalies admitted to neonatal intensive care units. *American Journal of Perinatology, 21,* 199–207. doi: 10.1055/s-2004-828604

Tapp, J. (2003). *Procoder for digital video.* Nashville, TN: Vanderbilt University.

Taylor, M., & Carlson, S. M. (1997). The relation between individual differences in fantasy and theory of mind. *Child Development, 68,* 436–455. doi:10.2307/1131670

Teddlie, C., & Yu, F. (2007). Mixed methods sampling: A typology with examples. *Journal of Mixed Methods Research, 1,* 77–100. doi:10.1177/2345678906292430

Ten Fingers, K. (2005). Rejecting, revitalizing, and reclaiming: First Nations work to set the direction of research and policy development. *Canadian Journal of Public Health, 96* (Suppl. 1), 60–63.

Thompson, L. S., Story, M., & Butler, G. (2003). Use of a university-community collaboration model to frame issues and set an agenda for strengthening a community. *Health Promotion Practice, 4,* 385–392. doi:10.1177/1524839903255467

Trancik, A. M., & Evans, G. W. (1995). Spaces fit for children: Competency in the design of daycare center environments. *Children's Environments, 12,* 43–58.

Trocme, N., Knoke, D., & Blackstock, C. (2004). Pathways to the overrepresentation of Aboriginal children in Canada's child welfare system. *Social Service Review, 78,* 577–600. doi:10.1086/424545

Tse, L., Mayson, T. A., Leo, S., Lee, L. S., Harris, S. R., Hayes, V. E., Backman, C. L., Cameron, D., & Tardif, M. (2008). Concurrent validity of the Harris Infant Neuromotor Test and the Alberta Infant Motor Scale. *Journal of Pediatric Nursing, 23*, 28–36. doi: 10.1016/j.pedn.2007.07.009

Turner, V (1969). *The ritual process: Structure and anti-structure*. Ithaca, NY: Cornell University Press.

UNICEF (1989). *United Nations convention on the rights of the child*. Retrieved from UNICEF website: http://www.unicef.org/crc

UNICEF. (2004). *Building child friendly cities: A framework for action*. Florence, Italy: UNICEF Innocenti Research Centre.

UNICEF (2007). *Child Friendly Cities*. Retrieved from UNICEF website: http://www.childfriendlycities.org/

UNICEF (2007). Child poverty in perspective: an overview of child well-being in rich countries. *Innocenti Report Card 7*. Florence, IT: UNICEF Innocenti Research Centre.

UNICEF. (2010). *Aboriginal children's health: Leaving no child behind*. Retrieved from the UNICEF website: http://www.unicef.ca/portal/SmartDefault.aspx?at=2063

Van Gennep, A. (1909/1960). *The rites of passage*. Chicago, IL: Chicago University Press.

Vrijheid, M., Dolk, H., Stone, D., Abramsky, L., Alberman, E., & Scott, J. E. S. (2000). Socioeconomic inequalities in risk of congenital anomaly. *Archives of Disease in Childhood, 82*, 349–352. doi: 10.1136/adc.82.5.349

Watamura, S., Donzella, B., Alwin, J., & Gunnar, M. E. (2003). Morning-to-afternoon increases in cortisol concentrations for infants and toddlers at child care: Age differences and behavioral correlates. *Child Development, 74*, 1006–1020. doi: 10.1111/1467-8624.00583

Weaver, L., & Pivik, J. (1997a). *Community participation among members of the Health Information Partnership*. Kingston, ON: Health Information Partnership.

Weaver, L., & Pivik, J. (1997b). *Out of the mouths of experts: A community participation reader and compilation of community participation how-to hints*. Kingston, ON: Health Information Partnership.

Weilbacher, R. (1981). The effects of static and dynamic play environments on children's social and motor behaviors. In A. T. Cheska (Ed.), *Play as context* (pp. 248–258). Newbury Park, CA: Leisure Press.

Weingart, P. (2000). Interdisciplinarity: The paradoxical discourse. In P. Weingart & N. Stehr (Eds.), *Practising interdisciplinarity* (pp. 25–41). Toronto, ON: University of Toronto Press.

Wells, N. (2000). At home with nature: Effects of "greenness" on children's cognitive functioning. *Environment and Behavior, 32*, 775–795. doi:10.1177/00139160021972793

Westheimer, M. (2003). *Parents making a difference*. Jerusalem: Hebrew University Magnes Press.

Williams, J., & Holmes, C. A. (2004). Improving the early detection of children with subtle developmental Problems. *Journal of Child Health Care, 8*, 34–46. doi:10.1177/1367493504041852

Wolin, S. J. & Bennett, L. A. (1984). Family rituals. *Family Process, 23*, 401–420. doi: 10.1111/j.1545-5300.1984.00401.x

World Health Organization (2007). *Constitution of the World Health Organization.* (Basic Documents, 46th ed.). Geneva, Switzerland: World Health Organization.

Yoshikawa, H. (2006). Placing community psychology in the context of the social, health and educational sciences: Directions for interdisciplinary research and action. *American Journal of Community Psychology, 38*, 31–34. doi: 10.1007/s10464-006-9068-x

Yoshikawa, H., Weisner, T., Kalil, A., & Way, N. (2008). Mixing qualitative and quantitative research in developmental science: Uses and methodological choices. *Developmental Psychology, 44*, 344–354. doi:10.1037/0012-1649.44.2.344

Contributors

Jessica Ball, M.P.H., PhD, is a Professor in the School of Child and Youth Care at the University of Victoria. She is the director of a grant-funded program of research and education on the cultural nature of child and family development (www.ecdip.org) and has led several innovative education programs and research projects involving community-university partnerships to cogenerate concepts and practices. Dr. Ball is the author or coauthor of over 100 journal articles and book chapters and three books.

Susan Dahinten, RN, PhD is an Associate Professor in the School of Nursing at the University of British Columbia. Dr. Dahinten's research program addresses the intersection of family and community factors that influence the health and developmental trajectories of children and youth, and the evaluation of public health screening programs and family-focused interventions designed to support healthy childhood development.

Laurie Ford, Ph.D. is an Associate Professor in the Department of Educational and Counselling Psychology and Special Education and a Research Fellow with the Human Early Learning Partnership (HELP) at the University of British Columbia. A former special education teacher, Laurie is a School and Child Clinical Psychologist. Her primary research interests are in early childhood assessment, family, neighborhood, and community factors that promote early school success and family/professional relationships.

Hillel Goelman, PhD, is Professor in the Department of Educational and Counselling Psychology, and Special Education and is an Associate Member of the Department of Paediatrics and the School of Public and Population Health at the University of British Columbia in Vancouver, BC, Canada. Dr. Goelman also serves as the Chair of the Interdisciplinary Studies Graduate Program at UBC. His research interests are in early childhood intervention programs, developmental trajectories of typical and atypical children, and interdisciplinary studies on children and childhood.

Martin Guhn, PhD, is a Michael Smith Foundation for Health Research Postdoctoral Fellow at the University of British Columbia, with a background in Human Development, Psychology, and Music. His main research interests are in the joint influences of social, cultural, and demographic factors on children's development and health; bioecological theories of development;

school reform; and validity theory for population-level child development assessment.

Michaela Gummerum, PhD, is a Lecturer (Assistant Professor) of Psychology at the University of Plymouth, UK. Her research focuses on children's and adolescents' social development, particularly the development of fair and moral behavior, cognitions, and emotions, development of relationship concepts, and economic socialization. She approaches these topics from a cross-cultural and interdisciplinary perspective.

Susan Herrington teaches in the School of Architecture and Landscape Architecture at the University of British Columbia. Her book, 'Cornelia Hahn Oberlander: Making the Modern Landscape,' will be published in 2012 by the University of Virginia Press. The book is a biography of the Landscape Architect who designed the first adventure playground in Canada at Expo '67.

Virginia E. Hayes, RN, PhD is Professor Emerita at the University of Victoria School of Nursing and recently retired as Senior Practice Leader for Nursing Research at the Children's & Women's Health Centre of British Columbia. Her research program centers on issues for children with chronic conditions and disabilities and their families in community and acute care settings. She led an interdisciplinary team that examined the impact of training community-based child health practitioners in early assessment of infants to promote early intervention for neuromotor delays.

Lucy Le Mare (PhD), a Developmental Psychologist, is an Associate Professor in the Faculty of Education at Simon Fraser University. Emphasizing the centrality of social relationships and cultural-historical context, her research focuses on risk and resilience processes and school adjustment in diverse populations (e.g., children-in-care; intercountry adoptees; and Indigenous children).

Mari Pighini completed her PhD in 2008 while working with The CHILD Project. Her graduate work focused on parents with children with disabilities and their experiences while transitioning between preschool and school services. Mari continues her work with vulnerable children and families through her postdoctoral research and work with the Including All Children: Expanding Partnerships Project funded by the Social Development Partnerships Program.

Jayne Pivik, PhD, is a community psychologist with a background in Developmental Psychology and environmental influences on health. Her research interests are in identifying how communities can positively influence child/youth health, development and well-being; services and interventions promoting child and youth development; human-environmental interactions; methods for engaging children and youth in services that impact them; and equitable access for individuals with disabilities and the elderly. She is Founder and CEO of Apriori Research (www.aprioriresearch.com) and an Honorary Associate of the Human Early Learning Partnership, University of British Columbia.

Mary Russell, PhD, is Professor of Social Work at the University of British Columbia, where she has been teaching since 1974, primarily in the areas of research methodology and family violence. Most recently, she has been engaged in developing online courses on family violence . Her research interests include children and poverty, and family violence.

Suretha Swart is a PhD candidate in School Psychology at the University of British Columbia, with a background in clinical psychology and child and youth mental health. Her current research and clinical interests revolve around supporting students with Fetal Alcohol Spectrum Disorder (FASD) and other disabilities in schools.

Anne Synnes, MD, is a clinical neonatologist at British Columbia's Women's Hospital, medical director of the Neonatal Follow-Up program, Clinical Associate Professor at the University of British Columbia, and member of the Child and Family Research Institute. Her clinical research interests are evaluating the clinical outcomes of neonatal intensive care unit (NICU) graduates and changing NICU practices to improve outcomes.

Lillian Tse received her Master of Science in Nursing from University of British Columbia in 2005. She was the recipient of the 2003 Sheena Davidson Fund for her study on Parents' Perceptions about a Behavioural Sleep Intervention. Tse is currently a public health nurse specialized in the health and development of young children.

Silvia Vilches is completing her PhD in Social Planning, focusing on the experiences of lone mothers with welfare reform under neoliberal regimes. Her past work focuses on community capacity development, the community benefits of early childhood education, gender issues in the social and economic structures available to low-income families, and equity issues for Aboriginal peoples and for gay, lesbian, bisexual, two-spirited, and transgendered people.

Index

Aboriginal communities 24, 38, 43, 83, 143, 144, 160
assessment 38, 43, 55, 69, 70, 71, 75–88, 93, 96–113, 132, 139, 149, 158, 161, 167, 171, 185, 186, 205, 211

bioecological theory 21, 27, 28, 29, 30, 118, 142, 180, 181, 182
Bronfenbrenner 21–24, 26–30, 32, 34, 49, 54, 71, 79, 118, 124, 139, 142, 143, 153, 154, 180–183, 198, 199, 201

child and youth well-being 7, 117, 121, 126, 129, 130, 132, 133, 135, 136, 209
child care 3–6, 40, 41, 66, 197, 204
collaboration 1, 2, 7, 9, 12, 14, 15, 33, 36, 37, 44–48, 50, 51, 71, 82, 85, 90, 91, 108, 110, 111, 114, 122, 141, 147, 149, 150, 152, 153, 155, 156, 157, 158, 159, 161–177, 189, 190, 203, 206, 208, 209, 210–217
  see also interdisciplinary collaboration, university-community collaboration
collaborative research 9, 11, 12, 15, 18, 70, 93, 156, 159, 179, 199, 238
community
  community access factors 162, 164
  community asset mapping 20, 127

community capacity building 41
community contexts 76
community-engaged research 93
community influences 21
community kitchens 60, 90
community mapping approach 127
community programs 61, 62
community psychologists 118, 139
community psychology 46
school community relationships 88
university-community collaboration study 7
university-Indigenous community research partnership 84
community-based
  community-based expectations 70
  community-based policies 17
  community-based screening study 4, 24, 39, 105, 107, 111, 143, 144, 184, 185, 187
  community-based service/ providers 13, 155
  community-based supports 77
  community-based team members 92
community partners
  community agencies 165, 214
  community based ECE/D practitioners 76
  community-based health and mental health clinics 23
  community-based researchers 202

community-partners—*Continued*
  community building
    activities 216
  community elders 107
  community professionals 3, 14,
    15, 35, 49, 50, 106, 111, 114,
    158, 173, 174, 176, 183, 186,
    213, 217
  community representatives 50,
    91, 190, 216
  community-university (research)
    partnerships 69, 70, 92,
    175
  see also university-community
    collaboration
conflict (resolution) 167, 176
culture 2, 9, 13, 17, 18, 19, 26, 27,
  71, 72, 78, 86, 107, 108, 137,
  142, 157, 203–205
  culture of research/
    researcher 13, 14, 157
  disciplinary cultures 204
  European-heritage culture 72,
    76
  health cultures 45
  indigenous culture 27, 77, 90
  organizational culture/s 45, 157,
    158
  subculture 26

early intervention 14, 20, 23, 24,
  74, 77–79, 82, 85, 87, 89, 90,
  95–97, 100, 102, 104, 105,
  108, 143, 205

First Nations 5, 12, 23, 24, 35, 48,
  55, 69, 72, 74, 75, 76, 89, 94,
  95, 107, 112, 115, 143, 152

graduate students 3, 6, 7, 10, 13,
  35, 37, 44, 46, 91, 150, 154,
  179, 183, 186, 189, 194, 195,
  196, 198, 213, 217

health care 11, 20, 21, 42, 73, 100,
  112, 114, 204

Indigenous people
  Aboriginal HIPPY
    Documentation Project 4, 5,
    24, 38, 43, 69, 74, 143, 144,
    151, 160, 205, 208
  Indigenous Child Project 4, 5, 24,
    38, 43, 69, 74, 104, 106, 108,
    110, 112, 143, 144, 151, 208
  Indigenous children 5, 7, 70,
    71, 72, 73–86, 88–90, 92, 93,
    106, 205
  Indigenous communities 3, 4,
    38, 70, 71, 73, 76, 78, 81–83,
    89, 90, 93, 106, 107, 151, 208
  Indigenous families/homes 22,
    72, 78, 80, 81, 84, 85, 86, 88
  Indigenous knowledge/s 71, 83,
    182
  Indigenous peoples 25, 28, 69,
    70–74, 78, 79, 81–83, 91, 93,
    94, 107, 204
interdisciplinarity 1, 7, 15, 36, 51,
  141, 142, 145–154, 180, 193,
  197, 203, 206, 207, 210, 211,
  212, 216, 217
interdisciplinary collaboration 33,
  44, 141, 150, 152, 189, 203,
  215
intervention
  child protection interventions 61
  clinical intervention 196
  colonial government
    interventions 71, 73, 77
  colonial interventions 79, 81
  early childhood intervention
    programs 5, 24, 40, 143, 144
  early intervention 14, 20, 23, 24,
    74, 77, 78, 79, 82, 85, 87, 89,
    90, 95, 96, 97, 100, 102, 104,
    105, 108, 143, 205
  ecodevelopmental
    interventions 54
  intervention environments 54
  intervention practices 76
  intervention specialists 14, 87
  intervention studies 6

public health interventions 97
social intervention 59
state interventions 66

language 12, 13, 18, 27, 30, 31, 42, 45, 46, 49, 71, 72, 74, 76–78, 80, 83, 86, 88, 89, 106, 107, 111, 113, 122, 146, 148, 153, 168, 170, 186, 189, 203–205, 208, 210, 211
lone-parents 3, 57, 65, 66

neighborhoods 20, 50, 122, 129, 135–138, 141, 187, 212

playgrounds 124, 130, 137, 138
policy 1–5, 8, 12–15, 17, 18, 20, 24, 35, 38, 40, 42, 43, 48, 49, 50, 53, 54, 65, 78, 79, 97, 103, 139, 141, 143, 144, 150–153, 157, 158, 160, 182, 187, 192, 197, 202, 203, 208, 211, 212, 214
poverty 3, 7, 12, 22, 24, 25, 27, 31, 53, 54, 55, 56, 57, 58, 59, 61, 63, 64, 65, 66, 67, 73, 77, 112, 121, 138, 143, 182

schools 12, 72, 73, 75, 81, 86, 106, 124, 126, 136, 180, 202
Shonkoff 2, 13, 14, 20, 50, 126, 129, 141, 157, 164, 173
studies in the CHILD project
  Aboriginal HIPPY Documentation Project 4, 5, 23, 24, 38, 43, 69, 74, 75, 83, 85, 92, 143, 144, 151, 160, 205, 208
  Child Care Policy Study 3, 4, 24, 38, 43, 143, 144, 151, 153, 160, 187, 208, 212

  Community-Based Screening Study 4, 24, 39, 105, 107, 111, 143, 144, 184, 185, 187
  Developmental Pathways Study 4, 6, 7, 24, 41, 43, 102, 103, 107, 111, 142, 143, 144, 152, 153, 160, 185, 191, 209
  Income Assistance Study 3, 4, 24, 25, 38, 43, 53, 54, 56, 59, 60, 63, 111, 112, 143, 144, 151, 160, 187, 194
  Indigenous Child Project 4, 5, 24, 38, 43, 69, 74, 104, 106, 108, 110, 112, 143, 144, 151, 208
  Infant Neuromotor Study 24, 39, 103, 104, 105, 107, 108, 111, 142, 143, 144, 185
  Outdoor Play Spaces Study 5–7, 24, 37, 40, 43, 46, 143, 144, 151–153
  Parent Counseling Study 5, 6, 24, 37, 40, 43, 53, 54, 56, 59, 62, 63, 142, 143, 144
  Safe Spaces Study 5, 6, 7, 24, 25, 40, 43, 46, 117, 143, 144, 151, 152, 153, 161
surveillance 27, 31, 55, 70, 71, 80, 81, 82, 84, 85, 89, 92, 105, 108, 111, 112, 113, 131, 152, 204

university-community collaboration 7, 14, 36, 37, 155, 157, 176, 177

vulnerability 25, 53–67, 122, 184, 208

GPSR Compliance

The European Union's (EU) General Product Safety Regulation (GPSR) is a set of rules that requires consumer products to be safe and our obligations to ensure this.

If you have any concerns about our products, you can contact us on

ProductSafety@springernature.com

In case Publisher is established outside the EU, the EU authorized representative is:

Springer Nature Customer Service Center GmbH
Europaplatz 3
69115 Heidelberg, Germany

www.ingramcontent.com/pod-product-compliance
Lightning Source LLC
LaVergne TN
LVHW011810060526
838200LV00053B/3718